Language Contact and the Ma]
Vernacular

Exploring creole studies from a linguistic, historical, and socio-cultural perspective, this study advances our knowledge of the subject by using a cohesive approach to provide new theoretical insights into language shift, language acquisition, and language change. It compares the legal system regulating black slavery in Chocó, Colombia with the systems implemented by other European colonial powers in the Americas, to address questions such as: What do Chocó Spanish linguistic features say about the nature of Afro-Hispanic vernaculars? What were the sociohistorical conditions in which Chocó Spanish formed? Was slavery in Chocó much different from slavery in other European colonies? Whilst primarily focused on Afro-Hispanic language varieties, Sessarego's findings and methodology can be easily applied and tested to other contact languages and settings, and used to address current debates on the origin of other black communities in the Americas and the languages they speak.

SANDRO SESSAREGO is an Associate Professor in the Department of Spanish and Portuguese at the University of Texas at Austin. He is author of a number of books including *La schiavitù nera nell'America spagnola* (2018), *Afro-Peruvian Spanish* (2015), and *The Afro-Bolivian Spanish Determiner Phrase* (2014).

Cambridge Approaches to Language Contact

Founding Editor
SALIKOKO S. MUFWENE, *University of Chicago*

Co-Editor
ANA DEUMERT, *University of Cape Town*

Editorial Board
ROBERT CHAUDENSON, *Université d'Aix-en-Provence*
BRAJ KACHRU, *University of Illinois at Urbana*
RAJ MESTHRIE, *University of Cape Town*
LESLEY MILROY, *University of Michigan*
SHANA POPLACK, *University of Ottawa*
MICHAEL SILVERSTEIN, *University of Chicago*

Cambridge Approaches to Language Contact is an interdisciplinary series bringing together work on language contact from a diverse range of research areas. The series focuses on key topics in the study of contact between languages or dialects, including the development of pidgins and creoles, language evolution and change, world Englishes, code-switching and code-mixing, bilingualism and second language acquisition, borrowing, interference, and convergence phenomena.

Published titles:
Salikoko Mufwene, *The Ecology of Language Evolution*
Michael Clyne, *Dynamics of Language Contact*
Bernd Heine and Tania Kuteva, *Language Contact and Grammatical Change*
Edgar W. Schneider, *Postcolonial English*
Virginia Yip and Stephen Matthews, *The Bilingual Child*
Bernd Heine and Derek Nurse (eds.), *A Linguistic Geography of Africa*
J. Clancy Clements, *The Linguistic Legacy of Spanish and Portuguese*
Umberto Ansaldo, *Contact Languages*
Jan Blommaert, *The Sociolinguistics of Globalization*
Carmen Silva-Corvalán, *Bilingual Language Acquisition*
Lotfi Sayahi, *Diglossia and Language Contact*
Emanuel J. Drechsel, *Language Contact in the Early Colonial Pacific*
Enoch Oladé Aboh, *The Emergence of Hybrid Grammars*
Zhiming Bao, *The Making of Vernacular Singapore English*
Braj B. Kachru, *World Englishes and Culture Wars*
Bridget Drinka, *Language Contact in Europe: The Periphrastic Perfect through History*
Salikoko Mufwene, Chistophe Coupé, and François Pellegrino (eds.), *Linguistic Ecology and Language Contact*
Ralph Ludwig, Peter Mühlhäusler, and Steve Pagel (eds.), *Linguistic Ecology and Language Contact*
Sandro Sessarego, *Language Contact and the Making of an Afro-Hispanic Vernacular: Variation and Change in the Columbian Chocó*

Further titles planned for the series:
Rakesh Bhatt, *Language Contact and Diaspora*
Gregory D. S. Anderson, *Language Extinction*
Ellen Hurst and Rajend Mesthrie (eds.), *Youth Language Varieties in Africa*
Cecile Vigouroux, *Migration, Economy, and Language Practice*
Agnes He, *The Voice of Immigration: Transcultural Communication and Language Shift*
Yaron Matras and Leonie Geiser, *Reading the Linguistic Landscape: An Ecology of Practices in the Multilingual City*

Language Contact and the Making of an Afro-Hispanic Vernacular

Variation and Change in the Colombian Chocó

Sandro Sessarego
University of Texas at Austin

CAMBRIDGE
UNIVERSITY PRESS

University Printing House, Cambridge CB2 8BS, United Kingdom

One Liberty Plaza, 20th Floor, New York, NY 10006, USA

477 Williamstown Road, Port Melbourne, VIC 3207, Australia

314-321, 3rd Floor, Plot 3, Splendor Forum, Jasola District Centre, New Delhi - 110025, India

103 Penang Road, #05-06/07, Visioncrest Commercial, Singapore 238467

Cambridge University Press is part of the University of Cambridge.

It furthers the University's mission by disseminating knowledge in the pursuit of education, learning and research at the highest international levels of excellence.

www.cambridge.org
Information on this title: www.cambridge.org/9781108724777
DOI: 10.1017/9781108661782

© Sandro Sessarego 2019

This publication is in copyright. Subject to statutory exception and to the provisions of relevant collective licensing agreements, no reproduction of any part may take place without the written permission of Cambridge University Press.

First published 2019
First paperback edition 2022

A catalogue record for this publication is available from the British Library

Library of Congress Cataloging in Publication data
Names: Sessarego, Sandro, author.
Title: Language contact and the making of an Afro-Hispanic vernacular : variation and change in the Colombian Choco / Sandro Sessarego.
Description: New York, NY: Cambridge University Press, 2019. | Series: Cambridge approaches to language contact | Includes bibliographical references and index.
Identifiers: LCCN 2019019726 | ISBN 9781108485814 (hardback)
Subjects: LCSH: Choco languages. | Creole dialects, Spanish – Colombia – Chocó. | Languages in contact – Colombia. | BISAC: FOREIGN LANGUAGE STUDY / General.
Classification: LCC PM5817 .C4 S47 2019 | DDC 306.44/60986151–dc23
LC record available at https://lccn.loc.gov/2019019726

ISBN 978-1-108-48581-4 Hardback
ISBN 978-1-108-72477-7 Paperback

Cambridge University Press has no responsibility for the persistence or accuracy of URLs for external or third-party internet websites referred to in this publication, and does not guarantee that any content on such websites is, or will remain, accurate or appropriate.

Per Strufulgin

Contents

List of Figures	*page* xi
List of Tables	xii
List of Maps	xiii
Series Editor's Foreword	xv
Acknowledgments	xvii

1 Introduction — 1
- 1.1 Why This Book? — 1
- 1.2 Methodology — 4
- 1.3 The Book's Structure — 5

2 The Place of Chocó Spanish in the Spanish Creole Debate — 7
- 2.1 Introduction — 7
- 2.2 Granda's Monogenesis-Decreolization Hypothesis — 10
- 2.3 The Missing Spanish Creoles — 38
- 2.4 Chocó Spanish as a Testing Ground for the Legal Hypothesis of Creole Genesis — 44
- 2.5 A Note on the Importance of Chocó to the Field of Creole Studies — 47

3 A Sketch of Chocó Spanish — 49
- 3.1 Introduction — 49
- 3.2 The Dialects of Colombia — 49
- 3.3 The Phonetics and Phonology of Chocó Spanish — 52
- 3.4 Chocó Spanish Morphosyntax — 74
- 3.5 Some Observations on the Status of Chocó Spanish Grammar — 99

4 Roots of Some Languages — 103
- 4.1 Introduction — 103
- 4.2 Afro-Hispanic Languages at the Linguistic Interfaces — 106
- 4.3 Bare Nouns — 108
- 4.4 Nominal and Verbal Morphology — 110
- 4.5 Overt Subject Pronouns and Subject-verb Inversion in Questions — 114
- 4.6 Prosodic Features — 121
- 4.7 Interface Phenomena at the Root of Chocó Spanish's Origin — 125

5 Black Slavery in the Pacific Lowlands of Colombia 127
5.1 Introduction 127
5.2 The Conquest of the Region (1500–1680) 128
5.3 *Cuadrillas* in Popayán c. 1680s 131
5.4 The Mineral Exploitation (1680–1851) 137
5.5 The End of Slavery and Underdevelopment in Present-day Chocó 146
5.6 Remarks on the Nature of Chocó Spanish in Relation to Its History 146

6 Testing the Legal Hypothesis of Creole Genesis on Colonial Chocó 149
6.1 Introduction 149
6.2 Key Aspects of the Legal Hypothesis of Creole Genesis 150
6.3 Slavery in Rome 151
6.4 A Comparative Analysis of Slave Law in the Americas 152
6.5 Spanish Slave Law during the Eighteenth Century 161
6.6 *Instrucción Sobre Educación, Trato, y Ocupaciones de los Esclavos* 164
6.7 The Development of the *Coartación* Institute 171
6.8 Law in Books versus Law in Action 174
6.9 The Colombian Case 183
6.10 Focus on Colonial Chocó 185

7 Final Considerations 190

Appendix 194
References 210
Index 229

Figures

2.1	Cover of *De Instauranda Aethiopum Salute*	page 12
2.2	Cover of Granda's (1977) book	27
3.1	Sample F0 contours from Chocó Spanish data for *Ya tenemos doce años* (We are already twelve years old)	70
3.2	Sample F0 contours from Afro-Bolivian Spanish data for *El patrón no sirve para nada* (The owner is useless)	71
3.3	Sample F0 contours from Chota Valley Spanish data for *Ese sango de dulce puesto canela* ([In] this sango dessert I put cinnamon)	71
4.1	Sample F0 contours from Afro-Bolivian Spanish data for *Ha vivido muchos años ese* (That guy has lived many years)	104
4.2	Sample F0 contours from Chocó Spanish data for *Porqué ya no da manera ... tengo propiedad* (Because there is no way ... I own property)	105
4.3	Jackendoff's language faculty architecture	107
4.4	Sample F0 contours from Afro-Bolivian Spanish data for *Yo siempre más harto que todos ellos* (I am always much more than all of them)	122
4.5	Sample F0 contours from Afro-Bolivian Spanish data for *Después había que hacer camani* (Later one had to do work)	123
4.6	Sample F0 contours from Chocó Spanish data for *Cayó la primer bomba en el río Támbora* (The first bomb fell in the Támbora River)	124
6.1	Cover of *Instrucción sobre educación, trato y ocupaciones de los esclavos*	165

Tables

2.1	Granda's (1968) monogenetic features	page 14
3.1	Main phonetic and phonological traits of Chocó Spanish	72
3.2	Main morphosyntactic traits of Chocó Spanish	100
4.1	Five commonly reported Afro-Hispanic features traditionally ascribed to a previous creole stage	104
4.2	Five commonly reported Chocó Spanish features traditionally ascribed to a previous creole stage	105
5.1	Composition of Don Antonio de Veroiz's *cuadrilla* in 1694 (Cantor 2000: 48)	130
5.2	Percentage of slaves sold in Popayán with respect to Cartagena's sales (Colmenares 1979: 56)	138
5.3	Slaves sold in Popayán 1690–1789 (% according to their age) (Colmenares 1979: 36)	138
5.4	Chocó population 1636–1856 (Sharp 1976: 199)	144
5.5	Black population in the Chocó, 1704–1843 (West 1957: 100)	145
6.1	African slave importations to European colonies in the Americas	161

Maps

1.1	Overhead view of the Department of Chocó, Colombia (shaded area)	*page* 2
2.1	The Afro-Hispanic linguistic areas reported by Schwegler (1999: 241)	16
2.2	Hispanic and Lusophone varieties presenting postverbal negation and potential routes of diffusion (Schwegler 1991a: 64)	26
3.1	Dialectal map of the Pacific lowlands of Colombia (Granda 1977: 40)	61
5.1	Slave trade route to Popayán	134

Series Editor's Foreword

The Cambridge Approaches to Language Contact (CALC) series was set up to publish outstanding monographs on language contact, especially by authors who approach their specific subject matter from a diachronic or developmental perspective. Our goal is to integrate the ever-growing scholarship on language diversification (including the development of creoles, pidgins, and indigenized varieties of colonial European languages), bilingual language development, code-switching, and language endangerment. We hope to provide a select forum to scholars who contribute insightfully to understanding language evolution from an interdisciplinary perspective. We favor approaches that highlight the role of ecology and draw inspiration both from the authors' own fields of specialization and from related research areas in linguistics or other disciplines. Eclecticism is one of our mottoes, as we endeavor to comprehend the complexity of evolutionary processes associated with contact.

We are proud to add to our list Sandro Sessarego's *Language Contact and the Making of an Afro-Hispanic Vernacular: Variation and Change in the Colombian Chocó*. In this book, the author "combines linguistic, sociohistorical, legal, and anthropological perspectives to shed light on Chocó Spanish (CS), an Afro-Hispanic language spoken by the descendants of enslaved Africans brought to the Colombian Department of Chocó during the colonial period to work in the rich gold mines."

Of all the Afro-Hispanic language varieties of the Americas, CS is one of the most enigmatic ones. Offhand, it is spoken in a region that appears to be the perfect colonial context for the emergence of a creole. It has been claimed to have reunited a high disproportion of Africans to Europeans, harsh slave labor conditions, a population growth driven more by massive introduction of Bozal slaves than by birth, and limited interactions with heritage Spanish speakers. Yet, it provides evidence of no drastic divergence from other colonial, non-creole Spanish vernaculars.

Traditional accounts of this evolution of colonial Spanish have invoked "decreolization" or claimed that CS is the logical outcome of language without an African pidgin ancestor. Sessarego rejects them in favor of what he calls the Legal Hypothesis of Creole Genesis (LHCG). According to this, the fact that the enslaved Africans in Spanish colonies were protected by laws that treated them as integral members of the colonial populations disfavored the emergence of a creole vernacular. Varieties such as Palenquero are exceptions that confirm the rule, because they emerged in contact ecologies in which the Spanish colonial world order did not apply. More specifically, Sessarego argues that there is "a common element, which was shared by all the Spanish colonies but was absent from other European colonies of especially the Americas": the enslaved Africans had a legal personality that granted them rights to not be abused, to own property, to maintain a family, and to receive Christian education. That is, Spanish American colonies had a population structure that was less segregationist and more culturally assimilationist than other European settlement colonies, which made it easier for the enslaved Africans to learn Spanish without extensive divergence from the lexifier.

This study shows how structural features of CS align with those attested across a number of other Hispanic American vernaculars. All the so-called "creole-like" elements of CS can actually be explained as common SLA features related to processability constraints at the core of linguistic interface processes. The Chocó region apparently never received massive importation of African-born slaves. The *Bozales* and the majority of the Blacks that worked in the mines were *Criollo*, locally born, captives, who, in all likelihood, must have spoken vernacular Spanish varieties. In addition, "due to the pragmatic management implemented by the local *administradores de minas*, manumission was common practice." Combined with the above factors relevant to the LHCG, the latter favored closer, or less divergent, approximations of heritage vernacular Spanish by the *Bozales*.

The sociohistorical evidence presented in this book suggests that slavery was implemented differently in Spanish American colonies than in other European settlement colonies. Spanish colonial rule apparently fostered more cultural, including linguistic, assimilation, which prevented the formation of creoles. An important strength of this book lies in how the author combines legalistic and sociohistorical approaches to help us understand why, in general, Spanish settlement colonies did not produce creoles, unlike especially their Dutch, English, and French counterparts. It definitely provides more food for thought regarding variation in the ecologies of the transmission of European languages in European settlement colonies that used slave labor.

SALIKOKO S. MUFWENE
Founding Editor, CALC

Acknowledgments

This study would not have been possible without the support of several people and institutions. I owe my gratitude to all of them. I wish to thank all the people who helped me during my fieldwork in Chocó in the winter of 2014–2015: informants and assistants. In particular, I owe my gratitude to Professor Alejandro Correa (Caro y Cuervo), who introduced me to some of his former students currently living in Quibdó, the capital city of the Department of Chocó: Yadira Murillo Valencia, Rocío Urrego Salazar and Wilson Mena. Without their support and experience in the region, it would have been almost impossible to carry out sociolinguistic interviews in certain not-completely-safe villages in the proximity of Quibdó. My gratitude also goes to Linda Rodríguez Tocarruncho, who had researched Chocó Spanish several years ago for her Masters' thesis and with whom I had exciting conversations concerning the language and culture of the inhabitants of this region.

I am obviously also indebted to Professor Armin Schwegler (University of California, Irvine), Professor Bettina Migge (University College Dublin), and Professor David Korfhagen (University of Virginia), who have commented on different drafts of this book and/or on other studies related to Chocó Spanish.

Special thanks go to all the institutions that have supported my research during the past few years. I wish to thank the University of Texas at Austin (UT), the Freiburg Institute for Advanced Studies (FRIAS), and the Helsinki Collegium for Advanced Studies (HCAS). My research has especially benefited from the following support: UT Research Grant, UT Summer Research Assignment, UT College Research Fellowship, UT Humanities Research Award, two UT Supplemental Research Fellowships, Marie Skłodowska-Curie FRIAS COFUND Junior Fellowship and HCAS Core Fellowship. Some of the ideas developed in this study have also been enriched by the feedback provided by a number of academic journals in which I have published studies related to this contact variety. In particular, I should thank the anonymous reviewers of *Diachronica*, *Lingua*, *Language Ecology*, and the *Journal of Pidgin and Creole Languages*.

Last but not least, I would like to thank Professor Salikoko Mufwene (University of Chicago), Ana Deumert (University of Western Cape Town), Helen Barton and all the Cambridge University Press team for their help and professionalism during all the steps of this publication process. Thank you!

1 Introduction

1.1 Why This Book?

Of all the Afro-Hispanic languages of the Americas (AHLAs), the one that more than any other has puzzled linguists interested in the origin and evolution of these contact varieties is definitively Chocó Spanish (CS) (McWhorter 2000; Lipski 2005). CS is the dialect spoken by the inhabitants of the Department of Chocó (Map 1.1), Colombia, a region where blacks represent more than 90 percent of today's total population (DANE 2005) and consist of the descendants of the slaves taken to this region during colonial times to work the rich gold mines of the area.

Even though CS presents certain morphological and phonological reductions, the grammatical restructuring encountered in this language is not as intense as the one found in Palenquero, a Spanish creole spoken in San Basilio de Palenque, Department of Bolívar (Colombia) or in the many other European-based creoles spoken in the Americas (Jamaican English, Haitian French, etc.). At first glance, this may appear a bit surprising, since the conditions that have generally been held to be responsible for the creolization of other European languages in the Americas appear to have also been in place in colonial Chocó, namely: (a) a high number of African-born slaves proceeding from all over the Western African coast, (b) a huge disproportion of blacks-to-whites, (c) extreme working conditions in gold mines, (d) a difficult-to-access region, isolated from the rest of Spanish-speaking Colombia (McWhorter 2000: 9).

Indeed, it is well known that colonial Chocó became an important mining center during the eighteenth century, when thousands of black slaves were introduced into the region to carry out forced labor (Sharp 1976; Colmenares 1979). Moreover, only a much-reduced number of Spaniards settled the Department, so that the ratio of blacks to whites has always been quite high. For example, in 1782 there were some 340 whites residing in this district, who represented about 2 percent of the total population (Sharp 1976: 19). For these reasons, CS has captured the attention of a number of scholars who have tried to

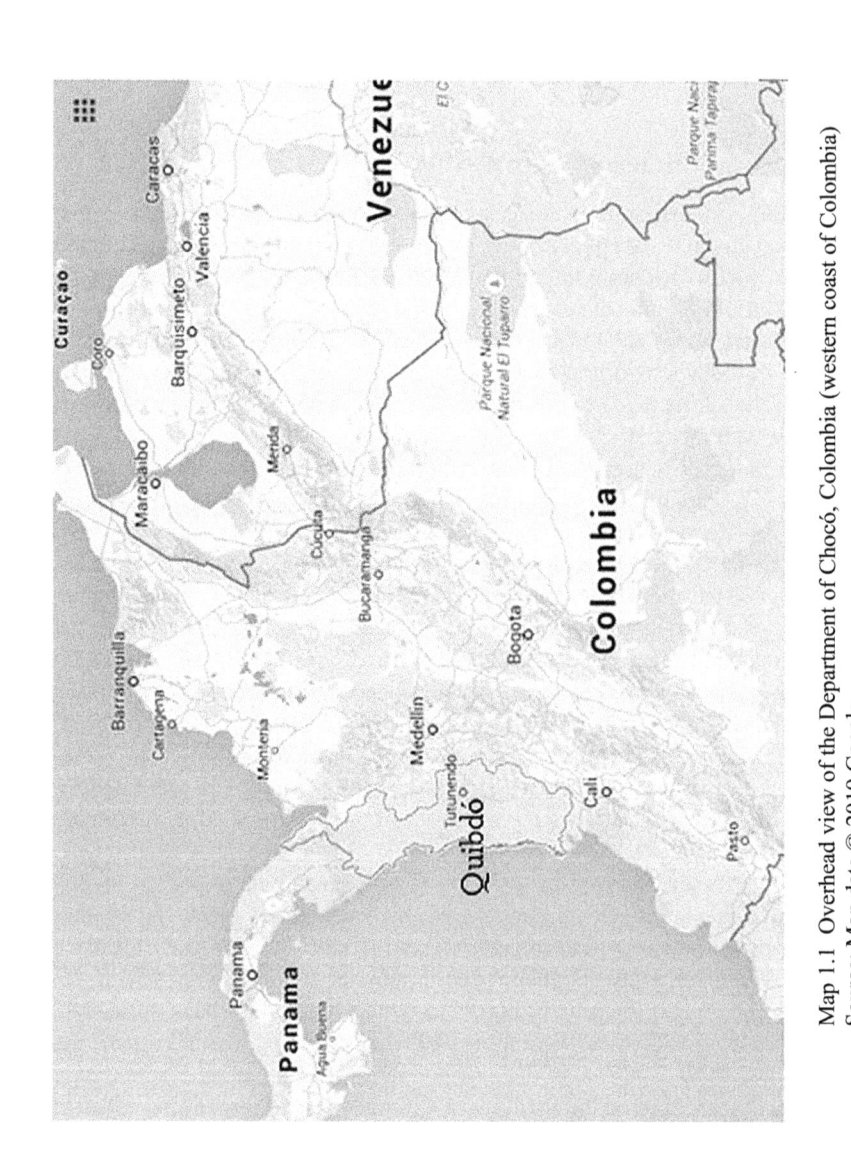

Map 1.1 Overhead view of the Department of Chocó, Colombia (western coast of Colombia)
Source: Map data © 2019 Google.

1.1 Why This Book?

account for its nature by offering different hypotheses on its evolution and the development of other Afro-European contact varieties in the Americas.

McWhorter (2000: ch.2), for example, in line with his Afrogenesis Hypothesis of creole formation, claims that the sociohistorical conditions for a creole to emerge were well in place in colonial Chocó, but due to the fact that a Spanish pidgin was not introduced into the Americas from western Africa, the linguistic bases for the development of a full-fledged creole language would have been missing in the Colombian Pacific lowlands, and in the rest of the Spanish colonies overseas. On the other hand, Granda (1977) and Schwegler (1991a, 1991b) indicate that a creole language may have existed in colonial Chocó, as well as in several other Latin American Spanish colonies, and that it would have subsequently decreolized due to more recent contact with standard varieties of Spanish. They suggest that several of today's AHLAs probably went through the same decreolizing path, and that they would have initially derived from one Portuguese-based pidgin/creole, originally formed in Africa and subsequently taken to the Americas.

Besides providing considerable ground for hypotheses on the genesis and evolution of Afro-European languages, CS also has much to offer to linguistic theory. In fact, some common features that have repeatedly been reported for CS (Ruiz García 2009; Rodríguez Tocarruncho 2010), and that in some cases have been identified as potential indicators of a previous creole stage for other AHLAs (Granda 1968 *et seq.*; Schwegler 1991a, 2014; etc.), represent deviations from standard Spanish that are extremely fascinating from a theoretical perspective (Sessarego 2012a), and testify to the instantiation in grammar of certain universal second-language acquisition processes, which appear to be at work in all cases of language contact (Sessarego 2013a, Sessarego & Rao 2016).

This project has two main goals. The first is to provide a linguistic description of CS, while the second is to assess the origin of this language and its implications for creole studies. The questions that this project addresses may be stated as follows: What are the main linguistic differences between CS and standard Spanish and what do they have to say about the nature of this and other AHLAs? What were the sociohistorical conditions in which CS formed? Was slavery in Chocó much different from slavery in other European colonies? How can we use this information to address current debates on the origin of other black communities in the Americas and the languages they speak?

There is plenty of research that has been carried out in other fields such as history and law, to which, so far, not much attention has been paid by linguists. In recent decades, some attempts to combine historical and linguistic data to cast light on the origin of certain AHLAs have been carried out for the Caribbean and the Andean Highlands (Mintz 1971; Laurence 1974; Díaz-Campos & Clements 2008; Clements 2009; Sessarego 2011a, 2011b, 2013b,

2013c, 2013d, 2014a, 2014b, 2014c, 2015a). Nevertheless, for the Colombian Pacific lowlands almost no research of this type has ever been done. This study explores the historical and linguistic evidence available for CS and challenges the traditional posture that would picture colonial Chocó as the perfect place for a Spanish creole to develop.

Findings indicate that the long-assumed creolizing conditions for CS might not have been in place in colonial Chocó and that the grammar of this language can be better analyzed as the result of advanced second-language acquisition processes, which do not necessarily imply any previous creole stage (Sessarego 2013a). In addition, this work provides an analysis of the evolution of CS in relation to the recently-proposed Legal Hypothesis of Creole Genesis (LHCG) (Sessarego 2015a, 2017a). In so doing, this study tests to what extent such a hypothesis makes valid predictions for a dialect like CS, which developed in a region described by many as "remote" and "on the frontier" (Whitten 1974; Sharp 1976), thus far away from legal courts and where the law was not likely to be properly enforced.

This project is meant to make a substantial advance in the frontier of knowledge of creole studies by laying down the foundations of a new, more cohesive, and interdisciplinary research program at the interface of linguistics, legal history, and colonial studies. It is primarily focused on CS and the other AHLAs, but its findings can be easily generalized, applied, and tested to other contact languages and settings. Thus, this will enable future researchers to better address current debates on the origins of other black communities in the Americas and the languages they speak.

1.2 Methodology

Linguistic data were collected during the winter of 2014–2015 in the capital city of Quibdó and in its surrounding areas. In particular, fieldwork was conducted in the village of Villa España, a recently built refugee camp hosting thousands of Chocoanos who escaped from guerrilla warfare taking place in both the northern and southern provinces of the Department. Given the very violent climate in Chocó at the time of my visit, it was not possible to travel across the Department to carry out fieldwork in other areas. Nevertheless, since the people interviewed in Quibdó and in Villa España came from a variety of locations (namely, Istmina, Condoto, Nóvita, Cértegui, Sipi, Opogadó, Iró, San Juan, and Río Sucio), the collected data may be taken as representative of the overall regional dialect. All of the informants were native speakers of their own CS variety and did not speak any other language spoken in the region, such as Emberá.

Sociolinguistic interviews were carried out with forty-five speakers of different ages (ranging from 19 to 95 years old) and levels of education (ranging from illiterate people to members of the community holding a college degree). Findings indicate – as expected – that the oldest and least educated informants use a variety that is quite rich in stigmatized features, while the youngest and most educated Chocoanos use more standard forms. Nevertheless, while research on other Afro-Hispanic dialects has shown that, even in rural communities, the youngest generations shifted almost completely to their respective regional standard varieties (see, for example, Sessarego 2013b, 2014a, 2015a for Ecuador, Bolivia, and Peru), in the case of CS, it is still possible to observe young speakers proceeding from rural areas who show morphosyntactic features remarkably divergent from what would be classified as "standard" Colombian Spanish.

This book not only presents linguistic data from CS. In fact, the linguistic information collected during the aforementioned fieldwork is here compared and contrasted with data proceeding from other studies, in particular with those analyzing other Afro-Hispanic varieties. In this way, it has been made possible to offer a perspective on where CS stands with respect to similar contact vernaculars. This investigation is also based on secondary literature on colonial history and law, which helped provide a broader and more comprehensive picture of the social background in which CS developed.

1.3 The Book's Structure

This book consists of seven chapters. Chapter 1 is the introduction to this work; it describes its objectives, methodology, and structure. Chapter 2 offers an analysis of the so-called "Spanish creole debate" (Lipski 2005: ch.9), or the pull of different models that have been suggested in the literature to explain the paucity of Spanish-based creoles in the Americas. In so doing, it situates CS within such a context and illustrates the hypotheses that have been proposed to account for the development of this Afro-Hispanic dialect. Chapter 3 provides a sketch of CS grammar. Chapter 4 consists of an analysis of the linguistic features shared by CS and several other AHLAs. It shows that a number of the grammatical elements found in these contact varieties can be conceived as the traces of advanced second-language acquisition strategies, which do not necessarily imply a previous creole stage – contrary to what has been traditionally indicated in the literature. Such phenomena, in fact, impose high processing demands on the linguistic interfaces (Sessarego 2013a; Sessarego & Rao 2016; Rao & Sessarego 2016, 2018; Romero & Sessarego 2018; Sessarego & Gutiérrez-Rexach 2018); thus, they tend to result in non-target-like constructions, commonly found in advanced interlanguages. Chapter 5 is a sociohistorical analysis of slavery in Chocó. It presents a variety of legal, economic, and demographic aspects of blacks' lives in colonial Chocó to show how certain social factors shaped CS grammar. Chapter 6 provides a new analysis on the evolution of CS in relation to the recently-proposed LHCG, which ascribes a prime importance in the development of Afro-European languages in the Americas to the legal evolution of slavery from the Roman times to the different colonial settings implemented by the Europeans in the "New World" (Sessarego 2015a, 2017a). In so doing, the chapter tests the validity of the LHCG for an isolated region like Chocó, where legal courts have never been present during the colonial period. Finally, Chapter 7 summarizes the content of the book and provides the conclusions.

2 The Place of Chocó Spanish in the Spanish Creole Debate

2.1 Introduction

For more than four decades now, scholars interested in the origin and evolution of Afro-European contact languages in the Americas have tried to figure out why Spanish creoles are only spoken in two very circumscribed regions of Latin America, in contrast to the much more widespread use of their English- and French-based varieties. In fact, it is a well-known fact that contemporary Latin American Spanish creoles can only be found in the former maroon community of San Basilio de Palenque (Colombia) – where Palenquero is spoken – and in the so-called ABC-triangle, the Caribbean islands of Aruba, Bonaire, and Curaçao (Netherlands Antilles), where Papiamentu is used.

If we consider that Spain was the European country that "discovered" the "New World" and that became one among the most influential powers in the colonization of the Americas, it may appear somehow surprising to observe that Spanish creoles are so reduced in number and size. Moreover, according to some scholars (Goodman 1987; Schwegler 1993; McWhorter 2000; Jacobs 2012; among others), Papiamentu and Palenquero should only be classified as Spanish creoles in a strictly synchronic sense, since – in their view – these languages most likely started as Portuguese creoles and only in a subsequent phase went through a process of Spanish relexification.

The relative paucity of Spanish creoles in the Americas has captured the attention of several researchers, who proposed a number of models to account for this state of affairs. The pull of different views on this issue has been labeled in the literature as the "Spanish creole debate" (Lipski 2005: ch.9). One early attempt to provide an analysis of the given facts is the hypothesis initially postulated by Granda (1968, 1970), and subsequently supported by a number of followers (Otheguy 1973; Megenney 1984a, 1984b, 1985, 1990, 1993; Schwegler 1991a, 1991b; Perl 1982, 1985, 1998; etc.). According to these authors, a once-widespread Afro-Iberian creole used to be spoken by the black communities of colonial Spanish America. This language would have derived from one single Portuguese-based creole (Monogenesis Hypothesis), which originally developed around the fifteenth century from the early contacts between the Portuguese merchants and the African groups found across the Western African coast. This hypothetical Pan-American creole would have approximated to Spanish over time (Decreolization Hypothesis), due to the pressure exerted by the standard norm and the stigmatization of this black vernacular. For this reason, according to the supporters of what may be called "the Monogenesis-Decreolization Hypothesis," besides Papiamentu and Palenquero, which preserved most of the original Portuguese-creole structure, all the remaining Afro-Hispanic varieties of the Americas would have converged towards Spanish to the point of presenting today only a few creole-like features. According to these scholars, such grammatical elements, which can also be found in colonial literary texts depicting black speech, represent a key piece of evidence in support of the monogenetic model, since their parallel existence in these black communities scattered across the Americas would be very difficult to explain in terms of independent developments (Schwegler 1991a: 77).

This early attempt to account for the current paucity of Spanish creoles has faced some criticism. Some researchers, in fact, have objected that due to a concomitance of historical factors, the Spanish Caribbean differed quite significantly from the English and the French Antilles, such that the demographic and socioeconomic conditions in colonial times would not have been ripe for Spanish creolization to take place in Cuba, Puerto Rico, and the Dominican Republic (Mintz 1971; Laurence 1974; Lipski 1986, 1994a; Chaudenson 2001; Clements 2009). For these reasons, the grammatical features attested in the colonial Spanish Caribbean for the speech of *bozales* (black captives born in Africa, who did not speak Spanish natively) should not be taken as evidence of a Pan-American Afro-Iberian creole, but rather as the traces of non-target-like, substrate-driven, learning strategies, "which arose spontaneously each time Spanish and African languages came into contact" (Lipski 1986: 171).

McWhorter (1997, 2000) acknowledges that the Spanish Antilles, especially before the sugar boom of the nineteenth century, did not present the conditions that have traditionally been considered to enable creole formation. However, he claims that in the mainland Spanish colonies, and particularly, in Veracruz (Mexico), Chincha (Peru), Chota Valley (Ecuador), coastal Venezuela, and Chocó (Colombia), the conditions for creole formation obtained, but yet Spanish creoles did not develop (2000: ch.2). In his view, the reason why this did not happen should not be sought in the Americas but rather on the other side of the ocean, in Africa, from where captives were shipped to the New World. McWhorter (2000) believes that the creole languages spoken today in the Americas developed out of the pidgins that formed on the Western African coasts from the contacts between European traders and the Africans involved in the slave trade (Afrogenesis Hypothesis). According to this model, the real

2.1 Introduction

cause behind the non-creolization of Spanish in the Americas would be that Spain, unlike the other European powers involved in the colonization of the New World, did not trade directly in African slaves, such that a Spanish pidgin never developed in Africa and, as a result, a Spanish creole could not possibly form in the Americas.

The Afrogenesis Hypothesis has also faced some opposition. Several authors, after taking a closer look at the regions described by McWhorter (2000: 7) as "canonical breeding grounds" for creole formation, have concluded that the sociohistorical conditions postulated by McWhorter were probably not in place in colonial times (see Díaz-Campos & Clements 2005, 2008 for Venezuela; Sessarego 2013b, 2013d, 2014b for Ecuador; Sessarego 2014c, 2015a for Peru). Nevertheless, besides this criticism, McWhorter's proposal has been generally prized for providing a unified account for all the Afro-Hispanic dialects of the Americas (Schwegler 2002: 121; Lipski 2005: 286).

Along these lines of reasoning, in recent works (Sessarego 2015a, 2017a) I have proposed a new hypothesis, which follows a common thread among all these varieties. I called it the "Legal Hypothesis of Creole Genesis" (LHCG). This proposal focuses on an aspect of the European colonial enterprise in the Americas that has never been closely analyzed in relation to the evolution of Afro-European contact varieties, the legal regulations of black slavery. The LHCG ascribes a prime importance to the historical evolution of slavery in the development of Afro-European languages in the Americas, from the legal rules contained in the Roman *Corpus Juris Civilis* to the codes and regulations implemented in the different European colonies overseas. Findings suggest that according to Spanish slavery, in contrast to any other system, slaves were legal persons and not mere "mobile chattel," as in Roman law. The presence of legal personality implied a corollary of rights for the Spanish captives, which were unknown or highly restricted for the slaves living in the colonies of other European nations. This factor, I claim, played a key role in the evolution of Afro-European relations in the New World, and consequently shaped the languages that developed from such a contact. A foreseeable critique of the LHCG regards the extent to which, in colonial time, "law in books" (what was stated in the legal rules) corresponded to "law in action" (the practical application of such rules to a specific social context) (Pound 1910), especially when such regulations concerned slaves living in remote plantations or mines, far away from legal courts and urban centers. Colonial Chocó represents the perfect place to test the LHCG against potential criticism of this sort, since it was a remote region, which never hosted either big cities or legal courts during the colonial period, and where formal legal rules could hardly be implemented by government's authorities (Whitten 1974; Sharp 1976).

10   The Place of Chocó Spanish in the Spanish Creole Debate

The current chapter will provide an overall analysis of the state of affairs concerning the Spanish creole debate by taking a closer look at the linguistic and historical evidence provided in support of, or against, the aforementioned hypotheses, all of which, in one way or another, acknowledge the relevance of Chocó as a region of fundamental importance to their respective models.

2.2   Granda's Monogenesis-Decreolization Hypothesis

Germán de Granda (1968, 1970, 1978a) was the first Hispanist to suggest a monogenetic connection among the Afro-Hispanic varieties of the Americas and the Portuguese-based creoles spoken in Africa. According to his view, an Afro-Portuguese pidgin would have formed in Africa between the fifteenth and sixteenth centuries from the contact of Portuguese traders, missionaries, and explorers and the local African populations (see also Thompson 1961; Valkhoff 1966). This early contact variety would have been exported to different regions of the world during a subsequent period of European colonial expansion, and only in a following phase would it have been relexified with the lexicon proceeding from the European languages spoken in the colonies (viz., French in Haiti, Spanish in Puerto Rico, English in Jamaica, etc.) (see also Whinnom 1965; Bailey 1965). Such a monogenetic evolution would be capable of accounting for the fact that a number of contact languages spoken in Asia, Africa, and in the Americas present similar linguistic features, a fact that could not be easily explained if such languages evolved independently, without sharing a common ancestor or proto-creole (Monogenetic Hypothesis) (Granda 1970). In addition, in Granda's view, the current paucity of Spanish creoles in the Americas should be conceived of as the result of a massive decreolization process, which supposedly took place in the nineteenth century after the abolition of slavery, when the Spanish creoles spoken in the black communities would have entered into closer contact with standard Spanish (Decreolization Hypothesis).

According to Granda (1978: 313), in fact, contrary to what has been suggested by some historians (Tannenbaum 1947; Klein 1967; Hoetink 1967), slavery in Spanish America was not that different from the forced-labor systems implemented by other European powers overseas. He provides four general working hypotheses, which would represent the foundation principles of his Afro-Hispanic research project (1978: 335):

a) Given the parallel social structures found in the Hispanic and non-Hispanic colonies, there is no reason to believe that Spanish creoles did not develop in Spanish America.
b) Spanish America must have had several Spanish creoles, which developed from a common Afro-Portuguese root.

2.2 Granda's Monogenesis-Decreolization Hypothesis

c) The majority of the Spanish creoles must have disappeared due to contact with standard Spanish in more recent times, after the abolition of slavery.

d) This decreolization process was not complete, so that some traces of such creole languages are left in the speech of black communities across the Americas.

He argues that – in line with the methods adopted in scientific research (Cohen & Nagel 1934) – these general hypothetical principles, in order to be valid, must find empirical support in the reality of the data. For this reason, on the one hand, there should be historical sources indicating the existence of such colonial creoles; while, on the other hand, linguistic traces of those contact varieties should be attested in the speech of contemporary Afro-Hispanic communities. Granda claims to have found both the historical and the linguistic evidence that would confirm his hypothesis.

As far as the historical data are concerned, he indicates that the well-known Jesuit treatise on slavery, *De Instauranda Aethiopum Salute* (Figure 2.1), written by Father Alonso de Sandoval between 1617 and 1619 and published in Sevilla in 1627, provides the evidence that would confirm the existence of a Portuguese-based creole language spoken by "masses of black slaves in Spanish America" (Granda 1970: 10). In particular, Granda (1970: 6) refers to a passage in Sandoval's (1627: 59–60) work where the Jesuit states:

And those that we call creoles and natives of São Tomé, due to the communication that they had with so many uncivilized nations during the period they lived in São Tomé, understand almost all varieties, with a sort of broken Portuguese that is known as the São Tomé language, so that now we can speak with all kinds of blacks with our corrupted Spanish, as it is usually spoken by all the blacks. (Author's translation)[1]

The aforementioned text, according to Granda, provides unequivocal evidence in favor of a once-widespread Afro-Iberian creole, originally formed on the Western African coast, and eventually spread across the Americas through the Portuguese slave trade (Granda 1970, 1978).

As for the linguistic proofs in support of his proposal, the author indicates that a cross-linguistic analysis of several Spanish- and Portuguese-based contact varieties spoken in the Caribbean and in Asia would clearly show that all of them share an Afro-Portuguese creole ancestor. Indeed, in his view, given the striking morphosyntactic similarities among Papiamentu, Palenquero, Puerto Rican Bozal Spanish, Macau creole Portuguese and the Spanish creoles of the

---

[1] Original version in Spanish: *Y los que llamamos criollos y naturales de San Thomé, con la comunicación que con tan bárbaras naciones han tenido al tiempo que han residido en San Thomé, las entienden casi todas con un género de lenguaje muy corrupto y revesado de la portuguesa que llaman lengua de San Thomé, al modo que ahora nosotros entendemos y hablamos con todo género de negros y naciones con nuestra lengua española corrupta, como comúnmente la hablan todos los negros.*

12   The Place of Chocó Spanish in the Spanish Creole Debate

Figure 2.1 Cover of *De Instauranda Aethiopum Salute*

2.2 Granda's Monogenesis-Decreolization Hypothesis

Philippines, the monogenesis account would be the only one capable of making sense of the data. Granda (1968: 202–3) states:

> The morphosyntactic similarities among languages so typologically different as Palenquero, Puerto-Rican-Spanish and Papiamentu 'Bozal' (with non-European, African, linguistic inputs), the 'creole' dialects of the Philippines (with Tagalog input) and Macau Creole (with non-European, Chinese, elements) do not lead to a coherent and uniform explanation of the parallel tendencies found in these non-European and extraordinarily different systems which, therefore, given their structurally-diverse bases, are incapable of producing such similar results as those that I have pointed out . . . . Nevertheless, it does not seem possible, as correctly indicated by Willam A. Stewart, Douglas Taylor, Albert Valdman, Jan Voorhove and Keith Whinnom, to find the independent evolution of the same simplifications in regions which are as geographically and culturally separated as Africa, Asia, America and Oceania. This fact would be as strange as the parallel invention of the same alphabetic system in multiple and distant geographic locations. (Author's translation)[2]

A summary of the features reported by Granda (1968: 195–201) as indicator of a previous Proto-Afro-Portuguese Creole ancestor is provided in Table 2.1.

2.2.1 Applying the Hypothesis to the Data

Even though in his 1968 study Granda did not include CS among the Afro-Hispanic varieties that would have been derived from this proto-Afro-Portuguese language, in several subsequent works he added this dialect to the list (e.g., Granda 1976: 20, 1978: 515, 1988a: 78, 1991: 112). In particular, he claimed that CS presents a morphosyntactic feature (double negation: *yo no como no* 'I do not eat'), which would be shared also by the Portuguese-based creoles spoken in São Tomé, Annobom, and Príncipe (Valkhoff 1966: 100). This grammatical element, which in his view would be compulsory in CS negative constructions and in the aforementioned creoles (Granda 1978: 517),

---

[2] Original version in Spanish: *La similitud de rasgos morfosintácticos entre modalidades lingüísticas como el palenquero, el habla 'Bozal' portorriqueña y el papiamento (con aportación no europea de tipo africano), los dialectos 'criollos' de Filipinas (con aportación tagala) y el macaísta (con elementos no europeos de origen chino) no permite apoyar una explicación coherente y totalizadora de sus tendencias paralelas en el influjo de estos sistemas lingüísticos no europeos extraordinariamente diferentes entre sí, por lo tanto, incapaces de producir partiendo de bases estructuralmente diversas, resultados tan similares como los que he constatado .... No parece, sin embargo, factible, como bien apuntan William A. Stewart, Douglas Taylor, Albert Valdmann, Jan Voorhove y Keith Whinnom, la producción independiente de procesos de simplificación, exactamente coincidentes, en ámbitos geográfica y socioculturalmente tan alejados como son África, Asia, América y Oceanía. Este hecho sería tan extraño como la invención paralela de un mismo sistema alfabético en múltiples y distantes puntos geográficos.*

Table 2.1 *Granda's (1968) monogenetic features*

Phenomenon	Examples [from Palenquero (Montes 1962)]	Contact languages reported by Granda as presenting similar phenomena
No plural marking on nouns	*Mucha gracia [muchas gracias]* 'thanks a lot'; *son mi sufrimienta [son mis sufrimientos]* 'they are my pains'	Palenquero, Papiamentu, Puerto Rican Bozal Spanish, Caviteño Spanish Creole, Zamboangueño Spanish Creole, Malayo Portuguese Creole, Macao Portuguese Creole
Invariable adjectives for gender and number features	*Mucho moka [muchas moscas]* 'many flies'; *luna ta muy claro [la luna está muy clara]* 'the moon is very bright'	Palenquero, Caviteño Spanish Creole, São Tomé Creole, Cape Verdian Creole, Macao Portuguese Creole
Single indefinite singular article *un*	*Un patada [una patada]* 'a kick'; *un batea [una batea]* 'a tray'	Palenquero, Puero Rican Bozal Spanish, Papiamentu, Caviteño Spanish Creole, Zamboangueño Spanish Creole
Vos as second person singular pronoun	*Bo comé [vos comés]* 'you eat'; *bo bailá [vos bailás]* 'you dance'	Palenquero, Papiamentu, Puerto Rican Bozal Spanish, Caviteño Spanish Creole, Zamboangueño Spanish Creole; Ermitaño Spanish Creole
Ele as third-person singular pronoun	*Ele comé [él/ella come]* 'he/she eat'; *ele bailá [él/ella baila]* 'he/she dance'	Palenquero, Caviteño Spanish Creole; Zamboangueño Spanish Creole
Elimination of syntactic linking elements (prepositions)	*Flo caña [flor de caña]* 'cane flower'; *planta mano [planta de la mano]* 'hand palm'	Palenquero, Papiamentu, Puerto Rican Bozal Spanish, Caviteño Spanish Creole, Macao Portuguese Creole
Use of *tener* 'to have' instead of *haber* 'to exist' to express existence	*Teneba cinco gende [había cinco personas]* 'there were five people'; *tiene un señora [había una señora]* 'there was a woman'	Palenquero, Caviteño Spanish Creole; Zamboangueño Spanish Creole
Constructions based on invariant *ta* + INFINITIVE to express present tense	*Aire tá quieto bué [el aire está quieto hoy]* 'the air is quiet today'; *pelo tá lairá [el perro está ladrando]* 'the dog is barking'	Palenquero, Papiamentu, Puerto Rican Bozal Spanish, Caviteño Spanish Creole; Zamboangueño Spanish Creole
Invariable forms for personal pronouns and possessive pronouns	*Miña cabeza ele [mira la cabeza de él]* 'look at his head'	Palenquero, Papiamentu, Caviteño Spanish Creole, Ermitaño Spanish Creole

2.2 Granda's Monogenesis-Decreolization Hypothesis

would be evidence of a *"estado criollo preexistente respecto a la modalidad actual de la lengua"* ('preexistent creole state with respect to the contemporary status of their language') (1978: 514).

Granda's Monogenesis-Decreolization Hypothesis has been embraced by several scholars, who reproposed it in different versions to account for the current status of a number of Afro-Hispanic dialects. One of the main advocates of this model is Armin Schwegler, who revisited Granda's hypothesis to propose a single Afro-Portuguese root for Palenquero (Colombia), Chota Valley Spanish (Ecuador), and nineteenth-century Caribbean Bozal Spanish (Schwegler 1999) (Map 2.1). In fact, the author departs from the original proposal that would ascribe a single Afro-Portuguese basis to all the transatlantic creoles (Schuchardt 1889; Voorhove 1953) and claims that, nevertheless, at least the three aforementioned varieties do share such a root (and more recently also Afro-Bolivian Spanish; Schwegler 2014). The linguistic evidence in support of this claim would be that these vernaculars, in Schwegler's (1999: 237) view, share a "deep" grammatical feature (viz., the Portuguese third-person subject pronoun *ele* 'he').

(1) Palenquero (Colombia):
 a. *Ele a-ta kumé ku ele.*
 he TMA eat with him
 He/she/it is eating with him/her.

 b. *Ele tan miní akí.* (archaic)
 they TMA come here
 'They will come here.'

(2) Chota (highland Ecuador):
 a. *Ele, él ta allí.*
 he he is there
 'He/she is there.'

 b. *¡Yo! con ele no fuera.*
 I with him no go
 'I! With him/her/it I would not go.'

 c. *Ele no les quiero dar.*
 him no to-them want give
 'I don't want to give it to him/her/it.'

(3) Bozal Spanish nineteenth century (Cuba/Puerto Rico):
 a. *Elle estaba en un mortorio.*
 they stay in a funeral
 'They were at a funeral.'

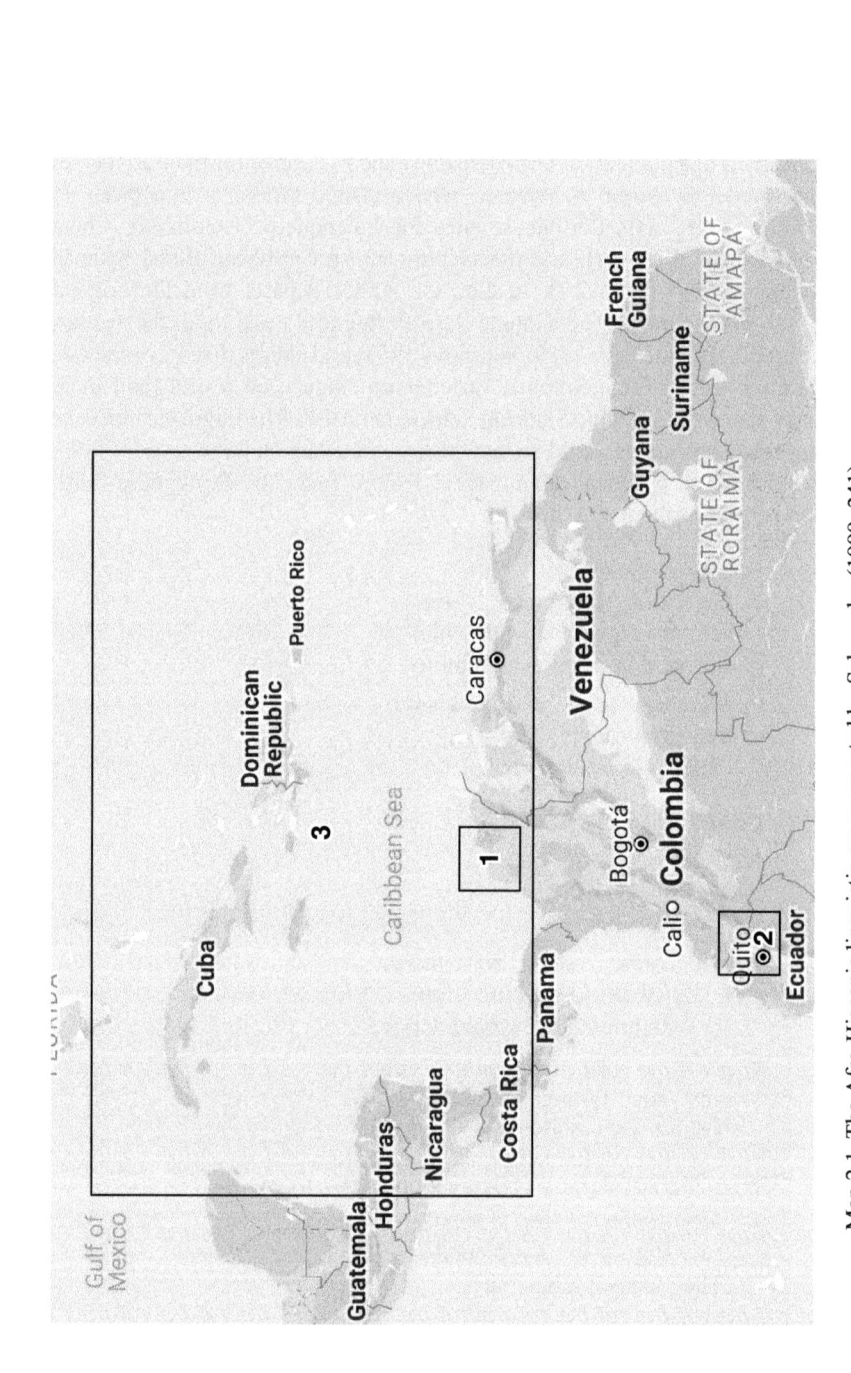

Map 2.1 The Afro-Hispanic linguistic areas reported by Schwegler (1999: 241)
①Palenquero; ②Chota Valley Spanish; ③Caribbean Bozal Spanish

2.2 Granda's Monogenesis-Decreolization Hypothesis

b. *Elle solito con su espá...*
   he   alone with his sword
   'He alone with his sword...'

Since structural elements of this kind would be hard to borrow through language contact, and since the Portuguese never really settled in Colombia, Ecuador, and the Caribbean, the presence of this Portuguese feature in three Afro-Hispanic varieties spoken across Latin America would represent "UNEQUIVOCAL evidence" (Schwegler 1999: 237) in support of the Monogenesis Hypothesis. In fact, according to Schwegler (1999: 252), this pronoun could not possibly have entered these dialects unless the slaves taken to these regions had a good command of the other functional and lexical domains of this supposed Proto-Afro-Portuguese Creole. In Schwegler's words, as he put it at a conference talk, this would be like finding a car on the moon and rejecting the idea that it arrived from the Earth (see also McWhorter 2000: 136–7; Schwegler 2014: 426; Rickford 2015: 36). In fact, according to the author's analysis, examples (1–3) provide clear evidence indicating that these three Afro-Hispanic varieties shared the same Afro-Portuguese ancestor. This would be the case since *ele* and *elle* could not possibly be related to Spanish *él/ella* 'he/she,' but must have been derived from Portuguese *ele* 'he.' To those who may consider this pronoun as the result of a paragogic process of final vowel insertion *él + e > ele* (quite common across the Afro-Hispanic world, according to Lipski 2005), he answers by indicating that *ele*, with a plural value in Palenquero, cannot possibly be explained on phonological grounds, through paragoge, which consists of a final vowel being inserted at the end of a given lexical item to create an open syllable, since Spanish *ellos/ellas* 'they' cannot lead to Palenquero *eles* 'they' (Schwegler 1999: 243–5). As for the origin of Cuba/Puerto Rico Bozal *elle*, Schwegler suggests that it would be the result of a "blend" between Afro-Portuguese *ele* and Span. *ella, ellos,* and *ellas* (1999: 250).

Moreover, in line with Granda (1976, 1978, 1991), Schwegler (1991a) also analyzes CS double negation as evidence of a clear link between this variety and a proto-Afro-Portuguese contact language. Nevertheless, he points out that Dominican Spanish (DS) also presents such a feature and provides a more detailed account of the sociolinguistic and pragmatic factors regulating its use in this dialect (see also Jiménez Sabater 1975: 170; Megenney 1990: 121–8; Lipski 1994b: 25–7; Ortiz López 2010: 181–212 for some considerations on DS double negation). In particular, he shows that in DS two different types of negation exist: a) the classic preverbal negation (NEG1), found in all Spanish dialects (see 4a); and b) double negation (NEG2), characterized by the co-occurrence of both a preverbal and a postverbal negator (see 4b)[3].

(4) Dominican Spanish

    a. *No   hablo   italiano.*
       no   speak   Italian
      'I do not speak Italian' (NEG1).

    b. *No   hablo   italiano   no.*
       no   speak   Italian   no
      'I do not speak Italian' (NEG2).

Schwegler (1991a: 33–47) shows that NEG1 and NEG2 in DS are not in free variation; rather, their use is significantly conditioned by sociolinguistic and pragmatic factors. As far as the sociolinguistic factors are concerned, NEG2 is more common in informal speech; it is most likely used by people without a college education, with reduced incomes, and living in rural areas (1991a: 48). Therefore, it may be said that NEG2 is almost unheard among the members of the upper class, so that NEG1 may be conceived as the only available negation form for the Dominican elite. Nevertheless, it would be a mistake to believe that NEG1 and NEG2 are two synonymous constructions used by two different social groups in categorical ways (viz., NEG1 for the upper class; NEG2 for the rest of society). On the contrary, while the upper class tends to use NEG1 almost exclusively, the rest of the Dominican social groups can express negation by recurring to both options (NEG1 and NEG2).

It is crucial to point out that NEG1 and NEG2, as used interchangeably by the Dominican lower and middle classes: NEG2 is felicitous only in those pragmatic contexts in which the speakers want to negate either an explicit or implicit presupposition held by the interlocutor. Thus, NEG1 can be uttered out of the blue, when a speaker just wants to express a negative statement, whereas NEG2 can only be used if certain pragmatic requirements are met. More specifically, speakers may resort to NEG2 if they want to negate something that the interlocutor has just said (explicit negation) or something that the interlocutor is probably thinking, even though it has not been uttered (implicit negation). Schwegler (1991a: 38) provides the following example to show how NEG2 is used in DS.

(5)   Situation: In the moment of entering an avocado orchard, the linguist Armin Schwegler (A.S.) and the Dominican speaker, J.M., have the following conversation:

---

[3] Schwegler (1991a: 61) also shows that NEG2 is not the only form of negation in CS, in contrast with Granda's (1978: 515) observations; rather, NEG2 alternates with NEG1 and would obey the same pragmatic principles applying in DS.

A.S. ¡Ahora sí vamos a comer aguacates! ¡Pero de los buenos!
      now   yes go   to eat   avocados but of the good
      'Now we will eat some avocados! Some good ones!'

J.M. ¡Aquí **no** hay [aguacates] **no**! No es la temporada. Solo hay a
      here no exist avocados   no no be the season   only exist to
      partir del   mes   próximo.
      begin of-the month next
      'There are no avocados! This is not the season. There will be beginning next month!'

In example (5) we can see how A.S.'s statement ¡Ahora sí vamos a comer aguacates! automatically implies the existence of avocados in the garden. The use of a NEG2 construction by J.M. would have two functions here: a) negating the fact that avocados are present in the garden, b) negating A.S.'s presupposition about the existence of such avocados. On the other hand, the use of NEG2 out of the blue, without the context introduced by A.S.'s exclamation, would have resulted in an infelicitous statement. Thus, while the use of NEG2 requires a presupposition background, the employment of NEG1 does not obey such a restriction and a single negation can appear in contexts where a specific presupposition is not in place, as illustrated in (6):

(6)   Situation: The speaker is walking down the street and suddenly remembers she forgot to turn off the stove:[4]
      ¡Caramba! ¡**No** he   apagado el fuego (#**no**)!
      damn   no   AUX   turn off the fire   no
      'Damn! I did not turn off the stove!'

After offering an account of the pragmatic factors regulating NEG1/NEG2 alternation in popular DS, Schwegler proceeds to provide a potential account for the origin of NEG2 and the genesis of Caribbean Spanish. He points out that such a construction is found in a variety of Afro-Iberian vernaculars in both Africa and the Americas; moreover, he highlights the fact that some of such varieties also present an additional form of negation (NEG3), characterized by a postverbal **no** (i.e., Brazilian Portuguese falo italiano **não** 'I do not speak Italian'). Examples (7–11) present parallel data for all the Afro-varieties directly investigated by Schwegler (1991a: 51–7) in relation to NEG2 and NEG3:

(7)   Brazilian Portuguese
      a. Não   falo   italiano.
         no   speak   Italian
         'I do not speak Italian' (NEG1).

---
[4] Example adapted from Schwenter (2005: 1434).

b. *Não falo italiano não.*
no speak Italian No
'I do not speak Italian' (NEG2).

c. *Falo italiano não.*
speak Italian No
'I do not speak Italian' (NEG3).

(8) Angolan Portuguese
a. *Não falo italiano.*
no speak Italian
'I do not speak Italian' (NEG1).

b. *Não falo italiano não.*
no speak Italian No
'I do not speak Italian' (NEG2).

(9) Chocó Spanish
a. *No hablo italiano.*
no speak Italian
'I do not speak Italian' (NEG1).

b. *No hablo italiano no.*
no speak Italian No
'I do not speak Italian' (NEG2).

c. *Hablo italiano no.*
speak Italian No
'I do not speak Italian' (NEG3).

(10) Cartagena Spanish
a. *No hablo italiano.*
no speak Italian
'I do not speak Italian' (NEG1).

b. *No hablo Italiano no.*
no speak Italian no
'I do not speak Italian' (NEG2).

(11) Palenquero
a. *Nu asé ablá italiano.*
no TMA speak Italian
'I do not speak Italian' (NEG1).

b. *Nu asé ablá italiano nu.*
no TMA speak Italian no
'I do not speak Italian' (NEG2).

2.2 Granda's Monogenesis-Decreolization Hypothesis

   c. *Asé   ablá   italiano   nu.*
      TMA   speak   Italian   no
      'I do not speak Italian' (NEG3).

In addition, the author reports second-hand data of postverbal negation for Cuban Bozal Spanish (12) and four Portuguese-based creoles spoken in Africa (13–16) (Schwegler 1991a: 56, 65–8).

(12)   Cuban Bozal speech (data provided by Lipski)

     a. *Yo   no   Bebe   guardiente [,]   no.*
        I   no   drink   aguardiente   no
        'I do not drink aguardiente' (Fernández 1987: 96).

     b. *El   Amo   no   quiere   matar   Eugenio [,]   no.*
        the   master   no   want   kill   Eugenio   no
        'The master does not want to kill Eugenio' (Malpica de Barca 1890: 61).

     c. *Si   yo   ta   i   cuando   judío,   yo va moja.*
        If   I   am   go   when   Jewish   I go wet
        'If I am going when Jewish, I get wet.'
        No   moja   no.
        no   wet   no
        'It does not get wet.'
        No e mío [,] no.
        no is mine no
        'It is not mine.'
        Cuidado Francisco, e cosa   mala,   no levanta no.
        careful   Francisco   is thing   bad   no lift up   no
        'Be careful Francisco, it is a bad thing, do not lift it up' (Cabrera 1976: 25, 44).

     d. *Yo   no   so   pobre [,]   no.*
        I   no   am   poor   no
        'I am not poor.'
        Yo no   so   planeta [,]   no.
        I   no   am   planet   no
        'I am not a planet.'
        Yo no   so   bueye [,]   no.
        I   no   am   ox   no
        'I am not an ox.'
        Yo no   so   purio [,]   no.
        I   am   no   pure   No
        'I am not pure.'

Yo no so brujo [,] no.
I no am wizard no
'I am not a wizard no' (Benítez del Cristo 1930: 132, 133, 135, 139, 140).

(13) São Tomé
a. *Bo   na   bila   mesé   kumé   fa?*
   You   no   yet   want   eat   no
   'Don't you want to eat already?' (Ferraz 1978: 254).

b. *Kuma   batata   na   tava   se   fa   n-kɔpla   losu.*
   eat   patato   no   TMA   there no   I-buy   rice
   'Since there were no patatos there, I bought rice' (Ferraz 1978: 245).

(14) Annobon
a. *Pedulu   na   sula   f.*
   Pedulu   no   cry   no
   'Pedulu does not cry' (Valkhoff 1966: 101).

b. *Bo   na   kesé   xosé   f   di   salá   f.*
   you   no   forget this   no   for   that   no
   'Do not forget this for that' (Valkhoff 1966: 101).

(15) Príncipe
a. *Ami   Na   sebe   fa.*
   I   No   know   no
   'I did not know it' (Günther 1973: 78).

b. *Zwa   sabe   landa   fa.*
   Zwa   know   swim   no
   'Zwa does not know how to swim' (Ferraz 1978: 11).

(16) Angolar (unpublished data provided by Lorenzino)
a. *Pɔtɔ   sikɔlá   na   thá   kí   thávi   wa.*
   door   school   no   stay with key   no
   'The school door does not have keys.'

b. *Kɔmpá-m   kié   wa.*
   friend-my fall   no
   'My friend did not fall.'

As far as CS is concerned, Schwegler offers a dialogue showing how NEG2 is used (17) and indicates that on one occasion he could also record an instance of NEG3 (18) (Schwegler 1991b: 113). Nevertheless, given the

2.2 Granda's Monogenesis-Decreolization Hypothesis

existence of only a single token of NEG3 in his Chocó corpus, no detailed account of its pragmatic features could be established. For this reason, he suggests that probably in Chocó and in the other varieties showing NEG3, the function of this negation is essentially the same as that of NEG2 (viz., negating a presupposition in the common ground); nevertheless, he acknowledges the possibility that certain stylistic differences – yet to be determined – exist between those two types of negation (Schwegler 1991a: 54–5).

Chocó Spanish

(17) I *El sei de enero nací yo... Nací*   {Implicit in the
      the six of January born I born   conversation is the
      yo... el seis de enero nací. El día   idea that the
      I the six of January born   illiterate informant
      [de] los Reyes pusieron 'Reyes'[Magos]. (I) knows the day
      Of the Kings put Kings Wizards   but not the year in
      Me pusieron 'Reyes.' La cedula así   which he was born.}
      me put Kings the ID like this
      [lo dice];... allí. sabe la gente
      It say there know the people
      cuantos años tengo yo.
      how many years have I
      'I was born on January sixth . . ..I was born on January sixth. On the day of the 'Reyes Magos' they called me Reyes. They called me Reyes. The ID says so . . .. there people know how old I am.'

A.S. *¿Pero Ud. no lo sabe?* {This is questioning the truth of the previous
                                assertion, in which I stated he does know the
                                year in which he was born. It implies, in the
                                mind of A.S., that I probably knows when he
                                was born.}
'But, don't you know it?'
I. *Yo no lo sé no. No lo sé,* {The double negation is rejecting the
ni el nacimiento.   affirmative implication by A.S 'yes, you know
                                 the year in which you were born.'}
'I do not know it. I do not know it, not even the birthday.'

(18) Situation: A.S. and the informant (F) are talking about the languages spoken by his wife, not present at the time of the conversation.

A.S. *¿Y qué más [lenguas habla ella]?*
     and what more languages speak she
     'And what languages does she speak?'

F. Ella..., bueno, más   no...   más   no   más   no
    She   well   more   no   more   no   more   no
    habla ella.   Castellano así   como   estoy speaking
    speaks she   Castilian   like   how   am   She...,
    hablando yo   ...así   Pero   ella   en   lengua
    speaking I   like   but   she   in   language
    Chiro no
    Chiro no
    'She..., well, no more...no more she does not speak more. She speaks Castilian, the language I am speaking now. But she does not speak Chiro.'

Schwegler (1991a: 70) also claims that while NEG2 is quite common across Romance varieties (Italian, Milanese, French, etc.), it is unknown in the history of Peninsular Spanish (Llorens 1929), even though it can be heard in Peninsular Portuguese (19) (see also Vázquez Cuesta y Mendes da Luz 1971: 546).

(19) Peninsular Portuguese
      Question: Você fala   alemão?
                you   speak   German
                'Do you speak German?'
      Answer: Não   falo   não.
                no   speak   no
                'I do not speak it.'

Moreover, in line with Megenney (1990: 126–7), he states that a variety of African languages in contact with Portuguese in colonial times present parallel constructions, as examples (20–3) show for Kikongo, Kimbundu, and Umbundu. In addition, a number of potentially similar structures would be found in other probable substrate languages: Kwa, Mande, Yoruba, Jaude (Boretzky 1983: 102–3; Stolz 1987: 14).

        Kikongo
(20)   Ke   tu-kuenda   ko
        No   we-go   no
        'We do not go' (Tavares 1934: 64–5).

(21)   Kimbundu
        Etu   ki   tu   nake   etu
        No   be   we   eight   no
        'We are not eight' (Chatelain 1888: 52).

2.2 Granda's Monogenesis-Decreolization Hypothesis

(22)   Umbundu
       Oviti ka-vi-nene-ko
       sticks no-be-big-no
       'The sticks are not big' (Valente 1964: 134–6).

After providing such a vast range of cross-linguistic data, Schwegler (1991a: 57–74) postulates what follows (see Map 2.2):

a) NEG2 and NEG3 are probably the result of contact between Portuguese and African languages. Since some instances of NEG2 are found in Peninsular Portuguese, it is not possible to exclude that it provided the model for this structure to emerge; nevertheless, with all likelihood this pattern was modeled on African substrate structures and, in any case, Spanish could not possibly provide it.
b) These constructions crystallized in an Afro-Portuguese creole, which was eventually taken to the Caribbean and used among slaves in the Spanish colonies.
c) NEG3 survived in the most conservative black regions (Brazil, Palenque, Chocó), while it disappeared elsewhere, due to decreolization processes driven by social stigma.
d) NEG2 is still associated with stigma and lower class society; for this reason, it already disappeared in other black regions (Panama, Ecuador, etc.).

Schwegler (1991a: 57) claims that the spread of postverbal negation in Spanish America was facilitated by economic and social relations, which were particularly strong in the Spanish Antilles, Cartagena, and Chocó:

> The postverbal negative structures must have been used, already in the seventeenth century (i.e., when Palenquero developed), especially among black people, in a vast geographic area, ranging from the Hispanic Caribbean to certain peripheral regions outside the Caribbean (e.g., Chocó) which, as we already know (Granda 1977) (Figure 2.2), were at that time socially and economically well-connected with the main Caribbean slave centers, such as Cartagena. (Author's translation)[5]

The claim Schwegler makes on the presence/absence of NEG3 in Afro-Latin America (see point (c) above) has important implications for the monogenetic theory. In fact, the author suggests that the disappearance of NEG3 in DS is related to the fact that, from a Spanish perspective, NEG3 looked like an *"anomalía morfosintáctica"* (morphosyntactic anomaly) (1991a: 58), which

---

[5] Original Spanish version: *Las estructuras negativas postverbales debían de tener, ya en el siglo XVII (i.e., en el momento de formarse el palenquero), una amplia distribución diatópica, extendiéndose, sobre todo entre negros, a gran parte del Caribe hispano e inclusive a ciertas zonas marginales extracaribeñas (e.g., el Chocó) que, como se sabe (Granda 1977), solían estar en aquel entonces en estrecho contacto social y/o económico con importantes centros esclavistas caribeños como el de Cartagena.*

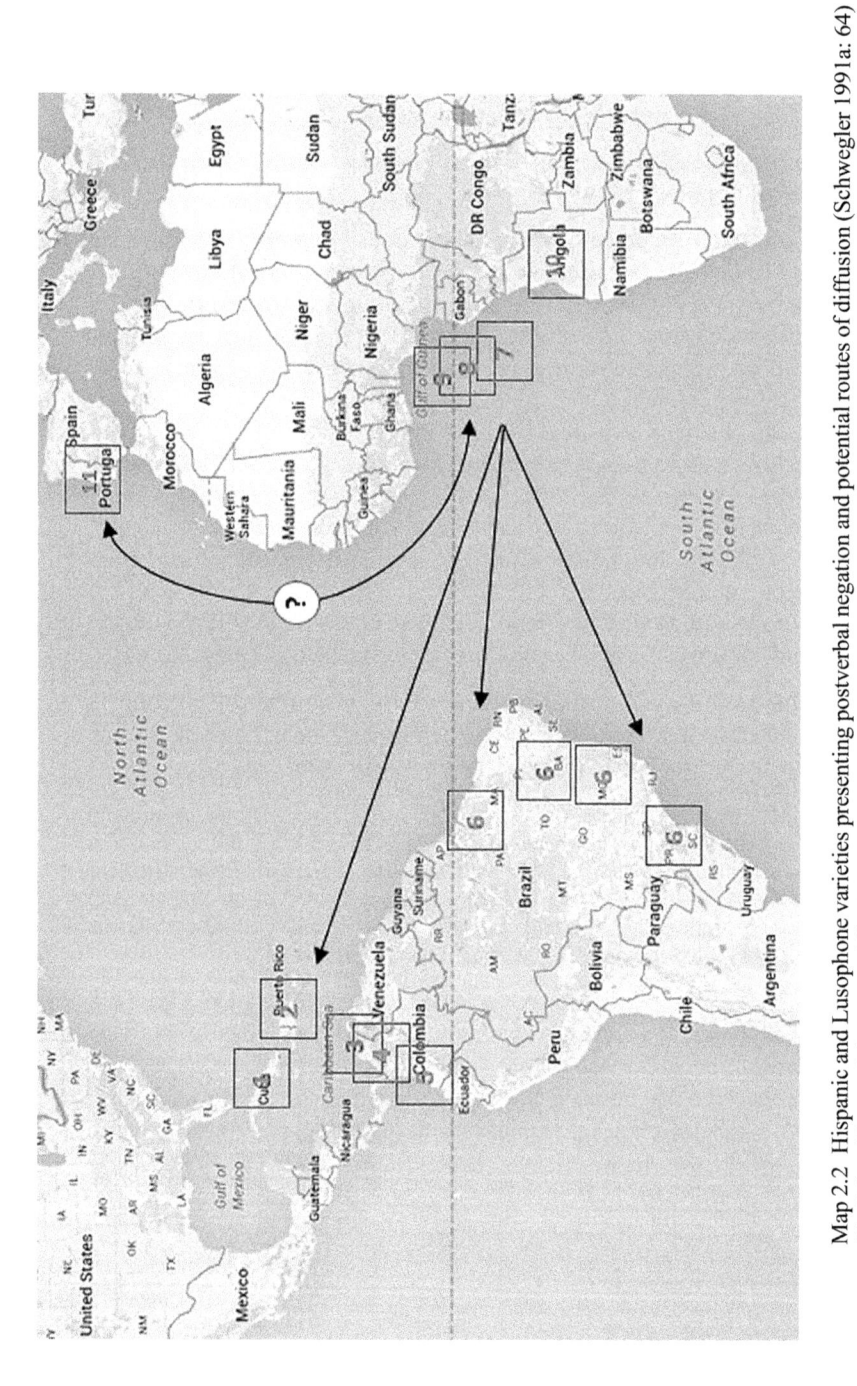

Map 2.2 Hispanic and Lusophone varieties presenting postverbal negation and potential routes of diffusion (Schwegler 1991a: 64) (1) Cuba, (2) Dominican Republic, (3) Cartagena, (4) Palenque, (5) Pacific lowlands of Colombia, (6) Brazil, (7) São Tomé, (8) Annobom, (9) Príncipe, (10) Angola, (11) Portugal.
(Schwegler 1991a: 64)
Source: Map data © 2019 Google, INEGI

Figure 2.2 Cover of Granda's (1977) book

could be readily identified as a stigmatized feature belonging to Bozal speech. As a result, it would have been progressively abandoned, but not completely, so that a compromised construction between standard NEG1 and Bozal NEG3 would have emerged: NEG2. In other words, from a diachronic perspective, the development of NEG2 would have derived from the retraction of NEG3. This would be the case not only for DS, where NEG3 disappeared completely, but also for CS, where only a few traces of NEG3 are left (1991a: 58, fn.33). On the other hand, NEG3 would have survived standard pressure in more conservative black communities (Brazil and Palenque), where it is still commonly found. The author states (1991a: 58):

> It is not difficult to see that, from a Hispanic linguistics perspective, the NEG3 pattern appeared, from early on, to be a morphosyntactic anomaly, which consisted of a notably identifiable Bozal speech feature. Naturally, it was subject to progressive standard pressure from an early stage ... The consequences of such prolonged pressure are not difficult to imagine: the NEG3 anomaly is abandoned, but not without preserving a negative marker (no + verb + no) whose form and morphosyntax coincide, at least partially, with standard negation no + verb. (Author's translation)[6]

Schwegler (1991a: 74) further highlights his position on this issue by saying that NEG2 in DS may not be the result of a linguistic calque on a substrate *no* + verb + *no* structure, but rather the byproduct of a *proceso combinatorio que habría acoplado la negación peninsular preverbal (*NEG1*) a la negación bozal postverbal (*NEG3*)* 'a combinatory process that would have merged prenominal Peninsular negation (NEG1) to the postnominal Bozal negation (NEG3).' He (1991a: 77) adopts a traditional dialectological approach and provides the following remarks to account for the nature of DS, the other Afro-Latino varieties of the Americas, and the linguistic features they share:

> When we examine related dialects, such as Dominican Spanish, Cuban Spanish, Chocó Spanish or Cartagena Spanish/Palenquero Spanish, all of which share the extra-Peninsular Spanish postverbal negation, the general dialectological and comparative historical linguistic practice is to assume that such dialects used to belong to an ancient diasystem, and that, for that reason, these constructions are not the result of independent innovations. As we have just suggested, the Afro-Portuguese creole hypothesis provides such an original diasystem and, at the same time, explains the marginal presence of

---

[6] Original Spanish version: *No es difícil ver que, partiendo de estructuras lingüísticas hispánicas, el patrón NEG3 habría resultado desde muy temprano como una anomalía morfosintácticas, constituyendo así un rasgo identificador muy notable del habla bozal. Es natural que haya debido de haberse sujetado tempranamente a las progresivas presiones de la modalidad estándar ... Las consecuencias de tales presiones prolongadas no son difíciles de imaginar: se abandona la anomalía NEG3, pero no sin conservar una marca de negación (no + verbo + no) cuya forma y morfosintaxis coinciden, por lo menos parcialmente, con la negación estándar no + verbo.*

2.2 Granda's Monogenesis-Decreolization Hypothesis

postverbal negation in some of the regions that we have examined. (Author's translation)[7]

In particular, Schwegler (1991a: 78–9) concludes by pointing out a list of features, which by co-occurring with postnominal negation in these varieties, would represent strong evidence in support of the Afro-Portuguese creole root for these vernaculars.

If there is no doubt that an atomistic perspective, excessively short-sighted from our point of view, has derived, up to this point, several Afro-Iberian quantitative and/or qualitative peculiarities such as the change [l] to [r] (lado>rado), the tendency towards open syllables (Dios>Dio – Dioso 'Dios'), the (almost) categorical elimination of plural redundancy within nominal phrases (la cosa buena 'las cosas buenas'), the (almost) systematic use of non-emphatic, non-contrastive subject pronouns (Yo hablo = hablo), syntactic invariability in interrogative constructions (¿Qué tú quieres?) or, to mention one additional example, the simplification of verbal conjugations (yo habla, tú habla, él habla, etc.), it is also true that postverbal negation, once accepted as clear evidence in favor of an Afro-Portuguese code spoken in the Spanish Caribbean, naturally provides greater credibility to those who have always linked such phenomena to the speech of black slaves. (Author's translation)[8]

Along with Schwegler, several other scholars have echoed Granda's proposal on the genesis and evolution of the Afro-Hispanic languages of the Americas. In fact, a number of authors have suggested that the linguistic features currently encountered in popular varieties of Cuban, Puerto Rican, and Dominican Spanish (Otheguy 1973; Perl 1982, 1985; Megenney 1984a, 1984b, 1985, 1993; Lorenzino 1993) should be seen as traces of a once well-established Afro-Iberian creole, which was spoken on these three Spanish

---

[7] Original Spanish version: *Cuando examinamos dialectos relacionados como el español dominicano, el cubano, el chocoano o el cartagenero/palenquero, que comparten todos como hemos visto, el rasgo extra-español (peninsular) de la negación postverbal, la general práctica de la dialectología y la lingüística histórica y comparativa es de suponer que tales dialectos pertenecían a un antiguo diasistema, y que, por lo tanto, no son el resultado de innovaciones independientes. Como acabamos de sugerir, la hipótesis criolla afroportuguesa proporciona tal diasistema de base, y a la vez permite explicar el carácter marginal de la postergación en algunas de las áreas examinadas.*

[8] Original Spanish version: *Si bien es cierto, pues, que una aproximación atomista, excesivamente corta de vista en nuestra opinión, haya permitido, hasta hoy, derivar de fuentes exclusivamente europeas peculiaridades cualitativas y/o cuantitativas negroíberas como el cambio de [l] a [r] (lado>rado), la tendencia hacia la configuración de sílabas abiertas (Dios>Dio – Dioso 'Dios'), la (casi) categórica eliminación de la redundancia de la marca de pluralidad en sintagmas nominales (la cosa buena 'las cosas buenas'), la (casi) regular adición de pronombres sujetos en contornos no enfáticos o contrastivos (Yo hablo = hablo), la invariabilidad sintáctica de interrogativos (¿Qué tú quieres?) o, para enumerar solo un ejemplo más, la simplificación desinencial del sistema verbal (Yo habla, tú habla, él habla, etc.), es también cierto que la postergación, una vez admitida como evidencia segura de la previa existencia de un código afroportugués en el Caribe negrohispano, naturalmente confiere mayor credibilidad a aquellos que desde siempre han tratado de relacionar tales fenómenos con el habla de los esclavos negros.*

islands, and potentially across other Caribbean regions. Such ideas, common – to different extents – to all of the supporters of the Monogenesis-Decreolization Hypothesis, are synthetized by Otheguy's words (1973: 334–5), who, after analyzing a variety of phenomena found in these dialects (viz., phonological reductions, non-inverted questions, etc.), states:

> In summary, the data presented here strongly suggest that the 'habla bozal' spoken in the Spanish Antilles (and possibly throughout the Caribbean) during colonial times was a Creole... Given this, the sample points of coincidence presented here between features which are shared by most Creoles but which are peculiar to Caribbean Spanish cannot be discarded as coincidence and must be taken into account in any explanation of the historical genesis of this major dialect type.

Although a number of scholars have embraced this view on the nature of *habla bozal*, on the other hand, there are others who have disputed it. For example, Lipski (1986, 1993, 1998, 2000) has repeatedly suggested that the features ascribed by some authors to this hypothetical Afro-Portuguese language spoken across the Caribbean may also be the result of common second language acquisition strategies, which do not necessarily imply the existence of a previous creole variety. Indeed, Lipski (1986) argues that for the most part those grammatical features should be seen as byproducts of non-target like acquisition phenomena that arose in every context in which African languages came into contact with Spanish.

His linguistic analysis finds historical support in a number of studies (Mintz 1971; Laurence 1974; Chaudenson 1992, 2001; Clements 2009), which show that the practice of slavery in the Spanish Antilles was quite different from the French and English Caribbean. According to these authors, in fact, a concomitance of social and demographic factors favored Spanish language acquisition by the enslaved sector of society. In particular, they point out that, while French Saint Dominique and English Jamaica received massive waves of African-born workers since the early days of colonization to supply sugarcane planters with an enslaved workforce, the massive use of African labor in the Spanish Caribbean took place much later, after the sugar boom of the nineteenth century – which affected for the most part only Cuba. Until that point, in fact, the Spanish Antilles were not "slave societies," but rather "societies with slaves" (Berlin 1997).

The sociodemographic scenario found in the early Spanish Caribbean would have allowed African slaves to acquire the language spoken by the white sector of the population, since for several centuries the black population was not the majority in the region. As a result, even when more African captives were introduced into the Spanish Antilles during the nineteenth and twentieth centuries, the recently arrived *bozales* did not creolize the Spanish dialect established in the islands, which was already spoken natively by a significant number of the blacks working in the local haciendas. Moreover, in sharp opposition to the French and

2.2 Granda's Monogenesis-Decreolization Hypothesis

English Caribbean, in the Spanish Antilles a significant sector of the black population was free. In fact, manumission was not only possible, it was indeed quite common. Spanish slavery allowed for a manumission system called *coartación*, which essentially worked as a mortgage on one's freedom. According to this mechanism, slaves could achieve freedom by paying their value to the masters by installments (Laurence 1974: 492). In addition, racial mixing was quite common from the very beginning of the colonial settlement, enabling a free mulatto group, which spoke Spanish natively, to emerge quite early.

The debate on the supposed (de)creolization of Spanish in the Americas has not concerned the Spanish Antilles only. Indeed, for almost all the Afro-Hispanic vernaculars scattered across this continent, there have been studies offering a (de)creolization hypothesis to account for their current linguistic status. One example is the proposal by Álvarez & Obediente (1998) on the creole origin of Barlovento Spanish, spoken in Venezuela. The authors suggest that some grammatical elements found in this variety such as the use of non-emphatic subjects, non-inverted questions, alternation between the phonemes /l/ and /r/, and /s/ weakening, may be seen as traces of a previous creole stage for this dialect. However, as Díaz-Campos and Clements (2005, 2008) have shown, a closer linguistic inspection of such grammatical phenomena reveals that the aforementioned features may be encountered in a variety of Spanish vernacular dialects, so that a creole hypothesis should not necessarily be invoked to account for their presence in Barlovento Spanish. Moreover, these authors were also able to back their linguistic analysis by showing historical evidence indicating that the introduction of an African workforce in the region was never massive, but rather strictly constrained by the Spanish Crown's monopoly on slave trading, and that the overall social conditions during the colonial period may have favored Spanish language acquisition by the black sector of the population (viz., interracial mixing, diffused Christian education, high rates of manumission, etc.).

Yungueño Spanish (YS), a black dialect from Bolivia, has also been classified as a decreolized language. On the one hand, Lipski (2006, 2008) has suggested that the morphosyntactic simplifications encountered across the nominal and verbal domains of this vernacular may have a Spanish pidgin ancestry (Lipski 2008: 186); while, on the other hand, Perez (2015) has proposed an Afro-Portuguese creole background for this variety. Nevertheless, a deeper sociohistorical and linguistic investigation has cast serious doubts on the possibility that contemporary YS passed through a previous pidgin/creole stage. On the contrary, YS seems to be a vernacular, which approximated quite closely to Spanish from its inception. It developed in isolated, rural valleys, far away from the social pressure imposed by formal education, standardization, and the linguistic norm. In such a scenario, advanced processes of second language acquisition could be crystallized and conventionalized in the YS speech community. For this reason, it is still possible to observe them today in the vernacular spoken by the oldest residents of these rural villages (Sessarego 2011a, 2011b, 2013c, 2014a).

Another Afro-Andean dialect for which the Monogenesis-Decreolization Hypothesis has been proposed is Chota Valley Spanish (CVS), a black vernacular spoken in the Provinces of Imbabura and Carchi, Ecuador. As we saw earlier in this chapter, as noted above, Schwegler (1999: 237) has argued that the presence of the pronoun *ele* in this dialect, in Cuban Bozal Spanish, and in Palenquero is "UNEQUIVOCAL evidence" showing that these three varieties developed from a common Afro-Portuguese creole ancestor, since claiming otherwise would be like "finding a car on the moon and refusing to allow that it had been brought there from the Earth" (see also McWhorter 2000: 137). Nevertheless, Lipski (2008) offers some data that appear to go against Schwegler's proposal. According to Lipski's (2008: 112) analysis, CVS speakers do not associate *ele* with a pronoun; rather, this element functions in this vernacular as a common interjection expressing "surprise, alarm, or other strong emotions" (see 23). Moreover, it is not only found in CVS; it belongs more generally to all the Highland Ecuadorean Spanish dialects, even those varieties spoken in regions that have never been populated by black communities (Córdova Álvarez 1995: 194).

(23) a. *Ele caray!*
hey damn
'Well, damn it!'

b. *Ele, la María!*
hey the María
'Hey, (it is) María!'

c. *Ele, a los tiempo te veo!*
hey at the time you see
'I haven't seen you for ages!'

Lipski (2008: 113), however, admits that, even though none of his informants classified *ele* as a pronoun, in a few instances in his linguistic corpus of recorded interviews, this element may look as such (see example 24). For this reason, the author proposes that these sporadic occurrences may be better classified as the result of paragoge processes, where a final vowel is added to a given lexical item to create an open syllable (CV). In fact, epenthetic [e] also applies to other words in this dialect: *ayer* → *ayere* 'yesterday,' *ser* → *sere* 'to be,' etc.

(24) a. *Ele ya puso una escuela aquí.*
he already put a school here
'He already put a school here.'

2.2 Granda's Monogenesis-Decreolization Hypothesis

b. *Si yo Ya   me apegaba,   eli ya   me hacía.*
   if I already me got closer he already me did
   'If I got closer, he did it to me.'

As indicated in Sessarego (2013b, 2013d, 2014b), my own research, carried out with more than fifty Afro-Choteños, confirms Lipski's account. My results suggest that there are two different types of *ele*: a) the exclamatory marker, and b) the pronoun resulting from sporadic paragogic processes. Moreover, a closer look at Schwegler's data appear to lead to an interesting syntactic generalization, which I was able to further verify thanks to my informants' grammaticality judgments. The data presented in (25) show the use of *ele* in CVS, as reported by Schwegler (1999: 244):

(25) a. *Ele, él ta allí.*
        he he is There
        'He, he is there.'

   b. *Ele El guagua se   torció el pie.*
      he The kid   REFL twisted the foot
      'He, the kid twisted his ankle.'

   c. *Ele Ese ya   le   chancó al puerco.*
      he this already to it killed the pig
      'He, this one already killed the pig.'

   d. *Ele ellas se van a   pasear.*
      they they go to walk
      'They, they are going for a walk.'

   e. *Ele No les   quiero dar.*
      they No to them want give
      'To them, I do not want to give it to them.'

   f. *Eli los pescados se   han muerto.*
      they The fish   REFL AUX died
      'They, the fish have died.'

   g. *¡Yo! ¡Con ele no fuera!*
      I   with him no go
      'I! With him, I would not go!'

As it can be observed in (25a–f), in all these examples *ele* acts as a dislocated topic. It occupies the left edge of the structure, where it is separated from the rest of the sentence by a sort of "comma intonation." Its function consists of pointing out to the listener that the speaker is about to make a statement about somebody. This person (or group) has almost certainly been mentioned at a previous moment in the discourse or is readily identifiable in the context (perhaps by pointing or by shared knowledge between the speaker and hearer). When used in this way, *ele* can refer to any grammatical position in the sentence from which it is dislocated. The only example provided by Schwegler in which *ele* does not act as a topic marker is (25f). In this case, *ele* might be interpreted as the result of a paragogic process. Alternatively, it could be analyzed as the focus of the sentence. That is, it introduces new information that can generally be thought of as an answer to a question. In (25f), we could think of the sentence as an answer to the question: "Who wouldn't you go with?" Answer: *Yo, con ELE no fuera*. This can be paraphrased in English with clefts: "As for me, it is with him that I would not go." Even though all the Afro-Choteños I interviewed had clear grammaticality judgments on the status of *ele* as a topic marker, I could not encounter the same positive reactions to the focalizing hypothesis. For this reason, I suspect that *ele* in (25f) may be better explained as a case of paragoge. In any case, this example is the only one provided by Schwegler (1999) that does not align with the topic analysis. It would be interesting to see if the author has more data of this type to better understand its syntactic properties. Since *ele* may relate to any DP constituent in the sentence, it can easily be confused with a singular and/or a plural pronoun. Nevertheless, data show it is not so, since it acts as a topic and (possibly) a focus marker.

Based on the available linguistic evidence, therefore, CVS *ele* should not be analyzed as a Portuguese-derived pronoun. This, however, leaves open the possibility that Palenquero *ele* and nineteenth-century Cuban/Puerto Rican *elle* might have such an origin. I think nobody would reject the possibility that some black captives speaking a variety of Portuguese might have been taken to Ecuador or to other Spanish territories in colonial times, especially because it is well-known that Portuguese traders provided African slaves to Spanish America until 1640 (Peralta Rivera 2005). What appears to be less convincing, unless backed by solid historical data, is that such captives could speak a Portuguese-based creole and that this contact variety could be adopted by the following generations of blacks, who – from the middle of the seventeenth century – were taken to Spanish America by English, French, and Dutch trading companies (Colmenares 1979: 34). Moreover, an analysis of the socio-historical background of Chota Valley does not seem to indicate that a creole language could be introduced or was likely to form in the region (Sessarego 2013b, 2013d, 2014b). In fact, a concomitance of social, economic, demographic, and religious factors facilitated the acquisition of Spanish by the black captives working in these Jesuit plantations (Coronel Feijóo 1991; Lucena Salmoral 1994; Bouisson 1997; etc.).

Besides *ele*, as we saw, the other "creole-like" feature for which Schwegler has proposed a (de)creolization process is double negation (viz., **no hablo**

2.2 Granda's Monogenesis-Decreolization Hypothesis

italiano no 'I do not speak Italian'). In his (1991a) study, in fact, he suggested that DS, CS, Cuban Bozal Spanish, Palenquero, and several Afro-Lusophone languages would have derived from the same Proto-Afro-Portuguese Creole. Nevertheless, for this grammatical element and the languages in which it can be found, a number of alternative analyses have also been offered. Lipski (1994b), for example, suggests that DS was never a creole language. However, given that during the colonial and postcolonial history of Hispaniola this dialect has been repeatedly influenced by the creole spoken in Haiti, it may be conceivable to believe that the double negative pattern found in DS developed perhaps under the influence of Haitian Creole (HC), rather than from an Afro-Portuguese creole (1994b: 24–7).[9] He also admits that the existence of such constructions in both Palenquero and CS may have a common root. In his view, it could be possible that some of the slaves who escaped from Cartagena and the surrounding areas eventually fled to the Chocó in colonial times and, in this way, introduced into the region this syntactic construction, which may ultimately have been based on Bantu structures, as in Brazilian Portuguese (1994b: 25). Ortiz López (1998) analyzes the speech of rural Afro-Hispanic communities in Cuba, and discovers that structures of this sort (26) can still be heard (1998: 113).

(26)   a. *No sé no.*
         no know no
         'I do not know.'

       b. *Yo no hablaba extraño no, no.*
         I no spoke strange no no
         'I do not know.'

However, based on the linguistic and sociodemographic data available for the history of the Spanish Antilles, he rejects Schwegler's model. Rather, he suggests that, while it is reasonable to claim that this negative pattern may have been influenced by African languages, it is somewhat *ambicioso* (ambitious) to postulate a creole hypothesis to account for it (1998: 116). Thus, he concludes (1998: 117):

We reject the proposal of a "creole diasystem" as the foundation of Caribbean Spanish, since the evidence presented until now, as well as the results of this study, rather than legitimating the existence of a "creole" on the Caribbean soil,

---

[9] In an analysis of the Spanish spoken by HC speakers in the Dominican Republic, Ortiz López (2010: 181–212) concludes that contact with this French-based creole is not probably the reason for the presence of double negation in DS. In fact, HC does not present such a structure and the Spanish spoken by the Haitian community living in the Dominican side of the island does not seem to present high rates of such a negative pattern.

appears to support the Afro-Hispanic contact ... that our people experienced. (Author's translation)[10]

Ortiz López's (1998) account is also indirectly supported by the information contained in the correspondence between two nineteenth-century scholars, one from Cuba, José de la Luz Caballero, and the other from the United States, Francis Lieber. Their letters, brought to the attention of the linguistic community for the first time by Clements (2009: 68–102), consists of analyses of the linguistic scenario found in Cuba at that time. Luz Caballero points out to Lieber the presence of several non-standard features – including double negation – in the speech of Cuban *bozales*. Nevertheless, when Lieber asked Luz Caballero about whether it was possible to find in Cuba a Spanish variety comparable to the French creole spoken in Haiti, Luz Caballero replied that no such language existed on the island. Based on this information, Clements (2009: 101) also reaches the conclusion that double negation may well be analyzed as an African-driven feature found in black speech; however, it should not be taken as the indicator of a previous creole stage for Caribbean Spanish.

Finally, for the Department of Chocó, the Monogenesis-Decreolization Hypothesis and the origin of double negation have also been questioned. Indeed, Ruiz García (2000, 2009), after analyzing the main phonological and morphosyntactic features found in this dialect, suggests that CS should be seen as the descendant of Bozal Spanish, a contact variety that never creolized in the Colombian Pacific lowlands (2009: 81–4). In her view, the features found in this dialect appear to be vernacular traits, which may suggest some restructuring, but should not be interpreted as the traces of a previous creole phase. She also addresses the issue of double negation brought up by Schwegler (1991a: 53–5) and concludes that the presence of this structure in CS (and in other black dialects) is not enough to justify the proposal of a shared proto-Afro-Portuguese root.

Besides the aforementioned linguistic and sociohistorical case studies on the different dialects for which the Monogenesis-Decreolization Hypothesis has been proposed, there have also been a couple of analyses that tried to provide a different interpretation of the *Instauranda Aethiopum Salute* excerpt provided by Granda (1970). In particular, Lipski (2005: 288–9) has pointed out that it is true that when Sandoval (1627: 59–60) talks about *"un género de lenguaje muy corrupto y revesado de la portuguesa que llaman lengua de San Thomé"* ('a sort of broken Portuguese that they called the São Tomé language'), he is probably referring to a Portuguese-based creole. Nevertheless, Lipski also

---

[10] Original Spanish version: *Rechazamos la propuesta de un "diasistema criollo" como base del español caribeño, ya que la evidencia presentada hasta la fecha, así como los resultados de la investigación, más que legitimar un 'criollo' en suelo caribeño, parece apoyar el contacto afrohispánico ... que vivieron nuestros pueblos.*

2.2 Granda's Monogenesis-Decreolization Hypothesis

highlights that the Spanish priest is not necessarily implying – as Granda assumes – that all the blacks proceeding from Africa would actually speak such a language or learn it upon arrival to the Americas. Conversely, Lipski interprets *al modo que ahora nosotros entendemos y hablamos con todo género de negros y naciones con nuestra lengua española corrupta, como comúnemente la hablan los negros* ('so that now we can speak with all kinds of blacks in our corrupted Spanish, as it is usually spoken by all the blacks') as an indicator that all the blacks, even those who arrived speaking a creole, would eventually acquire a Bozal variety of Spanish.

In a recent study (Sessarego 2013d: 146), I provided an analysis of Sandoval's work that goes beyond the paragraph extracted by Granda. The analysis reveals that the vast majority of the slaves arriving to Cartagena in the seventeenth century could not speak the language mentioned in that brief excerpt. In fact, it is important to consider that only part of the slaves arriving in Colombia during that period originated in São Tomé. Indeed, as Sandoval indicates on several occasions in his treatise, slaves were captured in many different regions of Africa and subsequently shipped to Cartagena from four main locations (and sometimes from other areas): Guinea, Cape Verde, São Tomé, and Loanda (called Angola). Sandoval (1627 [1956: 90]) writes:

> There are four main ports from which blacks are usually shipped to Cartagena de Indias, which is the main slave-receiving hub in the world. They come from the Guinea rivers and from the mainland, from the island of Cape Verde, from the island of São Tomé and from the port of Loanda or Angola, and sometimes also from other remote kingdoms from the western as well as the eastern regions of Ethiopia. (Author's translation)[11]

Sandoval's main goal was to convert, Christianize, and baptize the *bozales* arriving in Cartagena. In order to do so, he had to explain to them the principles of the Catholic faith. Needless to say, that was not an easy task. One of the most difficult challenges he had to face was the huge linguistic barriers. Giving the highly heterogeneous linguistic background of the slaves entering this Colombian port in colonial times, finding somebody capable of translating Spanish into one or more African languages was crucial to the success of Sandoval's project. This is a point the Jesuit priest makes on several occasions. Indeed, the second chapter of the third book comprising *De Instauranda* is exclusively dedicated to this topic: *De la precisa necesidad que tienen los obreros destos etíopes del uso de los intérpretes y lenguas ladinas y fieles* ('On

---

[11] Original Spanish version: *Cuatro son los más principales puertos de donde ordinariamente suelen venir negros a este puerto de la ciudad de Cartagena de las Indias, que es la principal y derecha descarga de todo el mundo. Vienen de los ríos de Guinea y puertos de su tierra firme, de la isla de Cabo Verde, de la isla de San Thomé y del puerto de Loanda o Angola; y cual de los otros recónditos y apartados reinos, así de la Etiopía Occidental como de la Oriental.*

the precise need for using interpreters and trustworthy Spanish speakers when working with the Africans'; see Sessarego 2013d: 147).

Sandoval states that finding a translator in such a multilingual context was extremely difficult and could take several days of intense research: *buscarles lenguas e interpretes días enteros* ('looking for languages and interpreters entire days'; 1627 [1956: 335]). In order to save time and energy when teaching *bozales*, Sandoval had to find *ladino* slaves who could speak Spanish as well as several African tongues (1627 [1956: 338]). Nevertheless, he further highlights that this was not easy at all. In fact, not only were the *bozales* generally unable to understand each other in Cartagena, a city that received captives from all over Africa, but also, quite often black captives did not even share a common language in the African points of departure, due to the fact that they were captured in regions far away from the actual shipping ports (Sandoval 1627 [1956: 100–1]; Sessarego 2013d: 148; see also Chaudenson 2001 on this point).

Given these data, the chances of a well-established Afro-Portuguese creole spoken in Cartagena and then eventually transplanted to the rest of Spanish America appear to be highly reduced. Moreover, it has to be said that the Portuguese supplied Spanish America with slaves until 1640 (Peralta Rivera 2005), while several regions of colonial Spanish America started relying on a black workforce much later (e.g., Chocó, Yungas, Chincha, and Chota Valley; Sessarego 2013b, 2013c, 2013d, 2014a, 2014b, 2014c, 2015a, 2016), when the *asientos* were in the hands of French, English, and Dutch traders. This factor further diminishes the likelihood of the introduction of a Portuguese-based variety in those territories. In addition, it has been shown that the so-called 'monogenetic features' – mentioned by Granda (1968) in relation to several Latin American and Asian contact vernaculars – (see Table 2.1) can be better explained as common contact-induced grammatical patterns, not necessarily related to either Portuguese or African languages (Sessarego 2013d: 139–41).

2.3 The Missing Spanish Creoles

The Afrogenesis Hypothesis, presented by McWhorter (2000) in his much-debated book, *The Missing Spanish Creoles*, proposes that the creole languages found in the Americas and in the Indian Ocean developed from pidgins, which were previously formed on the Western African coasts from the contact between the Africans and the Europeans involved in the transatlantic slave trade. In this work, McWhorter criticizes what he labels "the limited access model," or the assumption that African slaves developed creole languages in plantation contexts because they only had limited access to the European superstrate. According to McWhorter, creoles came to represent a symbol of black identity among the slaves. McWhorter's position is therefore in contrast with the proposals that describe American creoles as restructured versions of their European lexifiers (Mufwene 1996), or depict their development as the byproduct of cyclical squared approximations to the European superstrate (Chaudenson 2001). These models, in his view, would be misleading, since they do not account for a pidgin stage for these languages.

One of the key elements provided by McWhorter to support his thesis is the attested paucity of Spanish creoles in the New World. In fact, he argues that since Spain was the only European power involved in the colonization of the Americas that did not directly participate in the slave trade, no Spanish pidgin formed on the Western African coasts and, consequently, no Spanish creole could possibly develop in the Spanish colonies on the other side of the Atlantic Ocean. This would account for the fact that besides Papiamentu and Palenquero, which were originally Portuguese-based contact varieties, no Spanish creoles are found in the Americas.

Since in the New World plantations there could not possibly be an African-born Spanish pidgin, the linguistic foundations would have been missing for the creation of a Spanish creole. As a result, the African slaves in these colonies just learned Spanish, and managed to convey their black identity by recurring to phonological variation and African lexical borrowings (McWhorter 2000: 203–4). More precisely, McWhorter points out that if the limited access model were correct, then a number of mainland Latin American territories should host a Spanish creole today, but they do not. The regions he indicates as perfect colonial locations for creole formation are: Chota Valley (Ecuador), Veracruz (Mexico), Chincha (Peru), coastal Venezuela, and especially Chocó (Colombia). On the other hand, we would be able to find a variety of French- and English-based creoles in the Americas because these two colonial powers directly traded in slaves in Western Africa in colonial times.

According to the Afrogenesis Hypothesis, English and French pidgins initially formed in Africa, were transplanted to the American plantations, and eventually became creoles. McWhorter pushes the Afrogenesis Hypothesis even further by claiming that all the French and English creoles spoken in the Americas, Africa, and the Indian Ocean must have been generated from one single English and one single French pidgin respectively. The English pidgin would have developed around 1632 in Ghana, in the Cormantine Castle (Porter 1989: 128; McWhorter 2000: 111), while the French pidgin supposedly formed in Senegal, on the Île the Bieurt, when the French started their slave trade activities around 1638 (Delafosse 1931: 111; McWhorter 2000: 173).

The Afrogenesis Hypothesis has been received in the field of creolistics with some skepticism. Schwegler (2002), for example, points out a few issues related to the linguistic evidence provided by McWhorter to support his model, and suggests that claiming that all English- and French-based creoles would have developed from one single English and French pidgin is probably a bit too extreme (2002: 117). In addition, he indicates that given the lack of linguistic and sociohistorical evidence provided, it is really not possible to make any solid claim on the potential existence of Spanish pidgins/creoles in the colonial regions surveyed by McWhorter (Schwegler 2002: 120).

Lipski (2005: ch.9) also shows some perplexities. He indicates that McWhorter's model does not explain why pidgins would have formed in Africa but could not possibly develop in Spanish America, if the sociodemographic conditions in Spanish plantations/mines were as extreme as those depicted by McWhorter. Lipski concludes by highlighting that overall McWhorter's sociohistorical analysis does not appear to be solid, and that his hypothesis seems to be more driven by an ideological position willing to identify creole languages as a symbol of black identity, rather than by an accurate study of the real historical facts.

Indeed, it must be noted that McWhorter (2000) does not offer much historical data to back his model. On a case-by-case analysis, in fact, the Afrogenesis Hypothesis does not stand up to the sociodemographic evidence provided by a number of recent studies. For example, Díaz-Campos & Clements (2008) show that the racial disproportions envisioned by McWhorter for colonial Venezuela did not correspond to the historical reality. Indeed, many of the captives that he classified as "Africans" were actually *criollos*[12] and *mulatos* (mulattoes), born in Venezuela, who in all likelihood could speak Spanish natively. Díaz-Campos & Clements (2008) also show that several economic and cultural factors, such as the Spanish Crown's monopolization of the slave trade and the influence of the Catholic Church in society, conspired against a massive introduction of African-born workers and provided the captives with more chances to acquire the Spanish language through Christian indoctrination, thus indirectly reducing the probability of Spanish creole formation in the colony.

McWhorter's account for colonial Ecuador has proven imprecise too. In fact, the author pictures a plantation society consisting of massive introduction of African-born workers from the very outset of the colonial enterprise. Nevertheless, a closer sociohistorical investigation reveals that massive slave importations never happened in this region, especially during the early colonial phase, when the local settlers had to face significant financial restrictions (Coronel Feijóo 1991). For this reason, whenever possible, planters would rely on a cheaper Indian workforce, and when blacks were used, they consisted for the most part of *criollo* captives. Recent investigations have also shown that the living and working conditions of blacks in Chota Valley might not have been as harsh as those documented for other plantation settings elsewhere in the Americas. Indeed, social relations appear to have been more flexible and

---

[12] A *criollo* slave is a black captive that was born in the Americas.

2.3 The Missing Spanish Creoles

favored the acquisition of Spanish by the enslaved population (Sessarego 2013b: ch.2; Sessarego 2014b).

In line with the Ecuadorean scenario, also for Peru McWhorter depicts a colonial plantation setting that does not seem to match the available historical information we have. In particular, besides the Company of Jesus, only a few laymen had the financial resources to rely systematically on an enslaved workforce. Slave introduction in Peruvian plantations was never massive nor abrupt and involved a high percentage of *criollos* (Flores Galindo 1984). Moreover, a closer analysis of the Jesuit plantation system implemented in the coastal haciendas appears to indicate that the demographic, moral, and working regulations implemented by the Company of Jesus favored Spanish language acquisition (Macera 1966; Sessarego 2014c, 2015a).

Another "missing Spanish creole" indicated by McWhorter (2000: 11) in support of the Afrogenesis Hypothesis is the Afro-Mexican dialect of Veracruz, where – according to the author – masses of African slaves would have been introduced in colonial times to carry out agricultural work on sugarcane plantations. In this context, McWhorter envisions a canonical breeding ground for creole formation, and yet a Spanish creole is currently missing in Mexico as well. Indeed, the author shows that contemporary Afro-Mexican Spanish aligns quite closely with other vernacular varieties of Spanish; thus suggesting that a creole language probably never existed in this region. McWhorter (2000: 11) reports the following example (27), taken from Aguirre Beltrán (1958: 201), to show the similarities between Afro-Veracruz Spanish and other vernacular varieties of Spanish.

(27) *Ese plan   tubo   (<estubo) bien hecho   ... pero Si el gobierno*
     that plan   was   well done   but   if the government
     atiende (la) lej, ba   a   causá   (<causar) gran doló (<dolor).
     follows the law go   to   cause   big pain
     'That plan was well done, but if the government follows the law it will cause a lot of pain.'

It may be noted, though, that Aguirre Beltrán (1958) did not describe the black community of Veracruz; rather, his monograph, *Cuijla*, focuses on an Afro-Hispanic village in the state of Guerrero, on the Pacific coast of Mexico. Thus, the data used by McWhorter to exemplify Afro-Veracruz Spanish are actually taken from a different Afro-Mexican dialect.

Unfortunately, to date not much linguistic literature has been produced on Afro-Mexicans. In particular, no book has ever been written to cast light on the linguistic nature and sociohistorical background of Afro-Veracruz Spanish. To the best of my knowledge, the only book-length manuscript focusing on an Afro-Mexican dialect is the Ph.D. dissertation of Norma Mayén (2007), who analyzes the speech of two black communities in the villages of Collantes and La Boquilla, located in the State of Oaxaca. This study provides a grammatical account of the main phonological and morphosyntactic features found in this variety and concludes that a (de)creolization hypothesis is not viable to account for this dialect. Nevertheless, this work does not provide much historical information on the origin of this vernacular since, as the author states, due to the lack of published information on these villages, she had to rely mainly on "personal observation and on tape-recorded information from members of these Afro-Oaxacan communities" (2007: 66).

Chocó represents for McWhorter's model the most important black region of Spanish America where a Spanish creole is not spoken. The author, in fact, dedicates several pages to this Colombian Department, which – in his view – in colonial times presented all the sociohistorical parameters that have traditionally been held responsible for creole development. In particular, he states that (2000: 7–10):

Starting in the late seventeenth century, the Spanish began importing massive numbers of West Africans who spoke a wide variety of languages into the Pacific lowlands of northwestern Colombia to work their mines. This context shortly became one which, according to the limited access model, was a canonical breeding ground for a contact language of extreme structural reduction.

In the Chocó region, for example, there were no fewer than 5,828 black slaves by 1778, while there were only about 175 whites – a mere 3 percent of the total population (West 1957: 100, 108).

Some creolists might guess that the absence of a creole in the Chocó might be due to there having been a long initial period during which whites and blacks worked in equal numbers ...

However, in the Chocó, there was no period of numerical parity between blacks and whites. The nature of mining is such that relatively large numbers of slaves were needed from the outset, and they were immediately engaged in work arrangements ensuring little contact with whites ... Sharp disproportion of blacks to whites was not only established at the outset, but also increased by leaps and bounds throughout the 1700s: there were 600 slaves in the Chocó in 1704, 2000 in 1724, and 7088 by 1782 (Sharp 1976: 21–2) ...

Today, the descendants of the Chocó slaves live in the same lowlands where their ancestors toiled under the Spanish, subsisting via small-scale mining. Whites, having retreated to the urban centers after the slaves were emancipated, are a negligible presence in the lowlands (e.g., 8 percent by the 1950s; West 1957: 108–9). Relations between blacks and whites are, unsurprisingly, edgy and distant (Rout 1976: 243–9) ...

What is important is that creole theory predicts that the Chocó context would have generated not a second-language dialect diverging only slightly from the local standard, but a more radically reduced, pidginized register, with much higher levels of structural interference from West African languages. In short, the modern situation in the Chocó is a striking counterexample to current creole genesis theory, all strains of which would predict a Spanish creole in this region.

2.3 The Missing Spanish Creoles

Therefore, if the limited access model were correct, Chocó should have produced a Spanish creole. In fact, in colonial times this region was characterized by the sociohistorical conditions that are supposed to be ideal for creole formation: massive introduction of *bozal* slaves, high demographic disproportions between blacks and whites, harsh working conditions in labor-intensive mines, and minimal access to the outside Spanish speaking society. Nevertheless, CS is not a creole, thus the reasons behind the non-creolization of Spanish in the Pacific lowlands of Colombia (and elsewhere in the Americas) must be other, presumably, the fact that Spain did not have enslaving forts in Africa, where a Spanish pidgin could have formed and from which it could have been introduced into Chocó (and the rest of the Spanish territories overseas).

A number of studies over the past seventy years have provided dialectological descriptions of certain aspects of CS grammar. For example, Flórez (1950), after visiting Chocó for a few days during the winter of 1948, offers an impressionistic account of some vernacular features that characterize CS phonology, morphosyntax, and lexicon. Montes Giraldo (1974) and Manzini (1983) provide the results of their respective dialectological investigations carried out independently during the 1970s across the Department of Chocó and propose the existence of linguistic isoglosses, which would link certain (northern) areas of Chocó to the Spanish Caribbean, while relating other (southern) provinces of the Department to the Andean region of Popayán. Another study on CS is the one by Schwegler (1991b), who provides the phonetic transcriptions of the interviews he carried out during the same year in several villages scattered across the Atrato and San Juan Rivers.

Granda (1977) represents the first book-length study on the Spanish spoken in the Colombian Pacific lowlands. This work consists of two main parts: a) one devoted to structures (pp. 19–236) including a number of chapters primarily focusing on several aspects of the phonology and lexicon of the dialects spoken in the Departments of Chocó, Valle, Cauca, and Nariño; and b) the other dedicated to the local oral folklore (pp. 237–360), consisting of a recompilation of traditional songs and poems.

As previously observed, Granda (1977) postulates in this study – and in a variety of other works, along with Schwegler (1991a, 1991b; see also Granda 1988, 1994) – a potential (de)creolization process to account for the grammatical elements found in this Afro-Hispanic vernacular. However, Ruiz García (2000, 2009), after analyzing the main phonological and morphosyntactic features found in the speech of a group of elder informants from the village of Tadó, Chocó, concludes that CS may be better conceived as the result of second language acquisition strategies, more likely related to *habla bozal* than to a Spanish creole.

In recent years, CS has been investigated by a number of young Colombian linguists, who focused on several phonological and morphosyntactic aspects of this vernacular. Páez Acevedo (2009) analyzed the phonetic realization of stops in the speech of informants proceeding from Quibdó, Nóvita, Nuquí, and Bahía Solano. Rodríguez Tocarruncho (2010) has studied variable plural marking phenomena based on a linguistic corpus she collected in several rural communities along the San Juan River. Correa (2012) has investigated the supposed African influence on the phonetic alternation between [ð] and [ɾ] and the realization of voiceless stop /k/ as glottal [?] in the villages of Tutunendo, Cértegui, Condoto, Nóvita, and Santa Rita de Iró. Murillo Valencia (2013) has conducted a sociolinguistic study in the refugee camps of Futuro and Villa España, in the proximities of Quibdó, to understand the patterns of variation characterizing certain morphosyntactic variables found in these speech communities. Mena Mena (2014) has analyzed several prosodic patterns found in the Spanish spoken in Quibdó.

Even though CS has long been acknowledged as one of the most important pieces (if not the most important one) to solve the Spanish creole debate puzzle (Granda 1977, 1978; Schwegler 1991; McWhorter 2000; Lipski 2005), the linguistic investigations carried out during the past seventy years have never been combined with a detailed sociohistorical account of colonial Chocó to cast light on the genesis and evolution of this Afro-Hispanic vernacular. For this reason, as far as McWhorter's claims are concerned, none of the aforementioned studies either proves or disproves the Afrogenesis Hypothesis.

2.4 Chocó Spanish as a Testing Ground for the Legal Hypothesis of Creole Genesis

During the past two decades, a variety of authors have shown that, due to a concomitance of social, economic, and demographic factors, the historical scenario that led to the creolization of certain European languages in former English, Dutch, and French colonies in the Americas did not apply to several regions ruled by the Spanish Crown. Indeed, recent research on Afro-Caribbean Spanish (Lipski 1993; Clements 2009), Barlovento Spanish (Venezuela) (Díaz-Campos & Clements 2005, 2008), Yungueño Spanish (Bolivia) (Sessarego 2011a, 2011b; 2013c, 2014a), Chota Valley Spanish (Ecuador) (Sessarego 2013b, 2013d, 2014b) and Chincha Spanish (Peru) (Sessarego 2014c, 2015a) appears to point to such a conclusion. Nevertheless, a case-by-case analysis of the genesis and evolution of these contact varieties seems to miss the bigger picture or, as McWhorter has put it, "something broader was at work [in Spanish America] than just unconnected, local demographic constellations" (2000: 39).

2.4 Chocó Spanish as a Testing Ground for the Legal Hypothesis

Faced with this challenge, in recent publications I tried to find a common thread among all these colonial realities (Sessarego 2015a, 2017a). To do so, I relied on a comparative analysis of slave law in the Americas, an aspect of creole genesis that has been overlooked by previous hypotheses attempting to account for the paucity of Spanish creoles in the New World. This resulted in what I called the LHCG, which – without denying the importance of such demographic, economic, and social factors as those evaluated by the aforementioned studies – ascribes a prime importance in the development of the Afro-European languages in the Americas to the historical evolution of slavery, from the legal rules contained in the Roman *Corpus Juris Civilis* to the colonial codes implemented overseas.

Findings show that much heterogeneity was present across European slave laws, and that the reasons for such a varying legislation had to do with different degrees and modalities of reception of the Roman *Corpus Juris Civilis*, where the foundations of slave law were originally set in ancient times. In fact, the legal figure of the "slave/serf"[13] had been received by the Spanish system in Roman times; it had been gradually modified during the course of history and was eventually codified in the *Siete Partidas*, the Spanish medieval code. Over time, this figure was further adapted, through the *Leyes de Indias* 'colonial laws', to meet the needs of an evolving colonial society, so that slaves progressively acquired more rights. In particular, during the medieval era, the Spanish slave obtained a legal personality. Having a legal personality within a certain legal system implies the capacity of acquiring a series of legal rights and obligations, such as taking part in civil lawsuits, getting married, entering into contracts, etc. The presence of legal personality and its corollary, rights, is essentially what differentiated a Spanish slave from a Roman one. Roman slaves, in fact, were property; they had no rights, since they did not have legal status (Watson 1989).

The LHCG points out that Spain not only diverged from other colonial powers in that it did not run enslaving forts in Africa, as indicated by McWhorter; rather, in all likelihood, the most significant difference between

---

[13] It should be pointed out that in Roman law there did not exist any word similar to 'slave.' The Latin word was and is *servus*, which became *serf* in English and in French and *servo* and *siervo* in Portuguese and Spanish. *Slave*, in fact, is an adoption of the "tribal" name for Slavs. Slavs suffered attacks from neighboring peoples who used to sell them as serfs in markets around the Dead Sea, and so their ethnic name became a synonym of *serf*. "Slave" is documented in Arabic in the ninth century and in Latin in the tenth century (*slavus, eslavus, esclavus* ...); so it is a late designation. Also, it must be acknowledged that the *Siete Partidas* never mention *esclavo* ('slave' in Spanish), but *siervo* ('serf,' from the Latin *servus*). Nevertheless, in the current study we will not focus on the historical evolution of these two terms (which ended up being used as synonyms in the Americas); rather, we will follow Watson's (1989) work and thus refer to "Roman slave law," "Spanish slave law," etc. We will do this for the sake of clarity, even though it is understood that, from an etymological perspective, it would be more appropriate to talk about "Roman serf law," "Spanish serf law," etc.

Spain and the rest of the colonizing nations in the Americas had to do with the legal regulation of slavery. Owing to a concomitance of historical factors, the Spanish system was the only one that granted legal personality to slaves. This, I argue, is key to understanding the social dynamics that shaped the nature of the Afro-European relations in the Americas and, consequently, the languages that developed from such a contact.

The acquisition of legal personality in medieval times implied that Spanish slaves in the Americas had a variety of rights completely unknown to – or highly restricted for – their counterparts in other colonies. Spanish slaves could take part in legal lawsuits and, if punished too harshly, could sue their masters and ask to be sold to a different buyer. They had the right to be assisted during trials by a *protector de esclavos* 'slave protector,' a state lawyer who specialized in slave law. They had the right to get married and, once married, couples and their children could not be separated; families had to be preserved. They could own property, accumulate wealth, and pay for their own freedom.

A compensation for the slave's work had existed since Roman times; it was called *peculium* and consisted of a small payment the owner could decide to concede to the slave for his work. It functioned as an incentive to work harder. Slaves could accumulate the *peculium* over time and, eventually, use it to pay for their freedom. The *peculium* was not compulsory; rather, it was voluntary in the *Corpus Juris Civilis* and the *Siete Partidas*; it became obligatory in the *Leyes de Indias*, so that each slave owner had to provide a sort of recompense to his captives. The *peculium* could be paid in cash, with goods, or with time off and means of production (viz., a piece of land on which to grow their own crops) to carry out extra work and gain some money (Andrés-Gallego 2005: 60).

Obtaining legal personality provided slaves in Spanish colonies with a number of benefits, not only on the legal and economic aspects of their lives but also on the familiar level, as their living conditions improved significantly. Fundamental to this was the pressure exerted by the Catholic Church, which, by insisting on the fact that blacks had a soul, managed to take away some of the power that masters had over their captives. An example of this can be seen in the fact that the institution of marriage was originally conceded to slaves to avoid the sin of fornication. This, subsequently, implied that marriages had to be preserved, so that couples and their offspring could not be separated or sold as individual tokens (Watson 1989).

On the other hand, all these rights, deriving more or less directly from the concept of legal personality, were completely absent or highly constrained in the other European colonies. This had to do with the fact that the concept of "slave/serf" followed significantly different evolutionary paths in the other legislations, since in Roman times the *Corpus Juris Civilis* was not received to the same extent all over Europe. In particular, none of the other European slave laws recognized slaves' legal personality. As a result, the corollary of rights coming with this concept were, for the most part, missing from those legal systems (for a more detailed comparative analysis of European slave laws in the Americas in relation to the LHCG, see Sessarego 2017a, 2018a, 2018b, 2018c).

The main criticism that the LHCG faces is the skeptical observation of those who find it hard to believe that slaves working on plantations or mines in Spanish America actually had real access to legal courts to stand for their rights. The formal aspects of slavery, as it was stated in the legal rules, "law in books," were inevitably divergent from the practical application of such regulations to a specific social context, "law in action" (Pound 1910). As we will see in this book, Colombian Chocó represents the perfect place to test the LHCG exactly because it was on one of the most remote "frontiers" of the Spanish Empire, where "law in books" could hardly have been implemented by state authorities.

2.5 A Note on the Importance of Chocó to the Field of Creole Studies

As we have seen, several hypotheses have been proposed to account for the paucity of Spanish creoles in the Americas. Within such a complex puzzle, Chocó represents a fundamental piece. On the one hand, Granda (1977, 1978) and Schwegler (1991a) claim that the grammatical features of CS bring evidence to the Monogenesis-Decreolization Hypothesis, in that they would point to a previous creole stage for this vernacular. This model has, therefore, been primarily based on linguistic data. On the other hand, McWhorter (2000) interprets the current non-creole status of this variety as a sign that, even in a place where the sociodemographic conditions traditionally held responsible for creolization existed, Spanish failed to creolize (because a Spanish pidgin never formed in Africa), thus supporting his Afrogenesis Hypothesis. At the same time, colonial Chocó may be taken as the perfect place to test the LHCG against potential criticism. In fact, Chocó was a remote frontier region, where no legal courts or significant urban centers ever existed during the colonial period, and where law could hardly be enforced.

This book builds on the LHCG (Sessarego 2015a, 2017a). This hypothesis suggests that, from both the legal and the sociohistorical perspectives, being a slave in Spanish America was substantially different from being a slave in any other European colony overseas. As a result, Spanish slaves had higher chances of obtaining manumission, integrating into free society, and learning the colonial language, all factors that constrained the probabilities of creole formation and/or preservation in the territories under the rule of the Spanish Crown (Sessarego 2018b). The addition of a legal dimension to the debate on the genesis and evolution of creoles offers a novel approach to the study of these contact varieties–an approach that can be easily replicated and applied to other contact scenarios to advance the frontier of knowledge of the entire discipline.

Linguistic hypotheses on the formation and evolution of creole languages have rarely been built on detailed sociohistorical analyses, and have *never* relied on comparative colonial slave laws to cast light on the development of these contact varieties. The following chapters will offer a linguistic, historical, and legal account of CS to evaluate the aforementioned hypotheses on the genesis and evolution of the Afro-Hispanic languages of the Americas (AHLAs). In so doing, not only will this book cast light on the grammar of CS and on the sociohistorical questions that gravitate around the origins of the other AHLAs; more importantly, it will also set the bases for a new, more multidisciplinary, way of thinking about creole studies, which will enable other researchers and students to make their own discoveries.

3 A Sketch of Chocó Spanish

3.1 Introduction

This chapter consists of an analysis of the main linguistic features characterizing Chocó Spanish (CS), as encountered during my visits to the province of Quibdó during the winter of 2014–2015. Results will be presented, along with the data provided by other researchers, in an effort to offer a general picture of the grammatical status of this Afro-Hispanic vernacular in relation to other AHLAs and to standard Colombian Spanish. This will serve as a linguistic foundation, which will be combined with the historical and legal information presented in the following chapters, to address the hypotheses that have been provided in the literature on the origin of CS and the current paucity of Spanish creoles in the Americas. In the following section, before focusing on the grammatical analysis of CS, I will sketch a phonetic description of the main Spanish dialects spoken in Colombia. This will help us locate CS within its dialectal context.

3.2 The Dialects of Colombia

As indicated by Lipski (1994a: 206), there have been different proposals to classify the dialects of Colombia; for this reason, there is no universally accepted categorization of the different dialectal zones encountered in that country. For example, after describing the nature of a series of phonetic and lexical isoglosses, Flórez (1964) suggests that the Colombian territory may be divided into seven main dialectal zones, which would roughly coincide with the following regions: Atlantic/Pacific coast, Antioquia, Nariño/Cauca, Tolima, Cundinamarca/Boyacá, Santander, and the Eastern/Amazonian zone. Montes Giraldo (1982), on the other hand, tries to show how the traditional distinction – northern/central versus southern Peninsular Spanish varieties – finds in Colombia a parallel counterpart. Indeed, he proposes two main macro areas, the interior region and the Pacific/Caribbean coast. Thus, the dialect spoken in the interior of Colombia would share several features with northern/central Peninsular Spanish (/j, ʎ/ phonemic opposition, etc.); while the coastal variety would resemble in many aspects the dialects spoken in southern Spain and the Canary islands (syllable-final /s/ weakening and deletion, etc.).

Lipski (1994a: 204–17) offers an overview of the literature on Colombian dialectology and, based on a series of phonetic traits, opts for dividing the country into four main dialectal zones: central highlands, Caribbean coast, Pacific coast, and Amazonian region. The following sections will summarize the linguistic features provided by Lipski's dialectal categorization to offer a general perspective of the principal dialects spoken in Colombia.

3.2.1 Central Highlands

a. Retention of syllable- and word-final /s/.
b. /s/ may be aspirated in onset position (i.e., *necesario* [ne.he.ˈsa.rjo] 'necessary') (Flórez 1973: 82–3).
c. /s/ may also be aspirated in word-initial position (i.e., *una señora* [u.na.he.ˈɲo.ɾa] 'a woman'), but this phenomenon tends to occur only in lower-class speech (Flórez 1951: 193).
d. /x/ tends to be realized as [h] (Montes Giraldo 1966).
e. Word-final /n/ is usually realized as [n].
f. /r/ is usually pronounced as a weak trill. However, in the regions in which Quechua is Spoken, such as Nariño, fricative variants of /r/ may be heard.
g. /ɾ/ in coda position may be pronounced as a weak fricative.
h. The cluster /tɾ/ may be pronounced as an affricate (Albor 1984).
i. The preservation of the /j/ versus /ʎ/ phonemic opposition used to be more widespread throughout the region. During the past three decades, there has been a tendency toward merging such phonemes.
j. Intervocalic voiced stops may be weakened and deleted (Amastae 1986).
k. Postconsonantal voiced stops do not tend to undergo such a weakening process.
l. Voiceless stops may be aspirated (Rodríguez de Montes 1972).

3.2.2 Caribbean Coast

a. Syllable- and word-final /s/ tends to be weakened and elided.
b. Word-final /n/ velarization.
c. The phoneme /x/ is aspirated and may be deleted in intervocalic environment.
d. Intervocalic /d/ is frequently elided.

3.2 The Dialects of Colombia 51

e. /d/ may be pronounced as [ɾ]. This phenomenon used to be more common in the past; nowadays it is not that frequent (Flórez 1973: 72).
f. Strong tendency toward eliminating phrase-final /ɾ/, especially in verbal infinitives.
g. /ɾ/ in coda position may be pronounced as a weak fricative.
h. Stops preceded by a liquid sound tend to undergo a process of gemination, so that a word like *Cartagena* may be pronounced as [ka.tːa.ˈhe.na]

3.2.3 Pacific Coast

a. /s/ in word- and syllable-final position is often aspirated and elided. Rates of /s/ reduction tend to be lower in this region than on the Caribbean coast. Nevertheless, the Department of Chocó presents comparable levels of consonant weakening and deletion to those found on the Atlantic coast of Colombia.
b. Word-final /n/ tends to be velarized. In some cases it may be pronounced as a labial [m].
c. Intervocalic /d/ may be pronounced as [ɾ], especially in Chocó (Montes Giraldo 1974; Granda 1977; Schwegler 1991b).
d. /ʎ/ may be pronounced as an approximant. It may be an affricate in word-initial position.
e. Consonant glottalization may occur (Montes Giraldo 1974; Granda 1974, 1977). This has been reported for word-final prevocalic /s/ (i.e., *los amigos* [lo.ʔa.ˈmi.ɣos], 'the friends') and for the phoneme /k/ (i.e., *bocadillo* [bo.ʔa.ˈði.jo], 'sandwich').

3.2.4 Amazonian Region

Lipski (1994a: 212–13) points out that the native Spanish speakers of this region tend to have moved to the Amazon from other zones, especially from the Colombian highlands and from Peru, while the local populations speak Spanish, if at all, as a second language. For these reasons, it is difficult to identify a homogeneous Spanish dialect for the Amazonian region. Nevertheless, some studies have been carried out on the local varieties of Spanish (Alvar 1977; Rodríguez de Monte 1981); thus, Lipski summarizes the main phonetic traits encountered across this vast area:

a. /s/ is generally pronounced as [s].
b. /n/ might be velarized. This phenomenon is not usually encountered in the Colombian highlands; thus, it might have been introduced into the region by immigrants from Peru.

c. Intervocalic stops tend to be pronounced as occlusive rather than approximant sounds.
d. /ʎ/ is pronounced as a weak fricative.

3.3 The Phonetics and Phonology of Chocó Spanish

The Department of Chocó is located in the Pacific lowlands of Colombia. For this reason, CS aligns quite closely with the overall phonetic account provided in Section 3.2.3 for the Colombian Pacific coast. Moreover, given the geographic proximity of Chocó to the Atlantic coast, its historical connection to Cartagena de Indias (the most important slave market of Spanish America), and the numerous linguistic traits shared by all coastal dialects (Flórez 1950; Montes Giraldo 1982), CS presents several features that are also common to Caribbean Spanish varieties, particularly in the communities scattered along the Atlantic and Pacific littorals of the Department (Granda 1977). At the same time, given the overall economic and cultural isolation of Chocó, this dialect appears to have preserved certain conservative phonetic features, typically reported for Bozal Spanish and encountered in several other contemporary Afro-Hispanic vernaculars. Its linguistic isolation appears to also be responsible for certain grammatical innovations (Granda 1974; Correa 2012), which are peculiar to this vernacular and thus differentiate it from the surrounding Colombian dialects and the rest of the AHLAs.

3.3.1 Vowels

(I) Vowel Variation Unstressed mid vowels /e/ and /o/ may be raised and pronounced as [i] and [u]. My corpus presents several instances of this phenomenon (28), which align with the data reported for CS by other researchers (29). Unstressed vowel raising is a common phonetic trait across vernacular varieties of Spanish, and the AHLAs are no exception in this sense, as the examples in (30) show.

(28) a. *Nojotru <nosotros> fuimu <fuimos> a comé.*
we went to eat
'We went to eat.'

b. *Es como un asunto espirimental <experimental>.*
is like an issue experimental
'It is like an experimental issue.'

(29) a. *Pulicía* <*policía*>; *Séltiga* <*Cértegui*>; *dicir* <*decir*>.
   pólice   Cértegui   to say
   'Police; Cértegui; to say' (Flórez 1950: 111).

   b. *Riferente* <*referente*>; *dicían* <*decían*>; *pudía* <*podía*>;
      referent   said   could
      nu <no>   *más*.
      no   More
      'Referent, they said, he could, no more' (Ruiz García 2009: 78).

(30) a. *No mi* <*me*> *hizo caso*.
      no CL   made case
      'He did not pay attention to me' (Barlovento Spanish, Megenney 1999: 85).

   b. *Desde   ayel   tamo   peliando* <*peleando*>.
      from   yesterday are fighting
      'We have been fighting since yesterday' (Afro-Cuban Spanish, Ortiz López 1998).

Unstressed vowel raising has often been reported in relation to other instances of vowel variability found in CS, which appears to be characterized by tendencies toward vowel harmony (31) and vowel opening (32).

(31) *Cienega* <*ciénaga*>; *antiguidad* <*antigüedad*>; *exestian* <*existían*>.
   Swamp   antiquity   existed
   Cértegue <*Cértegui*>.
   Cértegui
   'Swamp; antiquity; they existed; Cértegui' (Ruiz García 2009: 78).

(32) [kiβ.'dɔ] <*Quibdó*>; ['sɛr.te.ɲi] <*Cértegui*>; [bɔ.rɔ.'xo] <*borojó*>;
   Quibdó   Cértegui   borojó
   [pwɛ] <*pues*>.
   then
   'Quibdó; Cértegui; borojó; then' (Montes Giraldo 1974: 410; Manzini 1983: 129).

These and other cases of vocalic instability have repeatedly been mentioned for this dialect – especially in regards to unstressed vowels – and for other present and past Afro-Hispanic varieties (Lipski 2005). As Megenney (1999: 103) points out, Flórez (1950: 111) classifies these cases of variation in CS as *trueques de inacentuadas* 'unstressed vowel alternations' and provides the following list of examples:

(33) *Polecía, pulicía <policía>; centurión <cinturón>; endevido <individuo>;*
police belt individual
Sertigue, Seltiga <Cértegui>; rigular <regular>; dicir <decir>;
Cértegui regular to say
Antusiasta <entusiasta>; restrojo <rastrojo>; boñuelo <buñuelo>.
enthusiastic stubble Donut
'Police; belt; individual; Cértegui; regular; to say; enthusiastic; stubble; donut.'

Megenney (1999: 102–3) compares such phenomena with his data from Palenquero (34) and concludes that, given certain similarities (/i/>/e/, /e/>/a/, etc.), these two Afro-Hispanic varieties might once have been the same creole language, or two very similar languages.

(34) *Kumé <comer>; kumo <como>; antonse <entonces>; wele <abuelo>;*
to eat like therefore Grandfather
Imahende <imagínate>.
Imagine
'To eat; like; therefore; grandfather; imagine.'

Indeed, Megenney (1999: 103–4) agrees with Granda's (1968, 1970) view on the genesis and evolution of the AHLAs. Thus, he supports the Monogenesis-Decreolization Hypothesis and states:

It can be observed that these two dialects are different today because Palenquero has been more isolated from the Spanish-speaking community than the Chocoan villages. Nevertheless, it is more likely that at a certain point, probably around the sixteenth or seventeenth century, they were the same dialect, or if they were not exactly the same, they were at least two very similar dialects, having in common the same Portuguese creole language spoken by the slaves arriving in New Granada. (Author's translation)[1]

(II) Diphthongs, Hiatuses, and Single-vowel Alternation Another phenomenon reported by several authors consists of the alternation between diphthongs, hiatuses, and single vowels. In my corpus, this phonetic trait is not very common, but a few instances were nevertheless detected (35). Flórez (1950: 111), Montes Giraldo (1974: 410), and Manzini (1983: 129), on the other hand, could find several examples of such divergent syllabification processes (36), which have also been widely reported for other contemporary AHLAs as well as for colonial Bozal speech (37).

---

[1] Original Spanish version: *Se reconoce que estos dos dialectos son diferentes hoy porque el palenquero ha estado más aislado de la comunidad de habla castellana que los pueblos del Chocó. Sin embargo, es más probable que en un tiempo, posiblemente en el siglo XVI o en el XVII, fueran un mismo dialecto, o si no exactamente el mismo, que por lo menos fueran dos dialectos muy semejantes, teniendo en común la misma base de lenguaje criollo portugués que hablaban los esclavos llegados a este territorio de la Nueva Granada.*

3.3 The Phonetics and Phonology of Chocó Spanish

(35) a. *Se trata de un tradición antigo <antiguo>*.
CL Treat of a tradition ancient
'It is an ancient tradition.'
b. *El Topo, persona tierce <terca> es*.
the Topo person stubborn is
'Topo is a stubborn person.'

(36) a. *Arriendada <arrendada>; endivido <individuo>;*
Leased individual
diferiencia <diferencia>; mantras <mientras>
difference While
'Leased; individual; difference; while' (Flórez 1950: 111).
b. *Caúcho <caucho>; críar <criar>; crúeca <cueca>*.
Rubber raise cueca
'Rubber; generate; cueca' (Montes Giraldo 1974: 410).

(37) a. *Engrio <engreído>; rir <reír>; queto <quieto>; nues <no es>;*
conceited to laugh quiet is not
quiora <que hora>.
what time
'Conceited; to laugh; quiet; it is not; what time' (Afro-Peruvian Bozal Spanish, Romero 1987: 102).
b. *Poto <Puerto> Rico; cuedate <acordarte>; criguellita <criollita>*.
Puerto Rico remenber small creole girl
'Puerto Rico; remember; small creole girl' (Afro-Puerto Rican Bozal Spanish, Álvarez Nazario 1974: 150).

(III) Vowel Nasalization CS is characterized by widespread vowel nasalization, even in contexts in which vowels are not either preceded or followed by nasal consonants (38). Schwegler (1991b: 91) points out this phenomenon and provides a variety of examples (39). These findings for CS parallel the data reported for several other present and past AHLAs (40)

(38) a. *[sĩ] <Si> es así es un problema.*
if Is such is a problem
'If it is like this, it is a problem.'
b. *Es un tramo [ðẽ] <de> dos kilómetro.*
is a stretch of two kilometer
'It is a stretch of two kilometers.'

(39) a. *No me [yũ. 'to] <gustó> eso ayá no.*
no CL liked that there no
'I did not like that one over there' (Schwegler 1991b: 95).

b. *Desde que la ['trũ.ho]* <*trujo*>.[2]
   since that CL brought
   'Since he brought her' (Schwegler 1991b: 105).

(40) a. *Si no lan* <*la*> *quiere creer.*
        if no CL   want to believe
        'If he does not want to believe her' (Afro-Peninsular Bozal Spanish, Lope de Vega 1893: 368, in Lipski 1992: 273).

   b. *[ma. 'ĩ]* <*maíz*>; *[krũ]* <*cruz*>; *[des. 'pwẽ]* <*después*>.
      Corn   cross   after
      'Corn; cross; after' (Afro-Venezuelan Spanish, Megenney 1999: 167).

3.3.2 Consonants

(I) Syllable-final Aspiration and Elision of /s/ The phoneme /s/ in coda position tends to be aspirated and deleted, especially when it occurs word-finally. My corpus is rich in examples of this type (41). They perfectly align with the data reported by other investigators working on CS (42), as well as with the well-attested weakening processes encountered in other AHLAs and, more generally, across Caribbean dialects (43).

(41) a. *Allí había doh arbole* <*dos árboles*>.
        there had two three
        'There were two trees there.'
     b. *¿Qué é* <*es*> *eso?*
        what is   this
        'What is this?'

(42) a. *Son lah doh* <*las dos*>; *son lah tré* <*las tres*>; *así é* <*es*>.
        are the two   are the three   such is
        'It is two o'clock; it is three o'clock; it is like that' (Flórez 1950: 111).

   b. *Mihma* <*misma*>; *despué* <*después*>; *tuvimo* <*estuvimos*>.
      same   after   were
      'Same; after; we were' (Murillo Mena 2005: 31–2).

---

[2] As pointed out by Flórez (1950: 113), and highlighted by Schwegler (1991b: 105), CS still preserves archaic Spanish verb forms (*vide, truje,* etc.), which disappeared from contemporary standard varieties (but see Cuba 2002 and Sessarego 2015a, for similar verb forms in Afro-Peruvian Spanish).

(43) a. *Dioh noh <Dios nos> llama cuando quiere él.*
      God CL   call when   wants he
      'God calls us whenever he wants' (Afro-Peruvian Spanish; Sessarego 2015a: 30).

   b. *Bueno en lo demá tamo <demás estamos> viviendo bien.*
      Well in CL rest are   living well
      'Well, as far as the rest is concerned, we are living well' (Afro-Cuban Spanish; Ortiz López 1998: 83).

(II) Conversion /d/ > *[ɾ]* and /ɾ/ > *[ð]* The phonemes /d/ and /ɾ/ tend to be neutralized in onset position (44), as several authors have shown (45) (Flórez 1950: 111; Montes Giraldo 1974: 417; Manzini 1983: 132; Granda 1988: 76; Schwegler 1991b: 91; Murillo Mena 2005: 33–5; Ruiz García 2009: 72; Correa 2012: 56–9; etc.).

(44) a. *Ta mo muy ocuparo <ocupados>.*
         are very occupied
         'We are very occupied.'

   b. *Se han escapao toro <todos>.*
      CL have escaped all
      'All of them have escaped.'

(45) a. *Merico <medico>; puere <puede>; Mosqueda <Mosquera>;*
         Doctor   can   Mosquera
         enedo <enero>.
         January
         'Doctor; he can; Mosqueda; January' (Flórez 1950: 111).

   b. *Merellín <Medellín>; toravía <todavía>; iro <ido>; ayura <ayuda>*
      Medellín   however   gone   help
      'Medellín; however; gone; help' (Ruiz García 2009: 72).

Montes Giraldo (1974: 413) indicates that Cuervo (1955) was the first linguist to mention this phenomenon in relation to the black vernacular dialect spoken on the Atlantic coast of Colombia. He highlights this by quoting Cuervo's (1955: 751) remarks on the presence of [ð]>[ɾ] in Bozal songs:

We do not know if this transformation has been generalized, except for the Atlantic Colombian coast, as shown by Obeso in his songs: *ros (dos), repué (después), ran (dan), recencia (decencia), rice (dice), añare (añade), eturio (estudio)*, etc.; a pronunciation due to the African influence. According to Pichardo, it is found among Cuban blacks, and already in the seventeenth century it was one of the features used by Quiñones de

Benavente to describe the speech of a black man (Entremeses, II, pp. 31–8). (Author's translation)[3]

Nevertheless, Montes Giraldo argues that this phonetic trait was probably not only found on the Caribbean coast; rather, it was also common in the Pacific lowlands, where it can still be heard today. The author indicates that this phenomenon consists of [ð] pronounced as [ɾ] (tap) or [ɹ] (fricative alveolar) and claims that it must have developed in CS due to the African substrate. In fact, he suggests that it would be quite common in a number of Afro-Hispanic dialects, and moreover, according to van Bulk (1952: 847–904), the sound [ð] would be rare across Bantu languages, while many of them would share [ɾ]. Montes Giraldo (1974: 415) provides also a phonological analysis to account for the complementary distribution of /d/ allophones in CS (46). He proposes that [ɾ] would be the CS counterpart of standard Spanish [ð].

(46) /d/ ⟶ [d]/ {n, s, ɾ, l} __ [4]
      ⟶ [ɾ]/ elsewhere

Montes Giraldo (1974: 417) provides an account of CS [ɾ] ~ [ð] alternation and suggests that it is significantly affected by a number of social factors (i.e., speaker's age, level of education, and exposure to standard Spanish). Overall, he believes that the stigmatized allophone [ɾ] tends to be substituted by more prestigious [ð] in the speech of young, more educated informants, especially those who are in contact with the standard dialect spoken in the surrounding cities outside Chocó (Antioquia, Cali, etc.). The author also points out several instances of hypercorrection, driven by linguistic insecurity, where standard [ɾ] is substituted by [ð] (*cuedo*<*cuero* 'leather,' *cuchada*<*cuchara* 'spoon,' *carbonedo*<*carbonero* 'coalman,' etc.; see also Manzini 1983: 130–1).

Granda (1988: 76) also proposes that the conversion [ð] > [ɾ] in CS is probably due to the African substrate. In particular, after analyzing historical documents indicating the origins of Bozal captives in Chocó, he concludes that several of those slaves were in all likelihood speakers of Kwa and Bantu languages, which, for the most part, would lack [ð], but present the

---

[3] Original Spanish version: *No sabemos que esta transformación ofrezca carácter general sino en la pronunciación de la costa atlántica de Colombia, según la representa Obeso en sus cantos: ros (dos), repué (después), ran (dan), recencia (decencia), rice (dice), añare (añade), eturio (estudio), etc.; pronunciación debida a influencia africana. Según Pichardo, ocurre entre los negros de Cuba, y ya en el siglo XVII era uno de los rasgos con que Quiñones de Benavente remedaba el habla de un negro (Entremeses, II, pp. 31–8).*
[4] Traditionally, the allophonic distribution of /d/ in standard Spanish diverges from the analysis provided by Montes Galindo. In particular, the allophone [d] is usually supposed to occur in the following contexts: [d]/ {##, L, N} __ (Hualde 2005: ch.7).

3.3 The Phonetics and Phonology of Chocó Spanish

articulatory-similar sound [ɾ] (Ladefoged 1964; Bal 1979). Granda (1977: 37) suggests that the alternation between these two sounds is primarily limited to the interior villages of the Pacific lowlands (San Juan de Micay, Nóvita, Cértegui, Tutunendo), while on the coastal zone it would not be that common. Thus, he suggests this phenomenon is almost absent from the dialects of Tumaco and Buenaventura, while in Coredó, Arusí, and Bahía Solano, it would be heard only in the speech of elderly informants. In addition, on the Atlantic coast (Riosucio, Turbo, Acandí), traces of this phonetic trait would be limited to a few specific, technical, lexical items (i.e., *caido*<*cairo* 'specific type of rope, employed for certain fishing techniques').

Granda (1977) divides the Pacific lowlands of Colombia into four dialectal subareas: A1, A2, B1, and B2, plus a transition zone (see Map 3.1). In line with traditional dialectology, he bases this analysis on the territorial distribution of linguistic phenomena. In this particular case, he focuses on the use of different lexical synonyms to refer to a list of activities and items concerning the most important means of transportation in the region, the canoe. He also suggests that several phonetic isoglosses – such as those concerning the [ɾ] ~ [ð] alternation – may match, to a certain extent, with the limits of the aforementioned subareas. Nevertheless, the main factor in this dialectal classification would be the distribution of lexical items. In particular, he distinguishes two main zones, A and B (see Map 3.1).

In zone A the concept of 'little canoe' would be expressed by the words *potro* or *potrillo*, while in zone B the item *champa* would be used instead. Besides this main subdivision, Granda (1977: 34) identifies within zones A and B four subareas (A1, A2, B1, B2). Zone A1 would differ from zone A2 in the use of certain lexical items employed to describe different parts of the canoe: *extremo delantero de la canoa* (prow), *extremo trasero de la canoa* (stern), and *superficies laterals de la canoa* (sides). According to Granda's data, the concepts of prow, stern, and sides would be respectively expressed by the words *punta, pilota/patilla,* and *costillas* in A1 and by *proa/proba, popa,* and *costados* in A2. As far as zone B is concerned, Granda (1977: 35) selects several lexical items that he identifies as representative of two different subareas: the Atlantic littoral (B2) and a more internal zone (B1). Among the terms he catalogs, he points out that in B2 the words to express the concepts of 'a relief on the canoe surface' and 'canoe bench' are *realce/sobrebordera* and *bancos*, while in B1 such items would be called *bordera* and *tablas*. The author also identifies a *zona de transición* (transition zone) (see Map 3.1), characterized by much dialectal variation, which would separate the Atlantic area (B2), in contact with the Caribbean dialects, from the remaining zones.

Granda (1977) suggests that the vernacular spoken in the Chocó hinterland (A1 and B1) would have preserved more conservative features, due to its isolation from the rest of Colombia. Conversely, the dialect used on the

Atlantic coast of the Department (B2), which is in direct contact with the Caribbean region, would have abandoned some of the most stigmatized CS traits, in favor of more socially acceptable Caribbean features. In between these two dialectological extremes, it would be possible to locate the vernacular spoken along the Pacific littoral (A2), which is not as closely connected to other regions as the Caribbean coast, but – given the existence of commercial ports along the littoral – is less isolated than the dialects spoken in the hinterland of Chocó.

Another account of the [ɾ] ~ [ð] alternation in CS is offered by Correa (2012), who analyzes the phonetic variants encountered for the phonemes /d, r, ɾ/ in intervocalic position and word-initially after a vowel. He focuses on the speech of a group of informants from Cértegui, Nóvita, Tutunendo, Condoto, and Santa Rita de Iró and detects the allophones [ð, r, ɾ, l, Ø], for which he provides detailed spectrographic analyses. Like other authors, since much articulatory variation between /d, r, ɾ/ and /l/ would be present in several western and central African languages (Jacquot 1962; Ladefoged 1964; Lindau 1980; Parkvall 2000; Hyman 2003), Correa (2012: 48) attributes the presence of this phenomenon in CS to the African substrate.

Cases of /d/ ~ /ɾ/ neutralization are common to several contemporary Afro-Hispanic dialects, and have also been systematically encountered in colonial texts depicting *habla bozal* (47).

(47) a. *Kon uno re ustere <de ustedes>.*
 with one of you
 'With one of you' (Palenquero; Megenney 1986: 108).

b. *Como ro <dos> vece.*
 Like two Times
 'Like two times' (Afro-Domenican Spanish; Megenney 1990: 109).

(III) *Neutralization of /l/ and /ɾ/* The alternation between /l/ and /ɾ/ is quite frequent, especially in coda positions (48). This phenomenon has been reported for CS by several researchers (49) and parallels the cases of neutralization found in a variety of other Afro-Hispanic vernaculars (50). Nevertheless, as correctly indicated by Ruiz García (2009: 76), this alternation is also common across the Caribbean, the Canary Islands, and parts of southern Spain; thus, it should not necessarily be ascribed to the African substrate (Canfield 1981; Lipski 1994b).

(48) a. *Me dijo que llegó talde <tarde>.*
 CL said that arrived late
 'He told me that he arrived late.'

b. *¿Hizo argo <algo> malo?*
 did something wrong
 'Did he do something wrong?'

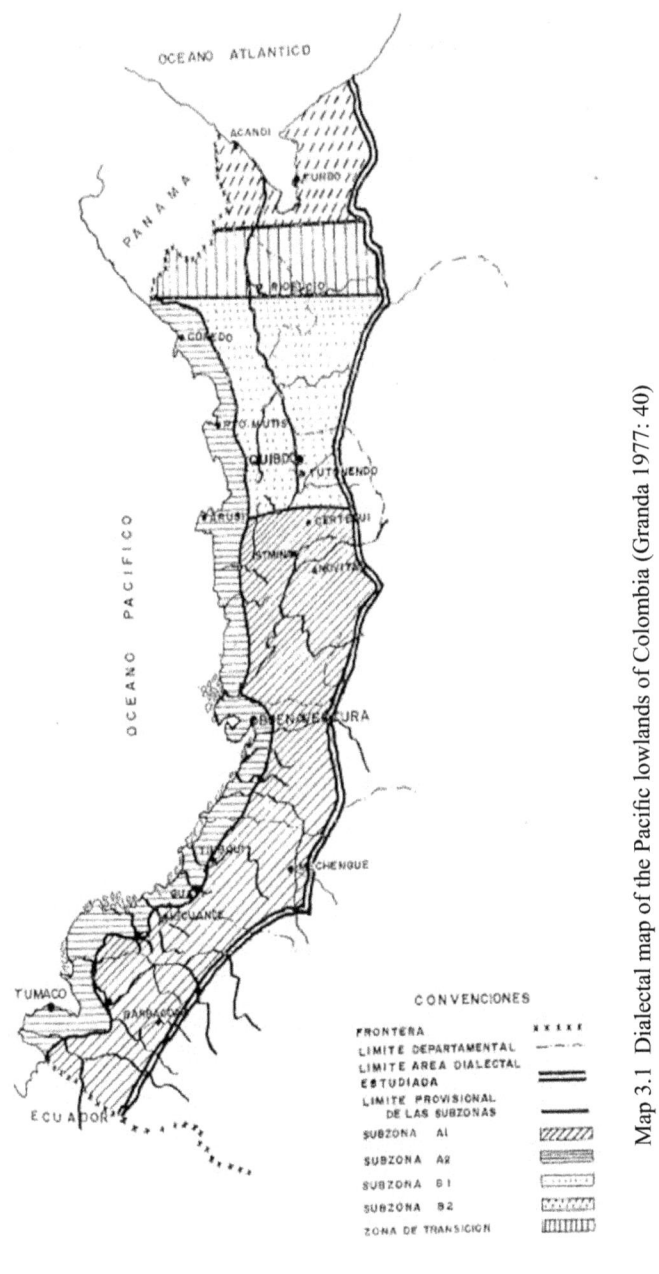

Map 3.1 Dialectal map of the Pacific lowlands of Colombia (Granda 1977: 40)

(49) a. *Autolidá* <*autoridad*>; *catolce* <*catorce*>; *cardo* <*caldo*>;
authority fourteen Soup
farta <*falda*>.
skirt
'Authority, fourteen, soup, skirt' (Flórez 1950: 111).

b. Colol <calor>; flol <flor>; malzo <marzo>; corchón <colchón>
heat flower March mattress
'Heat; flower; March; mattress; palm' (Manzini 1983: 132).

(50) a. *Ese chico vino a pol* <*por*> *pan.*
this guy came to for bread
'This guy came to get bread' (Afro-Peruvian Spanish; Sessarego 2015a: 33).

b. *Mier* <*miel*> *de abeja.*
Honey of bee
'Honey bee' (Barlovento Spanish; Megenney 1999: 74–5).

(IV) Loss of Syllable-final /r/ Syllable-final /ɾ/ may be elided, especially in word-final position on infinitive verb forms (51). My CS corpus aligns with the examples provided by other authors who studied this dialect (52), and with the data on /ɾ/ elision encountered across a variety of AHLAs (53).

(51) a. *Acá hace caló* <*calor*>, *siempre.*
here does heat Always
'It is hot here, always.'

b. *Ya no se puede trabajá* <*trabajar*>.
already no CL can work
'We cannot work anymore.'

(52) a. *Sí señó* <*señor*>; *ayé* <*ayer*>; *gobernaró* <*gobernador*>.
yes sir yesterday governor
'Yes sir; yesterday; governor; to discourage' (Flórez 1950: 111).

b. *Comé* <*comer*> *la yeba* <*yerba*>.
eating the grass
'Eating the grass' (Montes Giraldo 1974: 411).

(53) a. *Ese señó* <*señor*> *ya ta mueto.*
this man already is dead
'This man is already dead' (Afro-Peruvian Spanish; Sessarego 2015a: 31).

3.3 The Phonetics and Phonology of Chocó Spanish

b. *Le gusta   bailá <bailar> bomba con botella.*
   CL pleases to dance   bomba with bottle
   'She likes to dance bomba with a bottle' (Chota Valley Spanish, Sessarego 2013b: 64).

(V)   Yeísmo CS is perfectly in line with coastal Colombian dialects, where the opposition between /ʎ/ and /j/ has been lost in favor of /j/;[5] thus, it is a *yeísta* variety (54). On the other hand, in certain regions of the Colombian highlands, such an opposition may still be heard. For this reason, Highland Colombian Spanish has often been classified as a *lleísta* dialect (Canfield 1981: 36), even though /ʎ/ is rapidly disappearing from the Spanish spoken in Bogotá (Montes Giraldo 1969). CS *yeísmo* has been pointed out by several authors (55). In this respect, this vernacular matches the examples reported for several AHLAs, which, with the exception of a few cases (e.g., Chota Valley Spanish, Sessarego 2013b: 65), are for the most part *yeístas* (56).

(54) a. *Vamos   ayá <allá>.*
         go   There
         'Let's go there.'

      b. *Queda   en el   medio de la   caye <calle>.*
         stay   in the middle of the street
         'It is located in the middle of the street.'

(55) a. *Cayado <callado>; gayina <gallina>; tuyido <tullido>.*
         Silent   hen   crippled
         'Silent; hen; crippled' (Manzini 1983: 130).

      b. *Eyo <ellos>   se   fueron   ayer.*
         They   CL   left   yesterday
         'They left yesterday' (Schwegler 1991b: 99).

(56) a. *Hay que yamar <llamar> a señor del   Zarandango pa'*
         must   call   to man of the Zarandango for
         que   abra.
         that   open
         'We have to call the guy from Zarandango so that he will open' (Afro-Peruvian Spanish; Sessarego 2015a: 37).

      b. *Disi,   eyu <ellos>   habla   siempre   así.*
         they-say   they   Talk   always   such
         'They say, they always talk that way' (Afro-Bolivian Spanish; Lipski 2008: 101).

---

[5] In Castilian Spanish the phonemes /j/ and /ʎ/ are orthographically represented as <y> and <ll>, as in the minimal pairs *hoya* ['o.ja] 'hole' and *olla* ['o.ʎa] 'pot.'

64   A Sketch of Chocó Spanish

(VI)   Velarization and Labialization of Word-final [n]   Word-final /n/ in my corpus is often velarized [ŋ]. Occasionally, it is pronounced with a bilabial articulation [m] (57), in line with the cases reported by Flórez (1950), Montes Giraldo (1974), and Manzini (1983), among other authors (58). While velarization processes of this kind are frequently found across the AHLAs and Caribbean Spanish (59), final /n/ labialization is not commonly attested in these dialects. Montes Giraldo (1974: 427) indicates that this feature is quite sporadic in Chocó, while it is more widespread in nearby regions, especially in the Department of Cauca.

(57)   a. *Era una [na.'sjoŋ] <nación> de Europa.*
         was a   nation   of Europe
         'It was a European nation.'

       b. *Vamos pa' [po.pa.'jam] <Popayán>.*
         go   To   Popayán
         'Let's go to Popayán.'

(58)   a. *[saŋ.'xwam] <San Juan>; [ka.'xom] <cajón>.*
         San Juan   drawer
         'San Juan; drawer' (Montes Giraldo 1974: 412).

       b. *Corazóm <corazón>; maletím <maletín>; pam <pan>;*
         heart   Briefcase   bread
         tambiém <también>.
         too
         'Heart; briefcase; bread; too' (Manzini 1983: 132).

(59)   a. *Lo que dijo Sarli no me pareció [taŋ] <tan> amable.*
         CL that said Sarli no CL seemed so   lovely
         'What Sarli said did not seem to me so lovely' (Afro-Peruvian Spanish; Sessarego 2015a: 38).

       b. *Muy [βjeŋ] <bien>   hecho.*
         very well   done
         'Very well done' (Afro-Panamanian Spanish; Lipski 1989: 43).

(VII)   Gemination   Consonant stops in onset position may undergo gemination if preceded by a liquid sound or by /s/ in coda position (60). This phenomenon – reported for CS (61) and for other AHLAs (62) – is also encountered in Caribbean Colombian Spanish, as indicated by Lipski (1994a: 211) (see Section 3.2.3), as well as in a variety of other Caribbean vernaculars.

(60) a. *A mí me gutta <gusta> la fietta <fiesta> de San Pancho.*
to CL CL pleases the festival of San Pancho
'I like San Pancho festival.'

b. *Este señó vive en la sebba <selva>.*
this man lives in the forest
'This man lives in the forest.'

(61) a. *Pogke <porque>; aggo <algo>; pieddo <pierdo>.*
why Something lose
'Why; something; I lose' (Shwegler 1991b: 91).

b. *Le gutta <gusta> e chimme <chisme>.*
CL Pleases the gossip
'She likes the gossip' (Murillo Mena 2005: 31).

(62) a. *Tuetto <tuerto>; fuette <fuerte>; sebbesa <cerveza>.*
one-eyed strong beer
'One-eyed; strong; beer' (Afro-Puerto Rican Spanish; Álvarez Nazario 1974: 161).

b. *Pogque <porque>; sinveggüenza <sinvergüenza>.*
why shameless
'Why; shameless' (Afro-Cuban Bozal Spanish; Lipski 2005: 162).

(VIII) Weakening and Elision of Intervocalic Voiced Stops Voiced stops in intervocalic position are often weakened and elided in CS (63). This phenomenon is widespread in Afro-Chocoan speech (64) and in several other AHLAs (65); overall, it may be considered a common feature of vernacular Spanish.

(63) a. *Taban tomaos <tomados>.*
Were drunk
'They were drunk.'

b. *Hay como un lao <lago>.*
is like a laka
'There is something like a lake'

(64) a. *Amao <amado>; partío <partido>; auelo <abuelo>.*
loved left grandfather
'Loved; left; grandfather' (Manzini 1983: 131).

b. *Colorao <colorado>; pelaito <peladito>; naa <nada>.*
red child nothing
'Red; child; nothing' (Murillo Mena 2005: 33, 35).

(65) a. *En   la   mañana   ha   veníu <venido>.*
       in   the   morning   has   arrived
       'In the morning he has arrived' (Afro-Bolivian Spanish; Sessarego 2011a: 117).

   b. *Me   lo   roaron <robaron>.*
      CL   CL   stole
      'They stole it from me' (Afro-Peruvian Spanish; Cuba 2002: 26).

(IX) Consonant Cluster Simplification   Consonant cluster simplification is a frequent phenomenon in my corpus (66). Similar examples for CS have also been identified by Flórez (1950), Manzini (1983), and Ruiz García (2009), among others (67). This trait is commonly encountered in the AHLAs (68), and – more generally – across uneducated varieties of Spanish.

(66) a. *Así   jue   que   nosoto <nosotros>   arreglamoh   el   asunto.*
        such was   that we   fixed   the   issue
        'It was like this that we fixed the issue.'

   b. *Felipe es un ténico <técnico> de Quibdó.*
      Felipe is a technician   of Quibdó
      'Felipe is a technician of Quibdó.'

(67) a. *Prático <práctico>; produto <producto>; adatarse <adaptarse>.*
        Practical   product   adapting
        'Practical; product; adapting' (Flórez 1950: 111).

   b. *Ator <actor>; caráter <carácter>; diretor <director>.*
      Actor   character   director
      'Actor; character; director' (Manzini 1983: 132).

(68) a. *Ombe <hombre>; gande <grande>.*
        man   big
        'Man; big' (Palenquero; Megenney 1986: 115).

   b. *El   contato <contracto>   es   algo   pa'   ayudá*
      the contract   is   something   to   help
      a   los   peones   de   acá.
      to   the   peons   from   here
      'The contract is something to help the peons from here' (Afro-Peruvian Spanish; Sessarego 2015a: 35).

(X)   Conversion /f/ > gt; [hʷ, ɸ, x]   The phoneme /f/ may be pronounced as [hʷ], [ɸ], and [x] (69), especially when it occurs word-initially. This

3.3 The Phonetics and Phonology of Chocó Spanish

phenomenon is quite common across vernacular varieties. In particular, the /f/ > [hʷ, ɸ, x] conversion is frequently found in the dialects of Spanish that developed from contact with substrate languages lacking [f], and can also be conceived as the retention of a rustic pronunciation, which disappeared from standard varieties of contemporary Spanish (Lipski 1995, 2008: 71). This phonetic trait has often been reported for CS (70) and for a number of other AHLAs (71).

(69)   a. *Eso [ɸwe] <fue> algo raro.*
           this was   something strange
           'This was something strange.'

       b. *[a. 'hʷwe.ra] <afuera> los mandamoh.*
           Outside   CL sent
           'We sent them outside.'

(70)   a. *Ajuera <afuera>; jue <fue>.*
           Outside   was
           'Outside; it was' (Murillo Mena 2005: 37).

       b. *['hʷa.sil] <fácil>; [li.si.'ɸe] <Lucifer>.*
           Easy   Lucifer
           'Easy; Lucifer' (Montes Giraldo 1974: 410).

(71)   a. *Nosotros ['hʷwi.mos] <fuimos> al río.*
           we   went   to river
           'We went to the river' (Chota Valley Spanish; Sessarego 2013b: 50–1).

       b. *Cómo lo [ɸo.'ra.ba] <forraba>.*
           How   CL   covered
           'How he covered it' (Barlovento Spanish; Megenney 1999: 81).

(XI)   **Glottal *[ʔ]***   Apparently, the first linguist to notice /k/ glotalization in CS was Flórez (1950), who indicated the presence of this sound in the speech of some young Chocoanos. Nevertheless, as Granda (1977: 99–100) pointed out, Flórez did not seem to have realized that such a phenomenon was indeed a specific phonetic trait of this dialect; rather, he probably thought it had to do with some idiosyncratic pronunciation of a few informants. Granda (1974: 277; 1977: 99–100) highlights this situation by reporting Flórez's (1950: 161–2) words on this point:

In several Chocoan locations I have heard some people pronounce a strong *c* and *qu* as a little jump or light glottal occlusion. I have heard this articulation in the speech of some children from Condoto, who must be ten or twelve years old, the expressions *Córdoba, acomodar, cuando va a cobrar, queso, manteca.* We have observed similar phenomena in a child from Tadó, who must have been a bit older, in the expressions *una caja, una cajetilla.* We noticed something similar in the pronunciation of José Ángel Rivas, from Nóvita, who is forty-seven years of age: strong *c* or *qu* were replaced by a glottal occlusion in words like these: *coger, cantando, cuando, cualquier, aquí, mi querido.* Some teachers from Nóvita and Istmina said they had observed a similar pronunciation in *carne, queso, caro, callada, cálculo, miércoles, puerco, cerca, acercar, qué, quien, descolgaron,* etc. (Author's translation)[6]

Granda appears surprised by the fact that, given such an account of this phonetic trait, Flórez did not realize the systematic nature of [ʔ] in CS, and dismissed the phenomenon by saying that *"probablemente esta manera de articulación se deba a circumstancias anormales"* (this type of articulation is probably due to abnormal circumstances) (Flórez 1950: 162), thus suggesting those instances of [ʔ] would be the result of pronunciation errors. On the contrary, Granda stresses the fact that these glottal realizations are the systematic byproduct of a phonetic change affecting /k/ in onset position (1974: 228–9; 1977: 101). He suggests that the presence of [ʔ] in CS may be due to the fact that several substrate languages presented such a sound (see also Granda 1974: 252, 1977: 125, 1988: 77). In particular, he points out that a number of Kwa languages (Igbo, Kalabari, Kambari) would have implosive consonants, some languages belonging to the West-Atlantic family (Fula, Serer) have either glottal or preglottal sounds, while the Kwa group (Idoma, Bini, Isoko, Itsekiri) uses phonemes consisting of a combination of two stops (/k͡p/, /g͡b/), which require glottal occlusions for their realization (Ladefoged 1964: 5–13). In Granda's (1974: 252, 1977: 125–6) view, according to his Monogenetic-Decreolization model, the sound [ʔ] would have been transmitted from the African substrate languages to a colonial Latin American creole, which, in a subsequent phase, would have progressively approximated to Spanish:

It appears to be highly probable that the glottal articulation, frequent and general in these African languages, was transmitted from them, through a bilingual phase, to a "creole" phonological system that ... replaced them in the Latin American regions inhabited by black populations and that, subsequently, was transmitted, in turn ... to a more-recent

---

[6] Original Spanish version: *En varios lugares del Chocó he oído a algunas personas pronunciar la c fuerte y la qu como un saltillo o ligera oclusión glotal. A chicos de Condoto, con diez o doce años de edad, oí tal articulación en las expresiones Córdoba, acomodar, cuando va a cobrar, queso, manteca. Fenómenos semejantes observamos en un chico de Tadó, algo mayor que los anteriores, en las expresiones una caja, una cajetilla. Cosa parecida notamos en la pronunciación de José Ángel Rivas, noviteño de cuarenta y siete años de edad: la c fuerte o que se remplazaba con oclusión glotal en cualquier palabra que tuviera ese fonema: coger, cantando, cuando, cualquier, aquí, mi querido. Algunas maestras de Nóvita e Istmina nos indicaron que habían observado pronunciación semejante en carne, queso, caro, callada, cálculo, miércoles, puerco, cerca, acercar, qué, quien, descolgaron, etc.*

3.3 The Phonetics and Phonology of Chocó Spanish

variety of the language (of a creole base but progressively relexified and restructured by Spanish), and still remains in the present. (Author's translation)[7]

Granda (1977: 36) suggests that the presence of [ʔ] in CS would be concentrated in the region surrounding Nóvita and Cértegui (the most conservative zone). It would be only partially encountered in Tutunendo; while, in the northern region (Acandí, Riosucio and Turbo, closer to the Caribbean), it would be absent. Thus, this phenomenon would be parallel – to a good extent – to the territorial diffusion of the [ð]>[ɾ] process.

Of a different opinion is Correa (2012), who, after a detailed acoustic analysis of the glottalization phenomena occurring in CS, suggests that [ʔ] may be seen as the result of an internal change [k]>[ʔ], not necessarily driven by the African substrate. He highlights that a closer look at Ladefoged's (1964) data – originally reported by Granda in support of his thesis – indicates that the Kwa and Bantu varieties presenting [ʔ] in their phonological inventory are actually a small minority; while, on the other hand, the internal change by which a stop becomes a glottal sound would be quite widespread across the world's languages (Kohler 2001; Redi & Shattuck-Hufnagel 2001; Ladefoged 2001; Esling, Fraser, & Harris 2005), and even found across Spanish dialects (Chela Flores 1986; Zamora Munne & Guitar 1982).

Correa also points out that the instances of [ʔ] he encountered in his corpus should not just be analyzed as the allophonic realizations of /k/; rather, in several cases they act as intonation phrase markers (i.e., the phrase-initial marker in: *es muy poquito* [ˈʔe.ˈmuj.po.ˈki.to] 'it is very little'), a function that glottal stops seem to display also in a number of other languages – including English (Pierrehumbert & Talkin 1991; Dilley & Shattuck-Hufnagel 1995; Redi & Shattuck-Hufnagel 2001). Moreover, in other cases, [ʔ] appears prevocalically as an allophone of /s/ (i.e., *tres años* [tɾe.ˈʔa.ɲo] 'three years'), a phenomenon also recently reported for Puerto Rican Spanish (Valentín-Márquez 2006). Several authors have provided examples of glottalization in CS (72). In this respect, my corpus aligns with their findings (73).

(72)   a. *Nosotro lo [ʔul.ti.ˈβa.mo]* <cultivamos>.
        We   CL   cultivate
        'We cultivate it' (Montes Giraldo 1974: 421).

---

[7] Original Spanish version: *Parece, pues, altamente probable que la articulación glotal, frecuente y general en estas lenguas africanas, haya sido trasmitida desde ellas, y a través de un periodo de bilingüismo, al sistema fonológico 'criollo' que ... las reemplazó en las zonas de población negra de la América española y que, posteriormente, se haya transmitido, a su vez, ... a la modalidad de lengua (de base 'criolla', pero progresivamente reflexificada y reestructurada hacia el español) de las épocas más recientes, hasta llegar al momento actual.*

b. *Mis*   *[ʔo.'ne.ho]*   <*conejos*>.
   my   rabbits
   'My rabbits' (Murillo Mena 2005: 38).

(73)   a. *No me ['ʔa.e]* <*cae*> *muy bien.*
          no CL   falls   very well
          'I do not like him very well.'
       b. *Había ['u.noʔ]* <*unos*> *helicóptero del ejército.*
          was   Some   helicopter   of the   army
          'There were some army helicopters.'

3.3.3 Intonation Patterns

CS intonation significantly diverges from the prosodic patterns commonly attested in standard Spanish (Aguilar et al., 2009) and aligns with prosodic trends detected for other AHLAs (Lipski 2007). In fact, high (L+)H* tones, either rising from a low (L) tone associated with a valley or appearing as a plateau, are predominantly located within prenuclear stressed syllables and are exclusively aligned within stressed syllables in nuclear phrase position (see Figure 3.1) (Mena-Mena 2014; Knaff, Rao, & Sessarego 2018).

These results, in line with data reported for other AHLAs (see Figures 3.2–3.3), have been analyzed in previous works as the byproduct of conventionalized advanced second language acquisition processes, streaming from an incomplete mastery of the phonology/pragmatics interface (Sessarego & Rao 2016; Rao & Sessarego 2016, 2018). Similar prosodic features, in fact, have not only been detected for Spanish vernaculars in contact with African languages (which might have indicated a specific substrate effect); rather, they have also been encountered in dialects of Spanish in contact with Italian (Colantoni & Gurlekian 2004; Colantoni 2011), Veneto (Barnes &

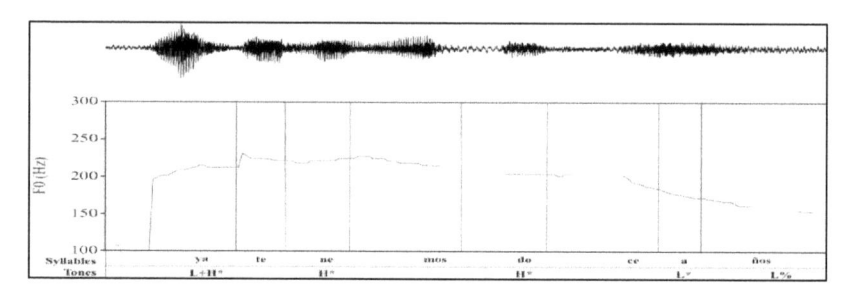

Figure 3.1 Sample F0 contours from Chocó Spanish data for *Ya tenemos doce años* (We are already twelve years old)

3.3 The Phonetics and Phonology of Chocó Spanish   71

Syllable	el	pa	trón	no	sir	ve	pa	ra	na	da
Tones			L+H*	H*	L+H*				L+¡H*	L-

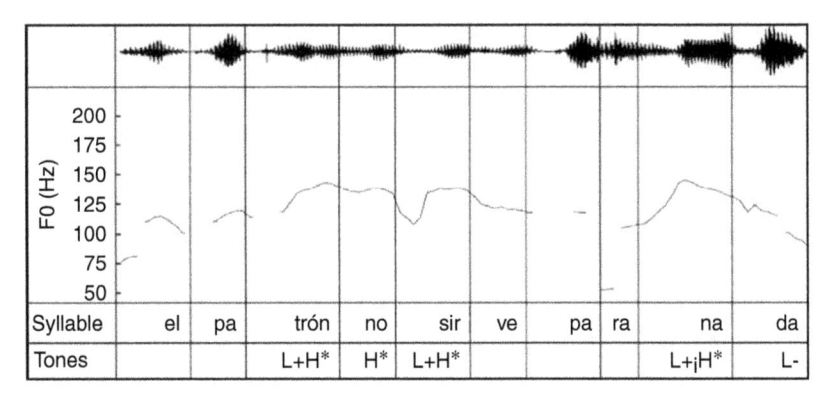

Figure 3.2 Sample F0 contours from Afro-Bolivian Spanish data for *El patrón no sirve para nada* (The owner is useless)

```
e  se    san go  de    dul  ce    pues to   ca    ne    la
L+H*      L+H*   L-    L+H*       L+¡H*           L%
```

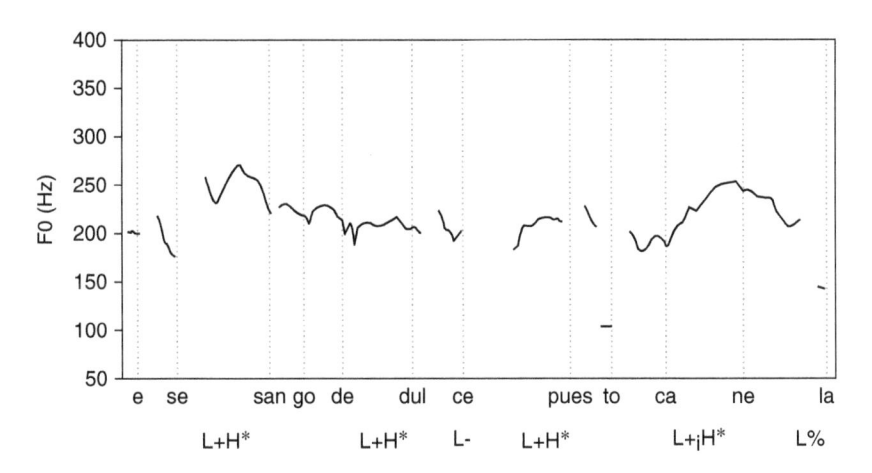

Figure 3.3 Sample F0 contours from Chota Valley Spanish data for *Ese sango de dulce puesto canela* ([In] this sango dessert I put cinnamon)

Michnowicz 2013), Basque (Elordieta 2003), Maya (Michnowicz & Barnes 2013), and Quechua (O'Rourke 2004, 2005); thus supporting the idea of a more widespread and universal second language acquisition mechanism (Sessarego & Rao 2016).

3.3.4   Summary of Chocó Spanish Phonetics and Phonology

The following table is meant to provide a schematic summary of the main phonetic and phonological traits detected for CS as well as their potential

Table 3.1 *Main phonetic and phonological traits of Chocó Spanish*

Phenomenon	SLA effect	Substrate (African) influence	Substrate (indigenous) influence	Internal change	Vernacular feature or Caribbean Spanish feature	Archaic form	Feature shared by other AHLAs
Vowel variation	✓						✓
Diphthongs, hiatuses and single-vowel alternation	✓						✓
Vowel nasalization		✓	?		✓ Caribbean Spanish		✓
Syllable-final aspiration and elision of /s/		✓		?	✓ Caribbean Spanish		✓
Conversion of /d/ > [r] and /ɾ/ > [ð]		✓					✓
Neutralization of /l/ and /ɾ/		✓			✓ Caribbean Spanish		✓
Loss of final syllable /ɾ/		?	?	?	✓ Caribbean Spanish		✓

Yeismo	✓	?		✓				✓
Velarization of word-final [n]		?	?		✓ Caribbean Spanish			✓
Labialization of word-final [n]			✓					
Gemination				✓	✓ Caribbean Spanish			✓
Weakening and elision of intervocalic voiced stops				✓	✓			✓
Consonant cluster simplification	✓			✓	✓			✓
Conversion /f/ > [hʷ, ɸ, x]		?			✓	✓		✓
Glottal [ʔ]		✓		?				
Early-aligned H* tones	✓							✓

origins: SLA effect, substrate influence, internal change, vernacular feature common to other Spanish varieties or encountered in Caribbean Spanish, archaic form, or feature shared by other AHLAs.

3.4   Chocó Spanish Morphosyntax

Besides presenting several phonetic traits that deviate from standard Spanish and align with other AHLAs, CS is also characterized by morphosyntactic phenomena that have been systematically reported for contemporary Latin American black speech and colonial Bozal Spanish. Some of these features have been at the center of the debate on the origin of this Afro-Hispanic dialect. Indeed, as we observed in Chapter 2, Granda (1974, 1977, 1988) and Schwegler (1991a, 1991b) claim that certain morphosyntactic patterns found in CS would represent the remaining traces of a now-decreolized colonial Latin American creole (Monogenesis-Decreolization Hypothesis), while, on the other hand, McWhorter (2000) argues that the grammatical elements detected for CS would not be that divergent from standard Spanish. Thus, in his view, they would show that, even in a scenario like colonial Chocó, where the sociohistorical conditions for creole formation were well in place, Spanish could not possibly creolize, since a Spanish pidgin did not previously form in Africa (Afrogenesis Hypothesis).

Casting light on this debate will inevitably require the combination of both linguistic and sociohistorical information. As for now, in the following sections we will concentrate on the most salient morphosyntactic patterns encountered in this Afro-Hispanic vernacular, as they emerged during my fieldwork and from the investigations of other researchers.

3.4.1   Nominal Domain

(1)   Reduced Number Agreement   Traditional CS is characterized by reduced plural marking across the Determiner Phrase (DP). Indeed, in sharp contrast with standard Spanish, in this dialect number is not marked redundantly; rather, plurality is indicated only on determiners, so that nouns and adjectives do not carry plural morphemes. DP plurality can be expressed either inherently – by recurring to quantifiers and numerals (74a–b), which do not take plural morphemes – or by inflecting possessives (74c), demonstratives (74d), and articles (74e–f). In this respect, pluralizing strategies in CS closely parallel the mechanisms adopted by several other Afro-Hispanic dialects (75). This phenomenon is also a well-known feature of Popular Brazilian Portuguese (PBP) (76) (Sessarego & Ferreira 2016), for which a (de)creolization hypothesis has also been proposed (Guy 1981, 2004).

3.4 Chocó Spanish Morphosyntax

(74) a. *Mucho* <*muchos*> *doctor* <*doctores*> *colombiano* <*colombianos*>.
Many doctor.SG Colombian.SG
'Many Colombian doctors.'

b. *Cinco doctor* <*doctores*> *colombiano* <*colombianos*>.
five doctor.SG Colombian.SG
'Five Colombian doctors.'

c. *Mis Doctor* <*doctores*> *colombiano* <*colombianos*>.
my.PL doctor.SG Colombian.SG
'My Colombian doctors.'

d. *Esos doctor* <doctores> colombiano <colombianos>.
this.PL doctor.SG Colombian.SG
'These Colombian doctors.'

e. *Los doctor* <doctores> *colombiano* <*colombianos*>.
the.PL doctor.SG Colombian.SG
'The Colombian doctors.'

f. *Unos doctor* <doctores> colombiano <colombianos>.
some.PL doctor.SG Colombian.SG
'Some Colombian doctors.'

(75) a. *Ella* tiene doce maceta <macetas> grande <grandes>.
she has twelve pot.SG big.SG
'She has twelve big pots' (Afro-Peruvian Spanish; Cuba 2002: 37)

b. *En idioma antigo de mis abuelo* <*abuelos*>.
the.SG language.SG old.SG of my.PL grandparent.SG
'The old language of my grandparents' (Afro-Bolivian Spanish; Lipski 2008: 93)

c. Mucho devoción tenían los afro <afros>.
Much.SG devotion.SG had the.PL afro.SG
'Africans used to be very devoted' (Chota Valley Spanish; Romero & Sessarego 2018: 68).

(76) *Meus/esses/os/muitos/quatro bom* <*bons*> *filho* <*filos*>
my.PL/this.PL/the.PL/many/four good.SG son.SG
trabalhador <*trabahadores*>
hard-working.SG
'My/these/the/many/four good hard-working sons' (PBP; Sessarego & Ferreira 2016: 292)

Granda (1988) also points out the aforementioned parallelism between CS and PBP. Nevertheless, in contrast to Guy's hypothesis on the origin of such a feature in this Lusophone vernacular, the author suggests that its source in CS –

as well as in some varieties of Caribbean and Paraguayan Spanish – may be explained in terms of internal processes driven by linguistic economy. Thus, for Granda, recurring to the (de)creolization hypothesis would not be the most explicative option in this case. Granda (1988: 79–80) states:

I do not think, on the other hand, that it is possible [to postulate an African origin] concerning ... the elimination of redundant plural marking across nominal phrases, even though this goes against the brilliant analysis by Gregory R. Guy in favor of an African genesis to account for this phenomenon in PBP ... I think that, as far as this concrete feature is concerned, it is better to ascribe its origin to internal factors, ... to preserve ... maximal economy in the use of ... number markers. (Author's translation)[8]

In the literature, in fact, some authors have suggested that non-redundant plural marking in PBP would be the direct result of African substrate influence (Guy 2004; Lipski 2006). Conversely, Naro & Scherre (2000) do not agree with this hypothesis and consider the number agreement differences between PBP and Peninsular Portuguese to simply be the result of internally motivated language change; thus, their perspective is in line with Granda on this point (see Schwegler 2010: 30–1 for an overview of this debate).

Owing to recent contact between traditional CS and more standard varieties of Spanish, much variation can be found in the speech of my informants. As a result, several DP categories (quantifiers, nouns, adjectives, etc.) may carry variable plural –s marking, thus generating a wide range of DP configurations, as shown in (77).

(77) *Hay unos muchacho <muchachos> que viven en el pueblo.*
is some.PL guy.SG who live in the.SG village.SG
we CL
Notro nos
mudamo acá Porque pueblo no había las cosas que hay en
moved here because village.SG no was the.PL thing.PL that is in
la ciudá.
the.SG city SG
Acá hay más trabajo Y entonce viven acá los trabajador
here is more work.SG and therefore live here the.PL worker.SG
<trabajadores>

---

[8] Original Spanish version: *No creo, por el contrario, que se pueda [postular un origen africano] respecto a ... la eliminación de la redundancia de la marca de pluralidad en sintagma nominales, a pesar de la brillante argumentación de Gregory R. Guy a favor de la génesis africana de este fenómeno en el portugués popular brasileño ... Pienso que, respecto a este rasgo concreto, es preferible remitirse a factores causales internos, ... para preservar ... la máxima economía en la utilización de los marcadores ... de número.*

pero los   trabajadores local <*locales*> *siguen allá en   las mina*
but the.PL worker.PL   local.SG   keep   there in the.PL
<*minas*>.
mine.SG
'There are some guys who live in the village. We moved here because in the village there were not the things that are here in the city. There is more work here and for this reason there are more workers living here, but the rural workers keep working there in the mines.'

The presence of reduced number agreement across the DP in CS has been described by a variety of authors, who have illustrated this process by providing several naturalistic examples (78). These CS phenomena strictly resemble the data reported for several other AHLAs (79).

(78)   a. *Hacen   unos   caney* <*caneies*>.
           Make   some.PL hut.SG
           'They make some huts' (Flórez 1950: 423).

          b. *Cuando   yo   era   niño,   eda   las*
           when   I   was   child   were   the.PL
           calle   barrosa <*calles barrosas*>.
           street.SG   muddy.SG
           'When I was a child, the streets were muddy' (Rodríguez Tocarruncho 2010: 36).

(79)   a. *Mis   hermano   joven* <*hermanos jóvenes*>.
           my.PL   brother.SG   young.SG
           'My young brothers' (Chota Valley Spanish, Sessarego 2013b: 70).

          b. *Cinco   trabajador   internacional* <*trabajadores internacionales*>.
           five   worker.SG   international.SG
           'Five international workers' (Afro-Peruvian Spanish, Sessarego 2015a: 41).

(II)   Variable Gender Agreement   Variable gender agreement is another feature commonly found in traditional CS. Elder informants, in fact, are those presenting the highest rates of lack of concord, while younger, more educated informants tend to present agreement configurations closer to the standard norm. Findings suggest that in the most traditional variety of this dialect only definite articles and demonstratives agree with the noun, while the remaining DP categories (indefinite articles, quantifiers, adjectives, etc.) are not specified for agreement features and appear in the default masculine form, as exemplified in (80).

(80) a. *Todo <toda> la   fiesta   colombiano <colombiana>.*
      all.M   the.F   party.F Colombian.M
      'All the Colombian party.'
   b. *Un <una> fiesta   colombiano <colombiana>.*
      a.M   party.F Colombian.M
      'A Colombian party.'

Nevertheless, a variety of gender agreement configurations can be encountered in contemporary CS. This is particularly evident in linguistic communities such as the refugee camp of Villa España, where informants of diverse ages and educational backgrounds, proceeding from different rural areas of Chocó, are now living together. Thus, the agreement patterns found in this camp are all but homogeneous and a lot of variation can be found, as (81) shows.

(81) a. *Esta   gente   es gente muy   educado <educada>,*
       this.F   people.F is people.F   very polite.M
       Dizque es gente de un <una> nación europeo <europea>
       apparently is people.F of a.M nation.F European.M
       'These are very polite people. Apparently these people are from a European nation.'
   b. *Todo <toda> esa   historia   es   un   asunto   de guerra.*
      all.M   this.F   history.F is   an.M   issue.M   of war.F
      Todas   las   trabajadoras   se   escaparon.
      all.F   the.F   worker.F   CL   Escaped
      All this history is a war issue. All the workers run away.'

Besides the fact that for some speakers certain DP categories (adjectives, quantifiers, etc.) may not be specified for gender features (80–1), another reason for the differences in agreement configurations between CS and standard Spanish is that certain nouns, classified as masculine in CS, are specified for feminine gender in standard Spanish, and vice versa. Montes Giraldo (1974) and Manzini (1983) identify this gender mismatch in the nouns *calor* 'heat' and *costumbre* 'habit' (82).

(82) a. *El <la>   costumbre   de   nosotros   aquíes   éste.*
       the.M   habit.M   of   us   here is   this.M
       'This is our habit here' (Montes Giraldo 1974: 423).
   b. *La <el>   calor   de   hoy.*
      the.F   heat.F   of   today
      'The heat of today' (Manzini 1983: 134).

3.4 Chocó Spanish Morphosyntax   79

Similar data on CS gender agreement have been detected by Ruiz García (2009: 43) (83) and are perfectly in line with the patterns reported for a number of other AHLAs (84). The presence of variation in CS and similar contact varieties, spoken in fairly isolated regions like the Colombian Chocó, should not be taken as a symptom of imminent decreolization. Contact languages, like any other languages, are not monolithic systems (Mufwene 1994); on the contrary, given the reduced pressure posed by standardization and schooling processes on these speech communities, these cases of language variability are to be expected.

(83) a. *Quieren   cosa   ligero <ligera>*.
         Want   thing.F   light.M
         'They want something light' (Ruiz García 2009: 43).

      b. *Como   negro.   somos   personas   contentos <contentas>,*
         as   black.M   are   person.F   happy.M
         alegres.
         joyful.M
         'We, as black people, are happy, we are joyful' (Ruiz García 2009: 43).

(84) a. *Siempre   contaba   algunos   cosa <algunas cosas>*.
         Always   told   some.M   thing.F
         'He always told some things' (Afro-Bolivian Spanish; Lipski: 2008: 90).

      b. *La   merluza   aquí   es   más   barato <barata>*.
         the.F   hake.F   here   is   more   cheap.M
         'The hake here is cheaper' (Barlovento Spanish; Megenney 1999: 46)

(III)   Bare Nouns Another morphosyntactic feature that makes CS diverge from standard Spanish is the presence of bare nouns, both in subject and object position (85), as Ruiz García (2009) showed in her study (86). A closer look at bare nouns' behaviors in CS seems to suggest that they obey syntactic, semantic, and pragmatic restrictions similar to those applying to other AHLAs (87) (Gutiérrez-Rexach & Sessarego 2011; Sessarego 2013b, 2014a, 2015a). Such patterns are also parallel, to a certain extent, to those encountered in PBP (88).

(85) a. *Ella   pica Ø <el>   pescao   así,   con Ø <el>   cuchillo.*
         she   chop   fish   such   with   knife
         'She chops the fish like this, with the knife.'

b. *Ø <los> soldados llegaban, Ø <la> gente escapaba.*
    soldiers arrived   people escaped
   'The soldiers arrived, the people escaped.'

(86)   a. *Yo*   trabajo *Ø <la>*   mina.
             I   Work   mine
          'I work the mine' (Ruiz García 2009: 45).

       b. *Ø <La> cabeza mía no es pa' eso no, maestro.*
               head   mine no is for this no sir
          'My head is not for this, sir' (Ruiz García 2009: 45).

(87)   a. *Ø <Los>*   chancho   come *Ø <las>*   papa.
              Pig   eat   potato
          'Pigs eat potatoes' (Afro-Bolivian Spanish; Sessarego 2014a: 70).

       b. *Ø <La>*   madre   quere   jugá   con *Ø <las>*   huawa.
                       mother   want   play   with   child
          'The mother wants to play with the child / Mothers want to play with children.' (Afro-Peruvian Spanish, Sessarego 2015a: 47).

(88)   a. PBP.
          Ele   *comprou Ø <o/os>*   *computador.*
          he   bought   computer
          'He bought a computer/ computers' (Schmitt & Munn 1999: 5).

       b. *Ø <Os>*   *cachorro*   *gosta*   *de Ø <da>*   *gente.*
                     Dog   likes   of   people.
          'Dogs like people' (Schmitt & Munn 1999: 7).

(IV) Adjectives The possessive *su* 'his/her' can be used in constructions in which standard Spanish would employ *nuestro* 'our' (89).

(89)   a. *El*   *caso*   *era*   *comer*   *su <nuestro>*   *pescao*   *y*   *comer*
             the   case   was   eating   his   fish   and   eating
             su <nuestro>   *caldo*   *ahumao*   *también, eso*   *era*   *lo*   *que*
             his   soup   smoked   too   this was   CL   that
             notro comíamo.
             we   ate
          'We used to eat our smoked fish and our soup, this was what we used to eat' (Rodríguez Tucarruncho 2010: 75).

3.4 Chocó Spanish Morphosyntax

b. *Nosotros allá tocamos su <nuestro> bombo.*
we there played his drum
'We played our drum there' (Dieck 1993: 21).

Flórez (1950: 112) also reports the use of *cuyo* 'whose' rather than *de quién* 'of whom' in interrogative constructions, as in (90).

(90)   a. *¿Estas sillas cuyas <de quién> son?*
         these chairs whose are
         'Whose chairs are these?' (Flórez 1950: 112).

       b. *¿Esto cuyo <de quién> es?*
         this Whose is
         'Whose is this?' (Flórez 1950: 112).

(IV)   **Subject Pronouns**   Traditional CS is characterized by *voseo*, so that the second person singular subject pronoun *vos* is used, along with its respective verb form (91).

(91)   a. *Vos sos jodona.*
         you are annoying
         'You are annoying' (Manzini 1983: 136).

       b. *Vo no tené no gana.*
         'You no have no desire'
         'You have no desire' (Manzini 1983: 136).

Nevertheless, in contemporary CS, the pronoun *tú* and its verbal conjugation (i.e., *tú comes* 'you eat') can be heard. Flórez (1950: 112) and Manzini (1983: 136) point out that *vos* and *tú* forms are often confused, so that they may be mixed together in the same construction (92).

(92)   a. *Vos, ¿qué me decís?* ~ *Vos, ¿qué me dice?s*
         you what CL say   you what CL say
         'You, what did you say to me?' (Manzini 1983: 136).

Montes Giraldo (1974) suggests that the presence of *voseo* in Chocó may be seen as an additional indicator of the conservative nature of this region, where certain linguistic changes that took place in the Caribbean were not completely adopted in CS. The author states (1974: 427):

While on the Atlantic coast these features appear to be at an advanced stage and high in frequency, in Chocó, and in the Pacific zone in general, they seem to have stopped at the beginning; this region does not appear to have adopted relatively modern changes such as *tuteo*, which is widespread across the Caribbean. (Author's translation)[9]

Another characteristic of CS is that overt subjects tend to be used in non-emphatic non-contrastive contexts, where covert subjects (*pro*) would be employed in standard Spanish (93). In a pro-drop language like standard Spanish, the difference between an overt subject pronoun and *pro* has to do with the specification of a [+topic shift] feature in the former category, which would be absent in the latter. Conversely, non-pro-drop languages, such as English, would not be endowed with *pro*, so that all subject pronouns must necessarily be overtly spelled out (Rizzi 1992; Grimshaw & Samek-Ludovici 1998). CS, in line with other AHLAs (94), Caribbean Spanish (95), and Brazilian Portuguese (96), is characterized by a hybrid system, so that overt subjects tend to be used redundantly, thus resulting in constructions that would sound pragmatically odd in standard Spanish (Sorace 2000, 2003; Rothman 2008; Sessarego & Gutiérrez-Rexach 2017).

(93) a. Ellos   decían que ellos querían estar   de acuerdo.
       they   said   that they   wanted   staying of agreement
       'They said they wanted to agree.'

   b. No,   pero   como yo   hace   rato   yo   ya   terminé
      no   but   since I   make   while I   already finished
      esa   jornada, yo   una vez   a   lo   mío   yo
      that   day   I   one time   to   CL   mine   I
      ya   no   tuve má.
      already no   had   more
      'No, because I had already finished my working day for a while, after having done my stuff, I was done' (Rodríguez Tucarruncho 2010: 61).

(94) a. Claro   yo como   fue   Chico   yo   no acorda.
       obviously I since   was   young   I   no remember
       'Obviously, since I was young I do not remember' (Afro-Bolivian Spanish, Lipski 2008: 101).

   b. Si uté no iba   a Songo, uté no veía la cara de un médico.
      if you no went to Songo, you no saw the face of a doctor
      'If you did not go to Songo, you did not see the face of a doctor' (Afro-Cuban Spanish, Ortiz López 1998: 106).

---

[9] Original Spanish version: *Mientras en la costa atlántica estos rasgos presentan carácter avanzado y frecuente, en el Chocó, y en el Pacífico en general, dan la impresión de haberse detenido en sus inicios; esta región parece no haber adoptado cambios relativamente modernos como el tuteo que sí se generalizó en el Caribe.*

(95) a. *Nosotros   a   veces nos   descuidamos,*
       we   sometime CL   neglect except
       salvo   que   no   sea   para
       that   no   is   for   a
       un   discurso, como por   ejemplo
       discourse as   for   example
       una   entrevista... En   eso   nosotros   nos
       an   interview in   this   we   CL
       descuidamos mucho, los   dominicanos específicamente.
       neglect   much   the   Dominicans   specifically
       'We sometimes are careless, except in cases of speeches, as for example an interview. In that regard we are careless, Dominicans specifically' (Dominican Spanish, Toribio 2000: 219).

   b. *Ellos me dijeron que yo tenía anemia ... Si ellos me dicen que yo*
      they CL said   that I had anemia   if they CL say   that I
      estoy en peligro cuando ellos me entran la aguja por   el
      was in danger when they CL enter the needle through the
      ombligo,   yo me voy a ver en una situación de estrés.
      belly-button I CL go to see in a   situation of stress
      'They told me that I had anemia ... If they tell me that I am in danger when they put the needle in my belly-button, I am going to find myself in a stressful situation' (Dominican Spanish, Toribio 2000: 219).

(96) BPB.
   a. *Você, no   Canadá, você pode ser o   que você quiser.*
      you   in the Canada, you can be   CL   that you want
      'In Canada, you can be whatever you want' (Duarte 2000: 191).

   b. *.O   Joãoi disse que elei comprou um computador.*
      the João Says that he   bought   a computer
      'João says that he bought a computer' (Barbosa, Kato, & Duarte 2005: 3).

Third-person pronouns in CS may also refer to inanimate referents (97), in contrast with standard Colombian Spanish, and in line with Caribbean Spanish and BPB (98).

(97) a. *Comenzaron a meterse pa' allá, lo soldao así, pero pa'*
       began   to put   to there the soldier such but   to
       Candelaria[10], como ellai no era popular la gente no, no
       Candelaria   like she no was popular the people no no

[10] Candelaria is the name of a local village.

84   A Sketch of Chocó Spanish

        corrieron por allá a buscarlo.
        run   to there to seek-him
        'They began going over there, the soldiers like this, but Candelaria, since it was not popular, people did not run there to look for him' (Rodríguez Tucarruncho 2010: 76).

    b. *Ese era un puebloi grande, éli fue capital, Nóvita viejo fue*
       this was a village big   he was capital Nóvita old was
       capital del   departamento del   Chocó.
       capital of the department   of the Chocó
       'This was a big village, it was the capital, old Nóvita was the capital of the Department of Chocó' (Rodríguez Tucarruncho 2010: 77).

(98)   a. [Re: *riveri*] *Éli tiene poca agua.*
          he has   little water
          'It has   little water' (Dominican Spanish Toribio 2000: 320).

    b. *A   casai virou   um filme quando elai teve de ir abaixo.*
       the house turned into   a movie when it had to go down
       'The house became a movie when it was demolished' (Brazilian Portuguese, Barbosa *et al.* 2005: 15–16).

(IV)   Object Clitics   Object pronouns may be omitted in CS. This is especially the case with reflexive clitics (99).

(99)   a. [*Mi hija   Ø <se> llama María.*
          my daughter   calls Maria
          'My daughter's name is Maria.'

    b. *Notro Ø <nos> ponemos a tocá   en un rato.*
       we   Start   playing in a bit
       'We will start playing in a bit.'

    Also Ruiz García (2009) and Rodríguez Tucarruncho (2010) reported this phenomenon for CS (100), a feature that is commonly found in other AHLAs too (101).

(100)   a. *Ahí donde   notro   Ø <nos>   bañamo.*
         there   where   we   bathe
        'There, where we bathe' (Rodríguez Tucarruncho 2010: 72).

    b. *No Ø <me> acuerdo   sino   que   llegaba.*
       no   remember   but   that   arrived
       'I do not remember anything but that he arrived' (Ruiz García 2009: 47).

(101) a. *Últimamente   la   gente Ø <se>   está   dedicando a   la*
       lately   the   people   is   dedicating to the
       agricultura
       agriculture
       'Lately people have turned to agriculture' (Chota Valley Spanish, Lipski 1992b: 33).

   b. *Eyus Ø <se>*   *llamaban*   *Sarvo*   *Sarvito.*
      they   call   Zambo   Salvito
      'They were called Zambo Salvito' (Afro-Bolivian Spanish, Sessarego 2011a: 96).

In regards to reflexive categories, a peculiarity of CS concerns the second person plural clitic pronoun *nos*, which may be pronounced as *los* (102).

(102) a. *El   ñame   es   el   cultivo que más resultado*
         the   ñame   is   the   crop   that more result
         los <nos>   ta   dando.
         CL   is   giving
         'The ñame is the crop that is giving us the best results' (Montes Giraldo 1974: 424).

   b. *Apenas   los <nos>   tomamos   por   Ahí   dos o   tres   tragos.*
      only   CL   drank   over there two or three   drinks
      'We only drank two or three drinks over there' (Montes Giraldo 1974: 424).

Variation in pronominal forms is also quite common for the first-person singular object pronoun, *mí* 'me,' and subject pronoun, *yo* 'I,' which may alternate in subject and object position (103).

(103) a. *Ésa   como   tuvo   Má   estudio   que   mí <yo>.*
         that   since   had   more   study   than   me
         'Since she studied more than me' (Rodríguez Tucarruncho 2010: 77).

   b. *Comprar   mi   cosita   ahí   pa   yo   <mí>.*
      to   buy   my   stuff there   for   I
      'To buy my stuff there for me' (Ruiz García 2009: 53).

3.4.2 Verbal Domain

(I) Regularization of Irregular Verb Forms Certain standard Spanish irregular verb forms appear to have been regularized in CS. This process is particularly visible for past participles, for imperfect past forms taking the *–ba* morpheme (rather than ending in *–ía*), and for stem-vowel-changing verbs

(104). In this respect, CS perfectly aligns with other non-standard vernaculars and L2 varieties of Spanish. Two other Afro-Hispanic dialects presenting such regularization processes are Afro-Bolivian and Afro-Peruvian Spanish, as the examples in (105) show.

(104) a. *¡Entonce lo ha víu <visto>!*
therefore CL have seen
'Therefore he saw it!'

b. *¿Cuándo vinió <vino>?*
when came
'When did he come?'

(105) a. *Dizque se ha muríu <muerto>.*
Apparently CL have dead
'They say he died' (Afro-Peruvian Spanish, Sessarego 2015a: 48).

b. *Lu joven saliba <salían> di fiesta.*
the young left of party
'The young people used to go out to party' (Afro-Bolivian Spanish, Sessarego 2011a: 53).

(II)   Archaic Forms The first author to detect archaic verb forms in CS was Flórez (1950: 113), who indicated that "*quedan todavía en el habla inculta formas del español antiguo como vide, vei, via, truje, tope, tar, etc.*" (in uneducated speech, it is still possible to encounter old Spanish forms such as *vide, vei, via, truje, tope, tar,* etc.). Schwegler has also reported their presence, as example (106) shows.

(106) a. *Dende que La trujo <trajo>.*
since that CL brought
'Since he brought it' (Schwegler 1991b: 105).

Verb entries of this type have also been detected for other AHLAs. Cuba (2002: 34–5), for example, found several archaic Spanish conjugation forms for the verb *ver* 'to see' in the black dialect of Chincha, Peru (107).

(107) a. *Yo lo vide <vi>.*
I CL saw
'I saw him.'

b. *Él también lo vido <vio>.*
he too CL saw
'He saw him too.'

3.4 Chocó Spanish Morphosyntax

Another sign of the conservative nature of CS is observed in the use of *ser* 'to be' as an auxiliary verb (108), a linguistic feature that survives in this dialect from Medieval Spanish (Aranovich 2003). In fact, in contemporary standard Spanish the only auxiliary verb employed in compound constructions is *haber* 'to have.'

(108) a. | *Que* | *se* | *fuera* <*hubiera*> | *puejto* | *a* |
| --- | --- | --- | --- | --- |
| that | CL | was | put | to |
| *recortá* | *marera* | *monte* | *adentro.* | |
| cut | wood | mountain | inside | |

'That he had begun to cut wood inside the mountain' (Manzini 1983: 134).

b. *No fueron* <*hubieron*> *hablado de la vida ajena.*
no were   spoken of the life of others
'They would not have spoken about other people's lives' (Ruiz García 2009: 53).

These elements are further indicators of the linguistic isolation of this Afro-Hispanic vernacular, which not only preserves phonetic traits that have already been lost in several other Colombian dialects, it also appears to be significantly conservative from a morphosyntactic standpoint.

(III)   Subject-verb Agreement   Subject-verb agreement tends to be robust; nevertheless, a few instances of third-person singular default forms can be heard in the speech of elderly informants.

(109) a. *Ellas dijo* <*dijeron*> *así, no sé   si é veldá.*
they said   so no know if is truth
'They said so, I do not know if that is the truth.'

b. *Esa vez vino* <*vinieron*> *catorce familias, catorce familias*
this time came fourteen families fourteen families came
'Fourteen families came this time, fourteen families came' (Dieck 1993: 21).

Instances of subject-verb lack of agreement are common across the AHLAs (110), and more generally, across contact varieties.

(110) a. *Yo quiele* <*quiero*> *sé diputá.*
I want   be deputy
'I want to be a deputy' (Afro-Peruvian Bozal Spanish, Lipski 2005: 253).

b. Yo   no   te   lleva <llevo>   a   casa   de   nadie.
   I   no   CL   take   to   home   of   nobody
   'I won't take you to anybody's house' (Afro-Cuban Spanish, Ortiz López 1998: 76).

(IV)   Lack of Subject-verb Inversion in Questions   CS presents lack of subject-verb inversion in questions (111). My results are in line with Ruiz García's (2009) findings for this dialect (112) and align with data from other AHLAs, Caribbean Spanish, and Brazilian Portuguese (113).

(111)   a. *¿Qué uté hace?*
           what you do
           'What do you do?'

        b. *¿Cómo ella se llama?*
           how   she CL calls
           'What is her name?'

(112)   a *¿Cuántos usted tuvo,   entre   vivos   y   muertos, cuántos*
           how many you   had   between alive   and dead
           hijos   usted llegó   a tener?
           how many sons   you   achieved to have
           'How many did you have, between alive and dead, how many sons did you have?' (Ruiz García 2009: 49).

        b. *¿Cómo, qué   diferencia usted ve   entre   el   bunde*
           how   what   difference   you   see   between   the   rhythm
           que   se   bailaba   hace unos 50 años, 60 año
           that   CL   danced   since some 50 years 60 year
           con   el   bunde   que   se   baila   ahora?
           with   the   rhythm   that CL   dance   now
           'What is the difference you see between the rhythm that used to be danced 50, 60 years ago and the rhythm that is danced now?' (Ruiz García 2009: 49).

(113)   a. *¿Qué   ella   dijo?*
           what   she   said
           'What did she say?' (Afro-Peruvian Spanish; Sessarego 2015a: 56).

        b. *¿Cuándo   ella   llega?*
           when   she   arrive
           'When does she arrive?' (Dominican Spanish; Jiménez Sabater 1975: 168).

3.4 Chocó Spanish Morphosyntax

c. Que   eles   tão   cantando?
   what   they   are   singing
   'What are they singing?' (Brazilian Portuguese; Rubio & Pine 1998: 55).

(V)   Adverb Duplication   One of the most reported morphosyntactic features of CS is double negation (NEG2) (i.e., *yo no como no* 'I do not eat') (114). As indicated in chapter 2, several authors have provided examples of NEG2 in this dialect (115), and some researchers have ascribed its presence to a proto-Afro-Portuguese creole origin.

(114)   a. *Yo eso no entiendo no.*
            I   that no understand no
            'I do not understand that.'

        b. *El trabajo no paga mucho no.*
            the job   no pays much no
            'The job does not pay much.'

(115)   a. *No voy p'allá no.*
            no go over there no
            'I am not going over there' (Flórez 1950: 113).

        b. *No lo Sé no.*
            no CL know no
            'I do not know it' (Manzini 1983: 135).

In fact, Granda (1978: 515, 1988a: 78) suggests that CS should be added to the list of AHLAs that would have derived from a colonial proto-Afro-Portuguese language, since NEG2, which – in his view – has never belonged to Peninsular Spanish (Llorens 1929), would be shared not only by CS and PBP, but also by the Portuguese-based creoles spoken in São Tomé, Annobom, and Príncipe (Valkhoff 1966: 100). This grammatical element, therefore, would be evidence for CS of an "*estado criollo preexistente respecto a la modalidad actual de la lengua*" (preexistent creole state with respect to the contemporary status of their language) (Granda 1978: 514).

More recently, the Monogenesis-Decreolization Hypothesis for CS has been reproposed by Armin Schwegler (1991a), who points out that NEG2 would also be shared by Dominican Spanish (DS) and other Afro-Iberian vernaculars. Moreover, he highlights the fact that some of those varieties also present an additional form of negation (NEG3), characterized by a single postverbal *no* (e.g., Brazilian Portuguese *falo italiano não* 'I do not speak Italian'). After proposing an analysis of the sociolinguistic and pragmatic factors regulating the use of double negation in DS and highlighting the systematic presence in several AHLAs of certain non-standard morphosyntactic phenomena (variable number concord across the DP, non-inverted questions, etc.), this author also concludes that all these dialects must have derived from a single proto-Afro-Portuguese creole language.

Schwegler (1991a: 58, 74) suggests that NEG2 would be the result of a 'blend' between standard NEG1 and the Bozal/creole-like NEG3, and that in certain conservative dialects such as CS, a few sporadic instances of NEG3 would still be preserved (116).

(116)   a. *Pero   ella   habla   en   lengua   Chiro   no.*
         but   she   speaks en   language Chiro   no
         'But she does not speak the Chiro language' (Schwegler 1991b: 113).

On the other hand, we observed that even if Ortiz López (1998) found instances of double negation in contemporary Afro-Cuban Spanish, based on the available sociohistorical information for the Spanish Caribbean (Mintz 1971; Laurence 1974), he rejects Granda's and Schwegler's hypotheses of a possible creole origin for this grammatical structure and he prefers to ascribe it to a non-creolized form of Bozal speech (Ortiz López 1998: 116).

As indicated in Chapter 2, Section 2.2.1, Ortiz López's account is also backed by the nineteenth-century letters exchanged by the scholars José de la Luz Caballero and Francis Lieber, who detected the presence of NEG2 in the speech of Cuban bozales, but rejected the possibility of a Spanish creole being spoken on the island (Clements 2009). For this reason, Clements (2009: 101) also concludes that the presence of this feature in certain dialects may be seen as the result of contact with African languages, but it should not be taken as evidence of Caribbean Spanish (de)creolization.

In a recent study, I have proposed a different hypothesis for the origin of NEG2 in CS and in other AHLAs (Sessarego 2017b). This hypothesis is based on new linguistic data, which had never been analyzed in relation to this debate. In such an investigation, I have suggested that Afro-Hispanic NEG2 may be the result of an internally-driven change, in line with the well-known proposal presented by Jespersen (1917).

In fact, since Jespersen's (1917) analysis on the diachronic development of negative constructions across languages, the evolution of negative forms has been at the center of intense linguistic investigations and a shared universal path of negation has been detected in a variety of language families, such as Romance, Germanic, Slavic, Semitic, and Celtic, to mention a few (Bernini 1987a, 1987b; Molinelli 1984; Ramat *et al.* 1986; Schwegler 1983; Larrivée &

3.4 Chocó Spanish Morphosyntax 91

Ingham 2011; Jäger 2008; Tsurska 2009; Biberauer 2009). Jespersen's analysis came to be known as the Jespersen cycle, which consists of a common evolutionary path of the sort NEG1➔ NEG2➔ NEG3.

The Jespersen cycle initially involves the doubling of a preverbal negation marker by a postverbal one, which acts as a reinforcement (i.e., French *je ne dis*➔*je ne dis pas* 'I do not say,' NEG1➔NEG2). Subsequently, such a postverbal element takes on an independent negative force, thus it first appears in co-occurrence with the preverbal negator and then by itself (i.e., French, *je ne dis pas* ➔ *je dis pas* 'I do not say,' NEG2➔NEG3) (Meisner *et al.* 2014).

The Jespersen cycle proved valuable to account for the development of negative structures cross-linguistically. In recent studies it has also been proposed to explain the variation currently attested in Brazilian Portuguese (BP), where NEG1, NEG2, and NEG3 co-exist. Indeed Schwegler (1991c) fully supports this analysis to account for BP negation, while Furtado da Cunha (2007: 1640) directly quotes Jespersen (1917) to analyze the Brazilian system:

> The variation attested in present-day BP between pre-verbal negation (*não V*), double negation (*não V não*), and post-verbal negation (*V não*) represents a common universal process which has been known as the "Jespersen cycle": "the original negative adverb is first weakened, then found insufficient and therefore strengthened, generally through some additional word, and this in its turn may be felt as the negative proper and may then in course of time be subject to the same development as the original word. (Jespersen 1917: 4)

In line with these observations, and knowing that NEG2 constructions can also be encountered in Peninsular Portuguese (see example 19, Chapter 2), it may be suggested that this feature was transmitted to the creole-based varieties spoken in Africa (i.e., São Tomé, Annobom, Príncipe, Angolar) by the Peninsular lexifier rather than the other way around, as Schwegler's (1991a: 64) model could lead one to believe (see Map 2.2).

The reason why the Jespersen cycle has never been applied to Afro-Hispanic varieties has to do with the fact that, so far, no cases of *no + V + no* constructions have ever been detected for Medieval Spanish, so that the roots of Afro-Hispanic postverbal negation have always been sought in Africa rather than in Spain.

Since Spanish NEG2 is a structure that tends to appear in speech only when specific pragmatic requirements are met in the common ground, its presence in historical written corpora is quite reduced. For this reason, Spanish philologists never reported NEG2 constructions in their linguistic analyses of Medieval Spanish negation (Llorens 1929; Camus Bergareche 2006; García Cornejo 2009). Nevertheless, with the advent of digitalized on-line databases of diachronic Spanish, it is today easier than before to search for low-frequency structures. The Davies' (2002) Spanish corpus has allowed me to search for

NEG2 patterns across a variety of Peninsular Spanish texts from the thirteenth to the twentieth centuries.

In what follows, I wish to show the results of my quest with the Davies' (2002) corpus for *no + V + no* patterns in Peninsular Spanish. My findings contradict the assumption that Spanish never presented such constructions. On the contrary, examples (90–4) indicate that NEG2 can be found in fifteenth- to nineteenth-century Peninsular Spanish. This shows that the presence of such structures in contemporary Afro-Hispanic vernaculars does not have to be necessarily ascribed to a previous Afro-Portuguese creole influenced by Kimbundu, Kikongo, Umbundu, or other African languages potentially presenting postverbal negation. Rather, the roots of Afro-Hispanic NEG2 can plausibly be tracked back to fifteenth-century Spanish.

(117) Fifteenth-century Spanish
 a. *Fabla del enperador que salio de nuestra tiera dela segoujana sierra porfazer en tu fauor **no** fue **no** por dormjdor delos romanos electo mas por diujno secreto non siendo mereçedor ....*
 '[He] speaks of the emperor who left our land of the Segovian Mountains to aid you; he was not chosen by the Romans for not being sluggish, but by a divine secret, since he was not deserving ...' (*Cancionero castellano de París*, 1444).
 b. *Mas hablar de tal virtud Su perdurable salud **No** quiero **no** quiero **no** Ca seyendo moço yo. Iniurio la iuuentud.*
 'But I do not want to speak of such virtue, Its long-lasting health, Because being a young man myself I do not want to do harm to youth' (*Coronación* by Juan de Mena, 1489).
 c. *... no puede ser que **no** sea **no** tus mercedes me nieges ...*
 '... it cannot be that it not be your mercy [that] you deny me ...' (*Arnalte y Lucenda* by Diego de San Pedro, c.1480).
 d. *No es para seruir por que **no** puede **no** para seruido por que rriñe.*
 'It is not for serving because he cannot serve since he tells people off' (*Letras de Hernando del Pulgar*, 1485).

(118) Sixteenth-century Spanish[11]
 *Las virtudes que aquí estamos, si todas juntas **no** vamos **no** que lo llevaría cualquiera viento.*
 'The virtues that here we represent, if all of us do not go together, any wind would carry it away' (*Coloquios espirituales y sacramentales* by Fernán González de Eslava, 1569).

(119) Seventeenth-century Spanish
 a. *... y assí, el infiel que vence coronado, tal vez **no** vence **no**, sino castiga ...*

---

[11] In a recent study, Schwegler (2018: 36–7) has questioned the validity of this token as a reliable instance of double negation.

3.4 Chocó Spanish Morphosyntax 93

'... and so the infidel who defeats Coronado, perhaps he does not defeat [him], but rather punish ...' (*Las lágrimas de David* by Felipe Godínez, 1622).

b. *Yo muero de vuestro olvido, Y os cansa que os ame yo; Si mi vida os ha ofendido, Quitármela habrá podido, Pero **no** quereros **no** ...*
'I am dying from your callousness, And it tires you that I love you; If my life has offended you, You will probably have been able to take it from me, But you do not want to ...' (*El poder de la amistad* by Agustín Moreto, 1644).

c. *Quando anda pobre y desterrado Telefo y Peleo **no** dize **no** palabras fanfarronas ...*
'When Telefo is poor and exiled and Peleo does not utter boastful words ...' (*Tablas poéticas* by Francisco Cascales, 1603).

d. *Bien es advertir, para declarar esto, que las carreras de la antigüedad **no** eran **no** encarecerlo, imitando a Dios ...*
'It is good to be aware, in order to declare this, that the roads of antiquity were not praising him, imitating God ...' (*Oraciones evangélicas y panegíricos funerales* by Hortensio Félix Paravicino y Arteaga, 1606).

(120) Eighteenth-century Spanish

a. *Marco Romano y Elvia Boloñesa **no** eran **no**, como son ciertos casados ...*
'Marco Romano and Elvia Boloñesa were not, as they are certainly married ...' (*El Cicerón* by Gian Carlo Passeroni, 1772).

b. *No hai que creer su gravedad austere, Porque **no** cede **no** a los más garbosos.*
'One should not believe his austere seriousness, Because he does not give in to the most generous [people]' (*El Cicerón* by Gian Carlo Passeroni, 1772).

(121) Nineteenth-century Spanish

a. *Pero por si alguno **no** posea **no** ya la colossal erudicion de usted ...*
'But in case someone does not already possess your colossal erudition ...' (*La ciencia española: polémicas, indicaciones y proyectos* by Marcelino Menéndez y Pelayo, 1884).

b. *Del alma vuestra la perversa fe pudo animar en vos tales recelos y **no** merecéis **no**, ¡viven los cielos! ni mi amor, si es verdad que yo os ame, ni el tiempo malgastado en mis desvelos.*
'From your soul the perverse faith managed to awaken in you such suspicions and you do not deserve, the heavens live! neither my love, if it is true that I love you, nor the time wasted in sleeplessness' (*Poesías* by Carolina Coronado, 1867).

c. *Aixá **no** iba **no** a derramar el placer en torno de su marido ...*
Aixá was not going to spill her pleasure around her husband ...' (*El suspiro del moro: Leyendas tradiciones, historias referentes a la conquista de Granada* by Emilio Castelar, 1866).

An analysis of the contexts from which examples (120–1) were extracted indicates that none of those instances of NEG2 occurred in an out-of-the-blue situation (Davies 2002). This suggests that the pragmatic function that NEG2 had in these texts may be essentially the same as that which it shows in contemporary CS and DS. Finding such pragmatic similarities between this corpus and contemporary Afro-Hispanic NEG2 constructions further enhances the possibility of an evolutionary connection between them. This claim finds additional support in the fact that CS has often been described as a conservative dialect preserving a number of archaic features (Granda 1977; Manzini 1983; Montes Girardo 1974), which have completely disappeared from standard varieties of Spanish, but that may still be detected in isolated Afro-Hispanic speech communities.

This situation has been pointed out in relation to several CS conservative phonetic and morphosyntactic traits (pronunciation of orthographic <h> as [hʷ], *voseo*, etc.) (Montes Giraldo 1974). Two other examples of the archaic nature of this vernacular, which appear to be highly relevant to NEG2 constructions since they too concern the verb phrase, are: a) the presence of archaic verb forms (see example 106); b) the use of *ser* 'to be' as an auxiliary verb (see example 108).

Moreover, it is worth pointing out that double negation is not the only form of adverb duplication encountered in CS. In fact, other adverbs may appear in pre- and postverbal position in this dialect (122).

(122) a. *Eso   sí   lo   hago sí.*
        this yes CL   do   Yes
        'Yes, I do this' (Manzini 1983: 135).

   b. *Sí   tengo   sí.*
      yes   have   yes
      'Yes, I have it' (Flórez 1950: 113).

   c. *Pero   ya   eso   cambió   Ya*
      but   already   this   changed   already
      'But this has already changed' (Rodríguez Tucarruncho 2010: 68).

   d. *Ella   ya   llegó   ya.*
      she   already   arrived   already
      'She has already arrived' (Montes Giraldo 1974: 425).

This feature can be taken as an additional indicator of the commonalities between CS and the Caribbean Spanish dialects mentioned above. In fact, when describing DC morphosyntax, Jiménez Sabater (1975: 170) states:

Even though this is not a real irregularity, it is worth indicating a typical syntactic feature of Dominican speech. I am referring to negative constructions with double negation–and

3.4 Chocó Spanish Morphosyntax

to a lesser extent, affirmative constructions with double affirmation–such as: *yo no voy mañana, no; Pedro no es bruto, no; Ellos no están aquí, no; Yo sí me quedo, sí* (Author's translation).[12]

This morphosyntactic phenomenon is only one out of the many other features that CS and Caribbean Spanish share (/s/ weakening and deletion, [l] ~ [ɾ] alternation, etc.). Indeed, this dialect has often been described as a coastal vernacular, closely related to the varieties spoken on the Atlantic coast (Flórez 1950; Montes Giraldo 1974, 1982). In particular, Montes Giraldo (1974: 427), after describing a number of morphosyntactic and phonetic features found in CS, concludes his analysis by stating that *"dentro del español de Colombia el habla del Chocó podría caracterizarse ... como de carácter fundamentalmete atlántico"* (within the Spanish spoken in Colombia, Chocó speech could be characterized as a variety that is essentially of an Atlantic type).

The existence of NEG2 constructions in Peninsular Spanish appears to further weaken the hypothesis that sees this feature in CS as necessarily derived from a now-decreolized Afro-Portuguese creole. In fact, while, on the one hand, for the genesis and evolution of NEG2 and NEG3 in a number of languages, such as BP (Schwegler 1991c; Furtado da Cunha 2007), it has been claimed that they developed by following the classic Jespersen cycle (NEG1➔ NEG2➔NEG3); on the other hand, as we have seen, for CS, DS, and several other Afro-Iberian varieties, Schwegler (1991a) has suggested that NEG2 would be the result of a 'blend' between preexisting NEG1 and NEG3. Indeed, if we maintain, as Schwegler does, that "the shift from strictly pre-verbal to embracing and ultimately post-verbal negation in BP [is] an ongoing linguistic change whereby the functional load of the pre-verbal negating particle is being shifted to the identical post-verbal particle" (Schwegler 1991c: 187–8), then it would make sense to expect that a similar internal change (maybe favored by external contact with African languages) might also have happened in CS, DS, and in other Afro-Iberian vernaculars.

In summary, a cross-linguistic evaluation of NEG2 has revealed that this negative form seems to have been common in the speech of Bozal slaves living in nineteenth-century Cuba (Clements 2009), can still be encountered in certain rural Afro-Cuban vernaculars (Ortiz López 1998), and represents a well-attested feature of DS, CS, and BP (Granda 1977; Schwegler 1991a, 1991b, 1991c; Schwenter 2005; Furtado da Cunha 2007; etc.). Thanks to the analysis

---

[12] Original Spanish version: *Aunque no constituye auténticamente una irregularidad, conviene indicar un uso sintáctico muy típico del habla dominicana. Me refiero a las oraciones negativas con doble negación – y en menor grado a las afirmativas con doble afirmación – tales como: yo no voy mañana, no; Pedro no es bruto, no; Ellos no están aquí, no; Yo sí me quedo, sí.*

of fifteenth- to nineteenth-century Peninsular Spanish texts (Davies 2002), it has been suggested, in contrast with previous claims (Granda 1977; Megenney 1990; Schwegler 1991a; etc.), that Afro-Hispanic NEG2 origins should not necessarily be ascribed to a number of African languages (Kimbundu, Kikongo, Umbundu, etc.), which eventually contributed to shaping a now-decreolized colonial creole spoken across the Americas. On the contrary, historical linguistic data have shown that such a construction was found in fifteenth- to nineteenth-century Spanish, where it probably presented similar pragmatic functions to those encountered in contemporary CS and DS. This is, I suggest, good evidence indicating that contemporary Afro-Hispanic NEG2 may be seen as an archaic morphosyntactic feature, on par with other conservative traits commonly encountered across these vernaculars (*ser* 'to be' used as an auxiliary verb, archaic verb forms, etc.); thus, the presence of NEG2 in CS and Caribbean Spanish does not necessarily entail (de)creolization for these dialects.

(VI)   Focalizing Ser   Another feature shared by CS (123) and Caribbean Spanish (124) is focalizing *ser*.

(123)   a. *Pagó   es   con   plata.*
         payed   FOC   with   money
         'It was with money that he paid.'

   b. *Yo   soy   es   de   acá.*
      I   am   FOC   of   here
      'It is here where I am from.'

   c. *Varias   son   e   lambía.*
      Several   are   FOC   Flirtatious
      'It is flirtatious that several of them are' (Murillo Mena 2005: 53).

   d. *No   me   gusta   bocachico   chiquito,   me   gusta   es   grande.*
      no   CL   like   bocachico   little   CL   like   FOC   big
      'I do not like the little bocachico, I like it big' (Ruiz García 2009: 45).

(124)   a. *Compró   los   libros   fue   Pedro.*
         bought   the   books   FOC   Pedro
         'It was Pedro who bought the books' (Caribbean Spanish, Camacho 2006: 14).

   b. *Mi   hermano   estaba   era   triste.*
      my   brother   was   FOC   sad
      'It was sad that my brother was' (Caribbean Spanish, Camacho 2006: 14).

c. *Llegamos   fue   ayer.*
   arrived   FOC   yesterday
   'It was yesterday that we arrived' (Caribbean Spanish, Camacho 2006: 14).

This construction is also widespread across several other varieties of Colombian and Ecuadorean Spanish. Méndez-Vallejo (2009) analyzed the use of focalizing *ser* in the dialect of Bucaramanga. She indicates that the verb *ser* in these constructions does not act as either a copula or an auxiliary; rather, it only intensifies the focalized element. Focalizing *ser* is not a common Afro-Hispanic feature, even though it can be heard in Chota Valley Spanish, a Black Spanish dialect from the Ecuadorean highlands (125).

(125) a. *Este   hombre   vino   Es   a   pie.*
          this   man   came   FOC   by   foot
          'It is by walking that this man came' (Chota Valley Spanish, Sessarego 2013b: 77).

       b. *Unos se vestía   es   con   falda.*
          some CL dressed   FOC   with skirt
          'It is a skirt that some people used to wear' (Chota Valley Spanish, Sessarego 2013b: 77).

3.4.3 Prepositional Domain

(I)   Preposition Omissions   In CS, prepositions may be omitted (126), as Ruiz García (2009) and Rodríguez Tucarruncho (2010) showed in their studies (127). These examples perfectly align with the patterns encountered in other AHLAs (128).

(126) a. *Porque Ø <en> un pueblo así   no hay mucho.*
          because   a   village like this no is   much
          'Because in a village like this there is much.'

       b. *No   se   sabe Ø <de>   dónde   viene.*
          no   CL   know   where   come
          'It is unknown where it is coming from.'

       c. *Dicen   misa Ø <a>   las   ocho.*
          say   Mass   the   eight
          'They say mass at eight o'clock.'

(127) a. *Ø <en> casi   todo el   Chocó llueve.*
          almost all   the Chocó   rains
          'In almost all Chocó it rains' (Rodríguez Tucarruncho 2010: 71).

98 A Sketch of Chocó Spanish

    b. *Ya   ni   me   recuerdo Ø <de>   mucha   pieza.*
       already   neither   CL   remember   much   token
       'I have already forgotten many things' (Ruiz García 2009: 46).

    c. *Viéndole   el   ojo Ø <a>   un   animalito.*
       seeing-it   the   eye   a   small animal
       'Seeing a small animal's eye' (Rodríguez Tucarruncho 2010: 72).

(128)   a. *Tengo   un   hermano   allá Ø <en>   Coroico.*
       have   a   brother   there   Coroico
       'I have a brother there in Coroico' (Afro-Bolivian Spanish, Lipski 2008: 111).

    b. *Pare Ø <de>   familia.*
       father   family.
       'Family man' (Afro-Peruvian Spanish, Cuba 2002: 36).

    c. *Atrás   hasta   que   llegué Ø <a>   el   llano.*
       behind   until   that   arrived   the   plain
       'Behind until I arrived to the plain' (Afro-Cuban Spanish, Ortiz López 1998: 111).

(II)   Divergent Use of 'Con'   The preposition *con* 'with' may be used in contexts in which *y* 'and' would be employed in standard Spanish (129).

(129)   a *Hablé a   Francisco con <y><a>   su   esposa.*
      spoke to   Francisco with   his   wife
      'I spoke to Francisco and his wife.'

    b. *Mi   mamá   con <y>   mi   papá   no   se   preocupaban.*
       My   mom   with   my   dad   no   CL   worry
       'My mom and my dad did not worry' (Ruiz García 2009: 51).

    These constructions find parallel examples in a number of other AHLAs, as (130) shows.

(130)   a. *Mi   tata   cun <y>   mi   mamá   nació   Mururata.*
       my   dad   with   my   mom   was born   Mururata
       'My mom and my dad were born in Mururata' (Afro-Bolivian Spanish, Lipski 2008: 55).

    b. *Yo con <y>   él   acabó   de   limpiar.*
       I   With   he   finished   of   clean
       'He and I finished cleaning' (Afro-Cuban Spanish, Ortiz López 1998: 90).

3.4.4 Summary of Chocó Spanish Morphosyntax

Here I provide a table to summarize the morphosyntactic feature characterizing CS and to offer a potential account for their origins, in a way that parallels the summary I proposed for CS phonetic and phonological traits in Table 3.1.

It is not always easy to draw inferences on the basis of pure linguistic data. The presence in several related contact varieties of common linguistic traits does not necessarily imply that they share a common diasystem (as some authors have suggested in the past for the AHLAs). On the contrary, as I have indicated in Table 3.2, and as I will explain in greater detail in Chapter 4, the so-called 'creole-like features' shared by several Afro-Hispanic vernaculars can also be explained as the result of universal SLA processes, common to a number of contact scenarios and certainly not only limited to creole languages.

3.5 Some Observations on the Status of Chocó Spanish Grammar

This chapter has provided a grammatical account of the main linguistics features characterizing CS. It was possible to observe that this Colombian Pacific variety shares several phonetic and morphosyntactic traits with other Afro-Hispanic dialects and Caribbean Spanish vernaculars. Indeed, CS aligns perfectly with several past and present AHLAs (Lipski 2005), while its linguistic connection to the Caribbean has been highlighted on several occasions (Flórez 1950; Montes Giraldo 1974, 1982).

Even though the linguistic similarities among CS, Caribbean Spanish, and the varieties of Black Spanish spoken across Latin America are clear, not so obvious is the origin of this Colombian vernacular. In fact, as we saw, some authors do not think that the features found in current CS, along with the ones of many other AHLAs, should be taken as evidence of (de)creolization (McWhorter 2000; Sessarego 2011a, 2011b, 2013b, 2014a, 2015a); while other researchers have classified the presence of certain CS traits as the linguistic traces indicating its previous creole stage (Granda 1977; Schwegler 1991a, 1991b). Even though the claims identifying CS double negation (NEG2) as an indicator of a previous creole stage do not seem to withstand the analyses and data provided by researchers who ascribe the origin of this construction to non-creolized Bozal speech (Ortiz López 1998; Ruiz García 2009; Clements 2009), CS presents a number of other creole-like features, often reported in the literature in relation to the Monogenetic-Decreolization Hypothesis (non-inverted questions, reduced agreement across the nominal and verbal domains, overuse of subject pronouns, etc.) (Granda 1968; Otheguy 1973; Perl 1982; Megenney 1990; Schwegler 1999), which still need a satisfactory explanation.

Table 3.2 Main morphosyntactic traits of Chocó Spanish

Phenomenon	SLA effect	Substrate (African) influence	Substrate (indigenous) influence	Internal change	Vernacular feature or Caribbean Spanish feature	Archaic form	Feature shared by other AHLAs
Reduced number agreement across the DP	✓				✓ **Caribbean Spanish**		✓
Variable gender agreement across the DP	✓						✓
Bare nouns in argument position	✓						✓
Peculiar use of possessive adjectives		?	?	?			
Non-emphatic, non-contrastive overt subject pronouns	✓				✓ **Caribbean Spanish**		✓

Variable omission of object clitics	✓					✓
Regularization of irregular verb forms	✓					✓
Vide, truje, etc. as conjugated verb forms				✓		✓
Variable subject-verb agreement	✓					✓
Lack of subject-verb inversion in questions	✓		✓ Caribbean Spanish			✓
Adverb duplication (*sí ...sí; ya ...ya*)			✓ Caribbean Spanish		✓	?
Doble negation (*no ... no*)			✓ Caribbean Spanish		✓	✓ Caribbean varieties
Variable preposition omission	✓					✓
Peculiar use of *con*	?	?				✓

In order to approximate a solution to this puzzle, it is fundamental to go beyond the pure descriptive analysis of the grammatical phenomena found in this and other Afro-Hispanic dialects and try to track the roots of such features. In particular, any model seeking to offer a convincing perspective to account for the genesis and evolution of this Afro-Colombian vernacular should be able to explain why this dialect and many other AHLAs have so many features in common, if they do not derive from the same proto-creole language, as Granda and Schwegler claim. The following chapter addresses this issue by providing a unified model to account for the linguistic traits shared by CS and the rest of the AHLAs.

4 Roots of Some Languages

4.1 Introduction

Besides providing considerable ground for hypotheses on creole genesis and evolution, CS and the rest of the AHLAs also have much to offer to linguistic theory, since these varieties are rich in structures and prosodic patterns that would be considered either ungrammatical or pragmatically infelicitous in standard Spanish and that may be used as a powerful testing ground for linguistic hypotheses, which have usually been built on standardized language data (Kayne 1996; Sessarego 2013a, 2014a). In fact, some common features that have repeatedly been reported for the vast majority of these Afro-Hispanic dialects, and that in some cases have been identified as potential indicators of a previous creole stage, represent deviations from standard Spanish that are extremely interesting from a microparametric point of view (Sessarego 2012a, 2013a, 2014a). Some of these recurring grammatical phenomena are: (a) presence of bare nouns in subject position; (b) variable number and gender agreement across the DP; (c) invariant verb forms for person and number; (d) use of non-emphatic, non-contrastive overt subjects; (e) lack of subject-verb inversion in questions; (f) earlier prenuclear peaks – corresponding with higher frequencies of the L+H* pitch accent. Table 4.1 reports features (a–e) with examples taken from some of the Afro-Hispanic dialects presenting them (Sessarego 2015b), while Figure 4.1 exemplifies phenomenon (f) in Afro-Bolivian Spanish (Rao & Sessarego 2016).

As we observed in Chapter 3, CS presents all of the grammatical features indicated in (a–f), which are here reproduced for this dialect in Table 4.2 and Figure 4.2, and that have been taken by the supporters of the Monogenesis-Decreolization Hypothesis as indicators of a previous creole stage for this and other Afro-Hispanic dialects (Granda 1976; Schwegler 1991a; among others). The main argument adopted by these scholars is that, given the simultaneous presence of these grammatical elements in several AHLAs, it would be difficult to accept that such linguistic patterns arose as the result of independent parallel developments; rather, these authors claim that a single proto-creole presenting those features must have existed in colonial times, and that the AHLAs

Table 4.1 *Five commonly reported Afro-Hispanic features traditionally ascribed to a previous creole stage*

Phenomenon	Example
a. Presence of bare nouns in subject position	*Niño no responde nara.* 'The kid does not say anything' (Afro-Peruvian Spanish, Lipski 1994c: 209). *Perro come carne.* 'Dogs eat meat' (Afro-Bolivian Spanish, Sessarego 2011a: 48).
b. Variable number and gender agreement across the DP	*Tan chicquito[s] puej mij nene[s].* 'My kids are little' (Afro-Mexican Spanish, Mayén 2007: 117). *Nuestro cultura antiguo.* 'Our old culture' (Afro-Bolivian Spanish, Lipski 2008: 89).
c. Invariant verb forms for person and number	*Yo sabe [sé]* 'I know.'; *yo tiene [tengo]* 'I have.'; *yo no pue [puedo]* 'I cannot' (Afro-Puertorican, Álvarez Nazario 1974: 194–5). *Tú jabla [hablas] y no conoce [conoces].* 'You speak and you do not know' (Afro-Cuban Spanish, Guirao 1938: 3).
d. Use of non-emphatic, non-contrastive overt subjects	*Mauricio fue también. Él se tomó una botella de cerveza y después él se fue de fiesta.* 'Mauricio went too. He drank a bottle of beer and afterwards he left to have fun' (Afro-Peruvian Spanish, Sessarego 2015a: 70). *Yo tando muy pequeña yo conocí a una señora.* 'When I was young I met a woman' (Barlovento Spanish, Megenney 1999: 117).
e. Lack of subject-verb inversion in questions	*¿Onde tú taba, mijito?* 'Where were you, my son?' (Barlovento Spanish, Megenney 1999: 118). *¿Qué ella dijo?* 'What did she say?' (Afro-Peruvian Spanish, Sessarego 2015a: 70).

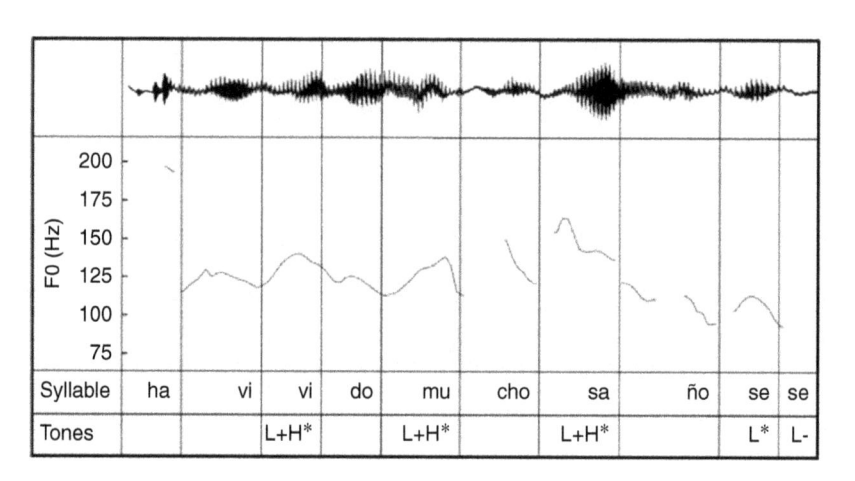

Figure 4.1 Sample F0 contours from Afro-Bolivian Spanish data for *Ha vivido muchos años ese* (That guy has lived many years)

4.1 Introduction

Table 4.2 *Five commonly reported Chocó Spanish features traditionally ascribed to a previous creole stage*

Phenomenon	Example
a. Presence of bare nouns in subject position	*Cabeza mía no es pa' eso no, maestro.* 'My head is not for this, sir' (Ruiz García 2009: 45). *Pollo vive allá.* 'Chickens live here' (current book, Chapter 3).
b. Variable number and gender agreement across the DP	*Hacen unos caney.* 'They make some huts' (Flórez 1950: 423). *Quieren cosa ligero* 'They want something light' (Ruiz García 2009: 43).
c. Invariant verb forms for person and number	*Ellas dijo <dijeron> así, no sé si é veldá.* 'They said so, I do not know if that is the truth' (current book, Chapter 3). *Esa vez vino <vinieron> catorce familias, catorce familias vinieron.* 'Fourteen families came this time, fourteen families came' (Dieck 1993: 21).
d. Use of non-emphatic, non-contrastive overt subjects	*Cuando él hace en la casa de él, me llama él.* 'When he makes it at his house, he calls me' (Rodríguez Tucarruncho 2010: 61). *Mi papá, yo casi no pasé con él no. Yo casi no me crié con él.* 'My father, I did not spend much time with him. I almost did not grow up with him'(Ruiz García 2009: 49).
e. Lack of subject-verb inversion in questions	*¿Cómo ella se llama?* 'What is her name?' (current book, Chapter 3). *¿Cuántos usted tuvo, entre vivos y muertos, cuántos hijos usted llegó a tener?* 'How many did you have, between alive and dead, how many son did you have?' (Ruiz García 2009: 49).

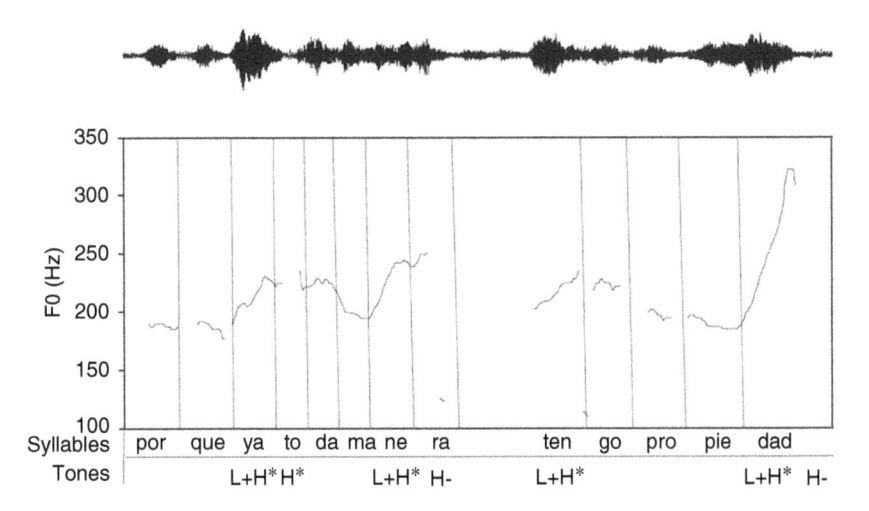

Figure 4.2 Sample F0 contours from Chocó Spanish data for *Porque ya no da manera ... tengo propiedad* (Because there is no way ... I own property)

showing such grammatical characteristics today should be seen as the direct offspring of such a linguistic ancestor.

The model proposed by the supporters of the Monogenesis-Decreolization Hypothesis, therefore, clashes with the analysis offered by Lipski, in which he claims that the aforementioned features "arose spontaneously each time Spanish and African languages came into contact" (Lipski 1986: 171). In the following sections of the present chapter, I wish to provide an analysis that not only diverges from the Monogenesis-Decrolization Hypothesis, but also – in part – from Lipski's account. In so doing, I claim that the grammatical features encountered in CS and shared – to different extents – by all of the AHLAs, should neither be seen as the result of a decreolization process nor as the byproduct of parallel substrate effects, driven, in each colonial setting, by the African languages that came into contact with colonial Spanish. On the other hand, I analyze all these features as the results of universal instances of advanced second language acquisition processes, which do not imply a (de) creolization phase for the AHLAs and appear to be, for the most part, independent from the specific substrate languages. In particular, I claim that those grammatical phenomena are the result of processability and language interface constraints. They are not only peculiar to the AHLAs; rather, they appear to be quite common in all cases of language contact.

4.2   Afro-Hispanic Languages at the Linguistic Interfaces

During the past few years, I proposed an analysis of the features reported in examples (a–f) that builds on recent theoretical models on the nature of the language faculty, its modularity, and the challenges that certain constructions may pose for the interaction between different language modules (Sessarego 2013a, 2015a; Sessarego & Gutiérrez-Rexach 2018; Romero & Sessarego 2018; Sessarego & Rao 2016; Rao & Sessarego 2016, 2018). In particular, I adopted Jackendoff's (1997, 2002) widely used model of linguistic interface architecture, seen in Figure 4.3, to account for the aforementioned data. Such a model assumes language modularity and allows for a parallel dialogue among different modules, without necessarily assuming the primacy of syntax over the others (for different views cf. Burkhardt 2005; Reinhart 2006).

In line with recent theoretical proposals within the field of language development, I assume that certain constructions involving high processing demands on the interface between different linguistic modules may be more difficult to master in second language acquisition (SLA) (Sorace 2003; Sorace & Serratrice 2009; Rothman & Slabakova 2011). Along these lines, I analyze the linguistic patterns found in several AHLAs as the result of advanced SLA strategies. I claim, therefore, that several

4.2 Afro-Hispanic Languages at the Linguistic Interfaces

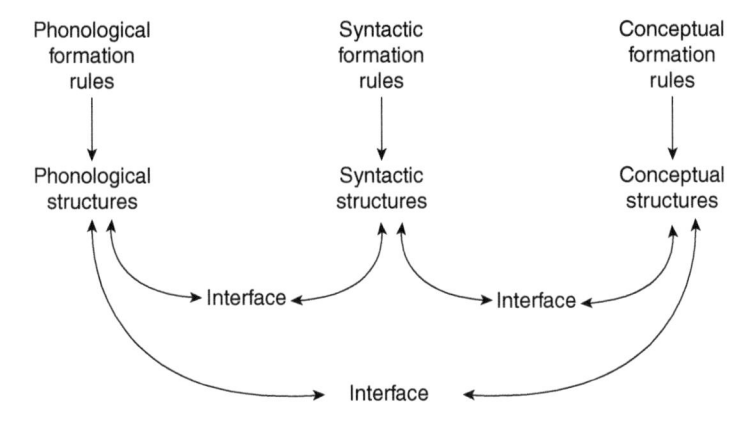

```
Phonological          Syntactic             Conceptual
formation             formation             formation
rules                 rules                 rules
   │                     │                     │
   ▼                     ▼                     ▼
Phonological          Syntactic             Conceptual
structures            structures            structures
```

Figure 4.3 Jackendoff's language faculty architecture

grammatical aspects of these contact varieties can actually be seen as *advanced, conventionalized L2 features* (Sessarego 2013a). This account combines SLA scholarship with creole studies to elucidate on the development of these contact varieties (see also Mufwene 2010), and contradicts the prototypical creole life-cycle, according to which pidgins became creoles and then eventually decreolized (Granda 1968, 1970). I wish to stress that the aforementioned path (viz., pidginization → creolization → decreolization) is only one of many potential forms of contact-induced restructuring, and that, as far as linguistic and sociohistorical data are concerned, there is no evidence implying that the vast majority of the AHLAs went through such a cycle (see Mufwene 2012, 2015 for a discussion on the putative creole life-cycle). On the other hand, based on the linguistic, legal, and sociohistorical findings of my investigations (Sessarego 2011a, 2013b, 2014a, 2015a), I would like to suggest that the structures found in the AHLAs may be better analyzed as *the result of L1 acquisition (nativization) of advanced L2 grammars*.

This proposal assumes that L1 and L2 acquisition are driven and constrained by Universal Grammar (UG). Children's L1 develops naturally and instinctively; however, L2 acquisition in adulthood operates somewhat differently, since biological and social factors impinge on the full proficiency of the target language (TL) (Herschensohn 2000). I propose that several AHLAs formed in colonial settings where African slaves had relatively good access to Spanish (the TL). In such a context, each individual developed a relatively advanced L2 grammar, which served as the primary linguistic data (PLD) on which the following generations of captives built their L1s, thus nativizing their parents'

L2 outputs. This process is exemplified in (131), where Grammar 1 (G1) and Grammar 2 (G2) consist of two different grammars, with dissimilar parametric configurations:

(131) a. Individual from Generation 1:
TLy → UG driving L2 acquisition → G1 → set of outputs X

b. Individual from Generation 2:
PLDx → UG driving L1 acquisition → G2 → set of outputs Z

According to the model provided in (104), the process of nativization consists of an L1 grammar (G2) built on L2 inputs (PLDx). Consequently, G2 will present crystallized aspects of an L2 grammar (G1). Thus, the patterns observed in these dialects can be analyzed as the traces of such a crystallization, in which advanced L2 strategies have been nativized by subsequent generations of speakers.

4.3 Bare Nouns

In recent studies, I offered an account of bare nouns (phenomenon a, Tables 4.1 and 4.2) in certain AHLAs (Gutiérrez-Rexach & Sessarego 2011, 2012; Sessarego & Gutiérrez-Rexach 2014; Sessarego 2014a). In so doing, I tested Chierchia's (1998) Nominal Mapping Parameter (NMP) and speculated on the nature of Afro-Bolivian Spanish (ABS), Afro-Ecuadorean Spanish (AES), and Afro-Peruvian Spanish (APS) nominal domains in light of Longobardi's (1994) generalization on the structure of DPs. My findings suggest that the NMP does not adequately explain the data. Indeed, these dialects do not fit into Chierchia's typological classification: they display plural morphology on D categories, the count/mass distinction is instantiated at the lexical level, and they present bare nouns in argument position.

As far as CS is concerned, it is possible to observe a system that very closely resembles the nominal configurations attested for the aforementioned Afro-Andean dialects. Indeed, number (plural/singular) is normally conveyed in CS by the determiner heading the DP (132).

(132) a. *Mucho <muchos> doctor <doctores> colombiano <colombianos>.*
much.SG   doctor.SG   Colombian.SG
'Many Colombian doctors.'

b. *Cinco doctor <doctores> colombiano <colombianos>.*
five   doctor.SG   Colombian.SG
'Five Colombian doctors.'

4.3 Bare Nouns

c. *Mis   doctor <doctores>   colombiano <colombianos>*
   my.PL doctor.SG   Colombian.SG
   'My Colombian doctors.'

d. *Esos   doctor <doctores>   colombiano <colombianos>.*
   this.PL doctor.SG   Colombian.SG
   'These Colombian doctors.'

e. *Los   doctor <doctores>   colombiano <colombianos>.*
   the.PL doctor.SG   Colombian.SG
   'The Colombian doctors.'

f. *Unos   doctor <doctores>   colombiano <colombianos>.*
   some.PL doctor.SG   Colombian.SG
   'Some Colombian doctors.'

Even though nominal and adjectival stems remain bare, plural morphology exists, since it clearly appears on demonstratives and possessives, and it is crucial for determining reference to plural or singular entities. The count/mass distinction is also present in CS (133).

(133) a. *Mucho   persona   vive   en   este   barrio.*
         much   person   live   in   this   neighborhood
         'Many people live in this neighborhood.'

      b. *Juan   toma   mucho   cerveza.*
         Juan   drink   much   beer
         'Juan drinks a lot of beer.'

While *persona* 'person' in (133a) has a plural reading, *cerveza* 'beer' in (133b) is understood as a mass term. This clearly shows that CS differs from languages like Chinese or Japanese, where a special classifier is required for count nouns, which would otherwise be interpreted as mass. What makes CS even more intriguing is the fact that bare-singular nouns can occur in subject and object position (134).

(134) a. *Niño   toma   pelota.*
         kid   take   candy
         'Kid(s) take ball(s).'

The presence in CS of plural morphology, count/mass distinction instantiated on Ns, and singular bare nominals in argument position make this dialect a language that does not fit into Chierchia's (1998) NMP typology (see Gutiérrez-Rexach & Sessarego 2011 for a similar analysis of the ABS nominal domain). Following Longobardi (1994), I assume that bare nouns are not structurally bare; rather, they are embedded into a DP, with an empty

D category (see also Contreras 1986). DPs can act as arguments, while NPs are predicates; thus they need to combine with a D head to be referential. The nom (∩) operation takes place in D to shift common nouns, which denote properties <s,<e,t≫, into individuals <s,e>. Covert determiners in these dialects encode a variety of functions (which vary according to the dialect), not only nom. Covert type-shifting operations can be seen as last-resort mechanisms that provide "bare" DPs with kind and quantificational interpretations. Such operations are not allowed if there is an overt determiner performing the same function. In the aforementioned Afro-Andean varieties and in CS, it is possible to observe the presence of definite and indefinite determiners, but bare nouns can still receive indefinite or definite-like interpretations without the presence of those items, although the resulting interpretations are not identical.

In such dialects bare nouns lack number specification. Number and quantificational force are encoded at the D level (Delicado-Cantero & Sessarego 2011). This particular configuration allows for a wider array of interpretive possibilities, depending on which operator is inserted. In general, these dialects instantiate very flexible systems, where the absence of overt morphological marking on nouns allows for contextual factors to determine the interpretation of bare DPs.

Bare nouns are commonly encountered in interlanguage grammars, even at very advanced levels of proficiency. This is particularly true when the L1 and the target L2 present very divergent determiner systems (García Mayo & Hawkins 2009). As far as Spanish is concerned, this phenomenon has been well-documented in a variety of cases (Sánchez & Giménez 1998; Montrul & Ionin 2010, 2012). In recent years, the presence of bare nouns in interlanguage grammars has been explained as the result of a syntax/semantics interface mismatch, which tends to persist at advanced stages of L2 acquisition (Ionin et al. 2004; Ionin & Montrul 2010; Park 2013), and therefore should not necessarily be taken as a sign of (de)creolization.

4.4   Nominal and Verbal Morphology

As for nominal and verbal morphology (phenomena b and c, Tables 4.1 and 4.2), linguistic theory has often considered the morphological richness of Spanish as a potential explanation for N-to-Num movement and V-to-Infl movement, among other phenomena (Pollock 1989; Picallo 1991). Nevertheless, the AHLAs, deprived of such morphological characteristics, show exactly the same noun+adjective and verb+adverb order combinations of standard Spanish (see Lipski 2005 for a survey). This indicates that agreement, at least in these clear cases, cannot be the trigger of movement, which may be driven by other mechanisms, such as the Extended Projection Principle (EPP)[1] or categorical features (Carstens 2001; Alexiadou 2001; Sessarego & Gutiérrez-Rexach 2011, 2012, 2015; Gutiérrez-Rexach & Sessarego 2011, 2014a, 2014b).

As for these instances of phi-(dis)agreement, in several studies I assumed current minimalist models of feature valuation (Pesetsky & Torrego 2007), which partially contrast with previous assumptions on the nature of *Agree* (Chomsky 1995). Cross-dialectal differences between the AHLAs and standard Spanish have been accounted for in a systematic fashion, as computationally determined by differences in the specification of lexical and functional items and by restrictions on syntactic operations (Sessarego 2013e, 2014a; Gutiérrez-Rexach & Sessarego 2014a).

These works also had the goal of enhancing a long-awaited dialogue between quantitative sociolinguistic methodology and syntactic generative theory. In fact, in line with several sociolinguistic studies, I recurred to statistical tools to analyze cases of variable phi-agreement. Nevertheless, unlike in traditional sociolinguistic investigations, results have been explained by adopting recent minimalist assumptions on agreement and feature valuation processes (Frampton & Gutmann 2000). In order to account for the variability encountered in the data and to formalize it, I followed the model proposed by Adger & Smith (2005), who argue for characterizing syntactic variation in terms of (un)interpretable features. According to this proposal, certain uninterpretable features may be present or active in one category or element but absent or inactive in another. Since they are uninterpretable, they would have no semantic repercussions. As a result, introducing in the numeration two items differing only in the presence/absence of uninterpretable features would have no effect on their semantic interpretation at Logical Form (LF), thus they will respect the principle of sameness, or the fact that speakers have more than one way of saying the same thing (Tagliamonte 2006: 6).

In this way, the real locus of variation is the lexicon, while syntax remains invariable. The phi-agreement variation observed in CS and in the other AHLAs can be pictured as the byproduct of different lexical items entering the numeration. This, however, does not exclude that a variety of social and idiolectal factors may affect such a variable lexical selection: ease of lexical access (probably linked to frequency of use), speaker-hearer relationships, social identity, etc. (Adger & Smith 2005: 164). Pesetsky and Torrego (2007) propose that the items selected by the syntactic computation may carry the following features:

(135)   uF[val] uninterpretable, valued
        iF[val] interpretable, valued

---

[1] This principle states that all verbs require a subject (Chomsky 1981, 1995, 2000; Lasnik 2001a, 2001b).

uF[] uninterpretable, unvalued
iF[] interpretable, unvalued
uF[val] uninterpretable, valued

Example (135) shows the annotations used to characterize the four possible feature specifications, which consist of two probes (uF[], iF[]) and two goals (uF[val], iF[val]) for a given feature F. Therefore, probes before participating in *Agree* will be annotated by a pair of empty brackets, and those brackets will receive a value only after such a syntactic operation has been applied. Moreover, I annotate elements that are not active for *Agree* and cannot participate as probes or goals as non-specified for a feature.

As a way of exemplifying one of these variable phi-agreement processes found across the AHLA nominal and verbal domains, (136) depicts how the number sharing/unification implemented by *Agree* would take place in the variable system we observe for CS. As it can be seen, in contrast with the agreeing items, the elements showing single default forms do not carry any Num feature specification.

(136) a. Variable number agreement across the Chocó Spanish DP
[DP *Mucho* [NumP [nP [NP *hijo* [AP *trabajador*]]]]]
iNum[PL]

b. [DP *Muchos* [NumP [nP [NP *hijo* [AP *trabajador*]]]]]
uNum[PL] ...... iNum[PL]

c. [DP *Muchos* [NumP [nP [NP *hijos* [AP *trabajador*]]]]]
uNum[PL] ...... iNum[PL] .... uNum[PL]

d. [DP *Muchos* [NumP [nP [NP hijos [AP trabajadores]]]]]
uNum[PL] ...... iNum[PL] .... uNum[PL] ....
uNum[PL]
Much.SG/PL   son.SG/PL   hard-working.SG/PL
'Many hard-working sons.'

Variable phi-agreement is a well-known feature of L2 Spanish varieties (Montrul 2004). In particular, the non-target-like acquisition of gender has been systematically documented – even for very advanced interlanguages (Franceschina 2002, 2005; Isabelli-García 2010). The use of variable number agreement across the DP does not just belong to L2 Spanish (Bruhn de Garavito & White 2000; White *et al.* 2004); rather, it is also one of the most widespread native features, encountered in the vernaculars of southern Spain, the Canary Islands, and the Caribbean to mention a few. Indeed, variable plural marking across the nominal domain is a well-studied phenomenon, known for obeying a variety of phonological, morphosyntactic, and sociolinguistic factors (Poplack

4.4 Nominal and Verbal Morphology

1979, 1980; Lipski 1994b). Also the use of default third-person singular verb forms (phenomenon c, Tables 4.1 and 4.2) has been amply documented in L2 Spanish (Montrul 2004; McCarthy 2008). For a formalization of such a process see examples (121–2) in the following section (4.5).

Current SLA theory identifies phi-agreement reductions of the sort found in the AHLAs as instances of grammatical simplification, recently modeled in terms of feature-geometry accounts (McCarthy 2008; Slabakova 2009; Sessarego & Ferreira 2016; Sessarego 2017c). The geometrical representation of morphological features relies on structured combinations of natural class nodes (Harley & Ritter 2002; Cowper 2005). In line with this view, more complex features involve more nodes, which, in turn, will be more difficult to process and acquire. Slabakova (2009: 59) provides a representation of number (see 137) based on Harley & Ritter's (2002) proposal. In this model, the default number is "singular," while plural is more complex, since it involves an additional node.[2]

(137) Number features:

```
SG      PL
#       #
        |
        >1
```

In line with current minimalist assumptions, lexical items can be viewed as elements containing feature bundles (Adger 2006). When we apply the feature geometry representation of number to the variable CS data, we obtain two different sets of lexical entries: (a) items lacking a Num feature specification, which surface as default singular forms and are characteristic of traditional CS vernacular speech (138); (b) items specified for Num features, which may present either plural or singular values, and are characteristic of standard Spanish (139).

(138) *hijo*
[iGen: -F]

(139) *hijos*   *hijo*
[uNum: +PL]   [uNum: -PL]
[iGen: -F]   [iGen: -F]

---

[2] For a feature-geometry analysis of default third-person singular verb forms in the AHLAs see Sessarego (2017c).

As Slabakova (2009: 60) highlights, the feature geometry framework not only accounts for the typological distribution of language universals (Greenberg 1963); it also predicts SLA steps. Here I would like to take this claim a step further and suggest that this model can also be used to account for the presence of default forms in vernacular dialects. More precisely, this framework is of particular interest to the study of (Afro-)Hispanic varieties, such as CS, since it provides a formal explanation for why these vernacular dialects present the impoverished number agreement system we analyzed in this section.

These phenomena, often mentioned in relation to high processing demands posed on the syntax/morphology interface (Montrul *et al.* 2008; Androutsopoulou *et al.* 2010; Arche & Domínguez 2011), have led SLA specialists to classify morphological reductions of this type as the "bottleneck" of acquisition (Slabakova 2008); thus, these features are common to all contact languages, not just to creoles, and therefore their presence in the AHLAs does not imply any (de)creolization phase for such contact varieties.

4.5 Overt Subject Pronouns and Subject-verb Inversion in Questions

With the advent of the Minimalist Program (Chomsky 1995), the prevailing view of linguistic variation within UG has undergone a shift from rigidly defined parameters – associated with clusters of properties (Chomsky 1981; Chomsky & Lasnik 1993) – to an approach in which features play a central role, are flexibly distributed, and originate in the lexicon, according to what Baker (2008) calls the "Borer-Chomsky conjecture" (Borer 1984; Chomsky 2001). A close cross-linguistic look at empirical data in the AHLAs seems to support this change in focus. For example, the Null Subject Parameter (NSP) (Chomsky 1981; Rizzi 1982), as originally formulated, had a number of shortcomings (Huang 1994; Holmberg 2005), and within the realm of Spanish and Portuguese, the analysis of Dominican Spanish (DS) and Brazilian Portuguese (BP) has already led to the postulation of new hypotheses to account for these new sets of data (Duarte 1993; Toribio 2000; Camacho 2008, 2013; etc.).

Sessarego & Gutiérrez-Rexach (2018) have explored the use of subject pronouns (phenomenon d, Tables 4.1 and 4.2) in APS. That study paid close attention to the alternation of overt and covert subjects in that Afro-Andean variety, which – similarly to DS and BP – does not conform to the NSP. In so doing, we provided an analysis of the data that partially deviates from previous accounts of similar pro-drop phenomena. In particular, that investigation appears to provide evidence for arguments questioning the validity of the NSP, or more broadly, for recent proposals that revisit the concept of

4.5 Overt Subject Pronouns and Subject-verb Inversion in Questions

'parameter' and suggest new potential paths of analysis (Boeckx 2011; Eguren, Fernández-Soriano, & Mendikoetxea 2016).

CS, in line with the Afro-Andean dialects I analyzed, may be classified as a partial pro-drop system, in that structures that belong to non-null subject languages (NNSLs) and null subject languages (NSLs) are both attested. Thus, CS is a hybrid system, where overt subjects are used redundantly, without signaling either emphasis or contrast, as in (140).

(140) a. *Ellos decían que ellos querían estar de acuerdo.*
       they said that they wanted staying of agreement
       'They said they wanted to agree.'

   b. *Y yo ya me salí con eso porque yo taba*
      And I already CL left with this because I was
      onde mi mamá y yo me salí con él de casa.
      left with him of home where my mom and I CL
      'And I left with that because I was at my mom's place and I left home with him' (Ruiz García 2009: 50).

   c. *No, pero como yo hace rato yo ya terminé esa*
      no but since I make while I already finished that
      jornada, yo una vez a lo mío yo ya no
      day I one time to CL mine I already no
      tuve má.
      had more
      'No, because I had already finished my working day for a while, after having done my stuff, I was done' (Rodríguez Tucarruncho 2010: 61).

Additionally, CS shows variable subject-verb agreement (141) (phenomenon 4, Tables 4.1 and 4.2). In fact, third-person singular forms may appear as default forms, especially in the speech of the oldest informants.

(141) a. *Ellas dijo <dijeron> así, no sé si é veldá.*
       they said so no know if is truth
       'They said so, I do not know if that is the truth.'

   b. *Esa vez vino <vinieron> catorce familias, catorce*
      this time came fourteen families fourteen
      familias vinieron.
      families came
      'Fourteen families came this time, fourteen families came' (Dieck 1993: 21).

CS also presents another property that has been traditionally ascribed to NNSL: overt pronouns can take an arbitrary reading (142) (Suñer 1983; Jaeggli 1986) and may refer to inanimate entities (143), as in BP and DS (Toribio 2000; Barbosa et al. 2005). This also implies a potential violation of Montalbetti's (1984) Overt Pronoun Constraint (144).

(142) a. *Dijeron que habían venido.* (Specific or arbitrary reading)
said that had come
'They said that they had come.'

b. *Ellos dijeron que habían venido.* (Specific or arbitrary reading)
they said that had come
'They said that they had come.'

(143) a. *Comenzaron a meterse pa' allá, lo soldao así, pero pa'*
began to put to there the soldier such but to
Candelaria_i, como ella_i no era popular la gente no, no
Candelaria like she no was popular the people no no
corrieron por allá a buscarlo.[3]
run to there to seek-him
'They began going over there, the soldiers like this, but Candelaria, since it is was not popular, people did not run there to look for him' (Rodríguez Tucarruncho 2010: 76).

b. *Ese era un pueblo_i grande, él_i fue capital, Nóvita viejo fue*
this was a village big he was capital Nóvita old was
capital del departamento del Chocó.
capital of the department of the Chocó
'This was a big village, it was the capital, old Nóvita was the capital of the Department of Chocó' (Rodríguez Tucarruncho 2010: 77).

(144) a. *Todo estudiante_i cree que pro_i es inteligente.*
every student thinks that pro is intelligent
'Every student thinks that (he) is intelligent.'

b. *Todo estudiante_i cree que él_{i/j} es inteligente.*
every student thinks that he is intelligent
'Every student thinks that (he) is intelligent.'

High rates of non-emphatic, non-contrastive overt subjects have not only been repeatedly attested across all the dialects of the Spanish Caribbean (Cameron 1996; Toribio 2000; Orozco & Guy 2008; Ortiz López 2010).

---

[3] Candelaria is the name of a local village.

4.5 Overt Subject Pronouns and Subject-verb Inversion in Questions

They also appear to be one of the most persistent grammatical features characterizing near-native grammars. This phenomenon has been ascribed to the challenging workload that the proficient use of subject pronouns exerts on the syntax/discourse interface (Sorace 2005; Sorace & Serratrice 2009). As a result, during the past decade, the study of subject pronouns has become one of the main foci of linguistic inquiry, and a number of articles, edited books, and monographs have been dedicated to the analysis of this phenomenon in advanced L2s and heritage varieties (Rothman & Slabakova 2011; Domínguez 2013). Therefore, encountering this feature in CS and in other AHLAs may be taken as another element supporting the advanced SLA model to account for their origins, rather than the (de) creolization or the African substrate ones.

The non-standard use of subject pronouns has also been related to the lack of subject-verb inversion in questions (phenomenon e, Tables 4.1 and 4.2) and to the acquisition of the pro-drop parameter (Toribio 2000; Camacho 2013). Generative studies have long inspected the nature of *wh*-questions crossdialectally to refine Rizzi's (1996) *wh*-criterion and the landing sites of subjects and *wh*-operators (Torrego 1984; Suñer 1994; Toribio 2000; Ordóñez & Olarrea 2006). While several formal approaches maintain that the presence/ absence of subject-verb inversion may be linked to the existence of a parametrized interrogative feature strength ([+wh/Q]) in C°, which would be difficult to acquire even in late L2 stages (Rizzi 1996; Cuza 2013; Guerra Rivera *et al.* 2015), linguistic theories that do not necessarily embrace the parametric/minimalist framework do acknowledge that subject-verb inversion is only mastered at advanced L2 levels of proficiency (Pienemann 1998, 2000), thus again indicating that this phenomenon is not necessarily related to a previous creole stage for the AHLAs.

CS data clearly indicate the presence in this dialect of questions in which subject and verb have not been inverted (145a,b). Nevertheless, I wish to mention that not all questions present such a pattern; thus verb inversion patterns are also attested in CS (145c,d).

(145) a. *¿Qué uté hace?*
what you do
'What do you do?'

b. *¿Cómo ella se llama?*
how she CL calls
'What is her name?'

c. *¿Cuánto vale {eso}?*
how-much worth it
'How much is it?'

d. ¿Qué compras {vos}?
what buy you
'What do you buy?'

The hypothesis I would like to advocate for here is that we should approach the phenomena associated with a hybrid NSP system such as CS as an instance of competing or evolving lexical and functional entries. What this means is that, for a variety of reasons, the inventory or feature specification of lexical and functional elements differs not only across languages but also across varieties, making room for a more fine-grained treatment of sociolectal and idiolectal variation. More specifically, lexical and functional items with two possible specifications may co-exist in a given variety. The choice of one or the other will have consequences in the word-order arrangements that might become available. Therefore, the instances of variable subject-verb agreement found in CS can be accounted for by relying again on the model proposed by Adger & Smith (2005), as in the case of number and gender agreement across the DP (Sessarego 2013e, 2014a). Specifically, we may envision a grammar in which two different Tense Heads (T) may be selected from the mental lexicon: T1 and T2. T1, like standard Spanish, would be endowed with tense, case, number, and person features, while T2 would not carry number and person features. If we conceive variation in these terms, we can now see how the application of the operation *Agree* between a subject pronoun and T1 will result in a fully conjugated verb form (as in examples 146–7).

(146)   T1 [tense:PRESENT, *u*case:NOM, *u*num:, *u*pers:] .... Pronoun [num:PL, pers:1, case:NOM] →T1[tense:PRESENT, num:PL, pers:1] ... .pronoun [num:PL, pers:1, case:NOM]

(147)   Spell-Out: *Nosotros   bailamos*
        we. NOM   dance.PRESENT.1.PL

In this scenario, the merger of the tensed verb form and the pronoun and the application of *Agree* derives the agreement configuration that is standard in Latin American and Peninsular Spanish. Adopting the probe-goal model of syntactic computation (Chomsky 2000), the T head acts as a probe with unvalued features. Such features get valued by co-valuation or unification (Pollard & Sag 2004) with the pronominal goal. Person and number features are valued by matching or co-valuation. Case is the feature that sets the goal as an active match and satisfies the EPP feature of the probe (Chomsky 2001).

Let us now look at the alternative "non-agreeing" configuration (148–9). In this alternative scenario, the probe is not specified for person and

4.5 Overt Subject Pronouns and Subject-verb Inversion in Questions 119

number. Thus, it targets the goal to satisfy its EPP (case) feature. Nevertheless, there is no co-valuation with the person and number features of the goal (pronoun) because T2 is not specified for them. Thus the agreement operation will not target such features of the pronoun. The system leads to default (third-person singular) values of the goal (Gutiérrez-Rexach & Sessarego 2014).

(148) T2 [tense:PRESENT, *u*case:NOM] . . . . pronoun [num:PL, pers:1, *u*case:]
→ T2[tense:PRESENT] . . . .pronoun[num:PL,pers:1,case:NOM]

(149) Spell-Out: *Nosotros baila*
we.NOM dance.PRESENT.3.PL

If we now analyze the position of subjects and verbs in interrogative environments, we can observe that in CS, in line with several other Afro-Hispanic dialects and with Caribbean Spanish varieties, it is possible to encounter both structures in which the fronted *wh*-operator (*wh*-op) is directly followed by a subject (*wh*-S-V), and cases in which the first element after the *wh-op* is the verb (*wh*-V-S), as in example (150).

(150) Afro-Hispanic/ Caribbean varieties
a. *¿Qué tú comes?*
what you eat
'What do you eat?'

b. *¿Qué comes {tú}?*
what eat you
'What do you eat?'

These subject-verb configurations partially diverge from the possibilities found in Mainland Spanish varieties, where the *wh*-S-V structure is not allowed (151).

(151) Mainland Spanish
a. *¿Qué tú comes?*
what you eat
'What do you eat?'

b. *¿Qué comes {tú}?*
what eat you
'What do you eat?'

The problem of subject inversion or lack thereof in questions has commanded much recent attention (summarized in Villa-García 2015), and I will not be analyzing it here. What is more relevant for our purposes is to focus on the connections with theories of SLA (Sessarego 2013a; Gutiérrez-Rexach & Sessarego 2014). A number of studies on formal syntax and SLA have tried to cast light on the mechanisms behind the acquisition of *wh*-fronting and S-V inversion in questions. Findings have suggested that target-like proficiency may be difficult to obtain for second language speakers, particularly when their L1 does not recur to such syntactic strategies (e.g., in Chinese, Korean, and Japanese) (Johnson & Newport 1989; Birdsong 1992; White 1992; Martohardjono & Gair 1993; White & Juffs 1998).

The fact that *wh*-S-V questions appear to be common among creoles (Holm & Patrick 2007) has led some researchers to postulate a potential creole origin for the Spanish dialects currently presenting such constructions (Perl 1998). While, in theory, such a connection is not impossible, we should keep in mind that lack of S-V inversion in questions is a very common phenomenon in SLA varieties of Spanish, and that it may be encountered even in very advanced interlanguages (Pienemann 1998, 2005). This suggests that *wh*-S-V questions should not necessarily be seen as a creole indicator. Moreover, it must be highlighted that, in the AHLAs and in the Spanish varieties spoken in the Caribbean, not only it is possible to find the *wh-S-V* order (see 150b); rather, *wh-V-S* constructions are common and recent quantitative analyses have actually shown that they are the most frequent ones (Gutiérrez-Bravo 2008: 227 for DS). Nevertheless, traditionally, linguistic studies have analyzed *wh-S-V* constructions as the Caribbean Spanish counterparts to Mainland *wh-V-S* structures. Gutiérrez-Bravo (2005, 2007, 2008) has repeatedly pointed out the importance of realizing that both patterns should not simply be seen as equivalent constructions in two different dialects; rather, they co-exist in Caribbean Spanish and their alternation obeys precise pragmatic constraints. Therefore, according to Gutiérrez-Bravo, while *wh*-V-S and *wh*-S-V are both possible structures in Caribbean Spanish, in Mainland Spanish the latter option is not allowed. Its equivalent form would be (152), where the subject is a sentence topic displaced to the left-peripheral position.

(152) Tú ¿qué comes?
       you what eat
       'What do you eat?'

Gutiérrez-Bravo (2005, 2008) proposed the Interrogative Clause Condition to account for the EPP in questions: a clausal Extended Projection is interrogative if the head of the highest phrase in the Extended Projection bears the feature [Q]. Given this proposal, in examples like (150b) and (151b), TP represents the highest projection. This allows *wh*-op to land in [Spec, T], and

T° to acquire a [Q] feature from Spec-Head agreement with *wh*-op. This movement operation satisfies the EPP requirement, and consequently allows the subject to remain in its VP internal position (153). Conversely, in (150a), *wh*-op moves to [Spec, C], and C° acquires its [Q] feature. In such a configuration, a topicalized subject will have to land on [Spec, T] to satisfy the EPP (154).

(153)   [TP *Quéi*   comes [VP *tú tj ti*]]?
        wh   T°
        [Q] → [Q]

(154)   [CP *Quéi*   Ø [TP *túj comesk* [VP *tj tk ti*]]]?
        wh   C°
        [Q] → [Q]

The existence in the AHLAs of two different word orders to express two different types of questions may be perceived as an additional complexity, not in line with the vast majority of contact linguistic phenomena, which tend to favor the acquisition of less complex/unmarked structures. This is definitely an issue that deserves to be studied in more depth. It requires a sociolinguistic analysis of the diachronic evolution of the *wh-S-V* order in the varieties presenting such a structure. Nevertheless, in the meantime, a speculative hypothesis to account for this phenomenon could be proposed if we suggest that at a certain point in the formation of these contact varieties, due to processability constraints on L2 production (Goodall 2004; Pienemann 2005), the linguistic output of a certain generation of L2 speakers may have been quite variable (including both *wh*-S-V and *wh*-V-S structures). Given such a context, it may be postulated that the acquiring children assigned two dissimilar interpretations to such constructions, so that in their L1 *wh*-S-V came to represent the topicalized subject structure traditionally expressed with (152) in the Mainland Spanish varieties.

4.6 Prosodic Features

Earlier prenuclear peaks – corresponding to higher frequencies of the L+H* pitch accent – (phenomenon f, Figures 4.1 and 4.2) have been reported for a number of contact varieties of Spanish (Barnes & Michnowicz 2013; Colantoni & Gurlekian 2004; Elordieta 2003; Michnowicz & Barnes 2013; O'Rourke 2004, 2005). In some relevant studies, such a pattern has been ascribed to a potential substrate influence. Indeed, Hualde & Schwegler (2008) suggest that Palenqueros reinterpreted Spanish stress as a lexical

122   Roots of Some Languages

Syllable	yo	siem	pre	má	s(h)ar	to	que	to	do	c	llos
Tones	L+H*	¡L+H*		H+L*	L+H*	L-		L+H*	L+H*		L%

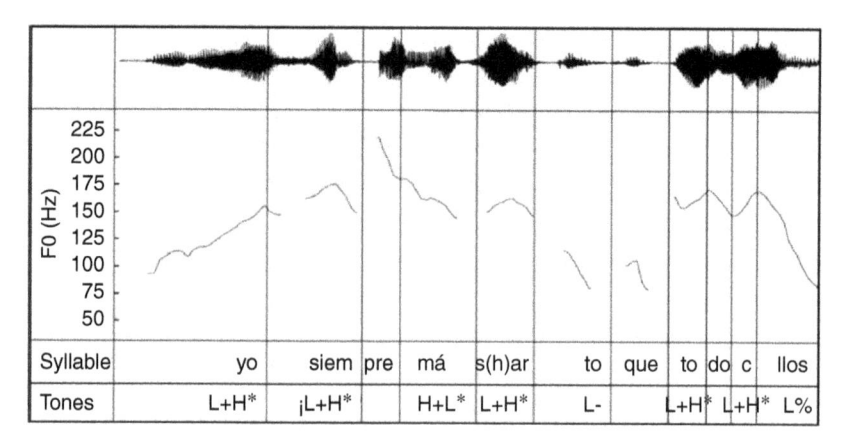

Figure 4.4 Sample F0 contours from Afro-Bolivian Spanish data for *Yo siempre más harto que todos ellos* (I am always much more than all of them)

H tone, in line with Bantu patterns, while O'Rourke (2004, 2005) has suggested a similar substrate effect for the Spanish of Cuzco in contact with Quechua. In this Andean Spanish dialect, in fact, high tones coincide with prenuclear stressed syllables, a pattern also encountered in the regional variety of the indigenous language. Similarly, prenuclear peaks are commonly observed within Italian stressed syllables, which has been a reason mentioned behind the unique alignment patterns found in Argentine Spanish (Colantoni, 2011; Colantoni & Gurlekian 2004). On the other hand, other investigations have repeatedly reported the same feature for varieties of Spanish in contact with languages that do not present such a prosodic pattern in their tonal inventory: Veneto, Basque, and Maya (Barnes & Michnowicz 2013; Elordieta 2003; Michnowicz & Barnes 2013). In particular, Michnowicz & Barnes (2013) suggest that earlier prenuclear peaks could be thought of as a sort of default strategy, generalized from nuclear position, or prosodic phrase heads, which tends to appear in contact varieties of Spanish and that should not be necessarily ascribed to any specific substrate effect (Gooden *et al.* 2011 for a broader-scoped discussion of closely related issues).

In the case of ABS and CS, as well as for the rest of the AHLAs, it is tempting to claim that such a feature may be seen as the result of some African substrate effect. Nevertheless, if we approach this issue from a broader perspective, which acknowledges the linguistic findings of this latter group of researchers, the hypothesis of a general default/simplification (of pitch accent inventory) strategy may provide some interesting insights. If we look at the L+H* pattern in this way, we may tentatively hypothesize that it consists of an advanced L2 feature, which was conventionalized and nativized by following generations of

4.6 Prosodic Features 123

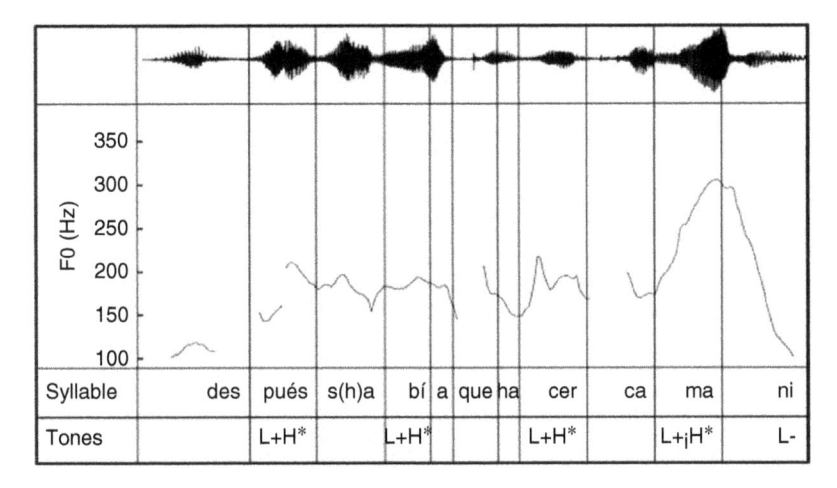

Syllable		des	pués	s(h)a	bí	a	que ha	cer	ca	ma	ni
Tones			L+H*	L+H*				L+H*		L+ᵢH*	L-

Figure 4.5 Sample F0 contours from Afro-Bolivian Spanish data for *Después había que hacer camani* (Later one had to do work)

AHLAs speakers, along with many other advanced SLA strategies that left an undeniable imprint on the morphosyntactic systems of these contact varieties (Sessarego 2013a, 2015b).

In addition, if we contextualize this feature within the list of the other prosodic patterns identified by Rao & Sessarego (2016) for ABS, the default strategy hypothesis acquires further momentum. I report such patterns here: g) L tones commonly appear at both the intermediate phrase (ip) and the Intonational Phrase (IP) boundaries (Figure 4.4); h) a general lack of downstep and some observed uses of upstep as a means of signaling emphasis (Figure 4.5, upstep takes place on the word *camani* 'work').

Combining phenomena (f–h) implies the potential perception, by speakers of dialects that do not implement these features, of a generalized use in ABS of narrow focus intonational tendencies. The proficient use of the inventory of pitch accents and phrase boundary tones of standard native varieties (Aguilar *et al.* 2009) by L2 speakers requires the mastery of the (intonational) phonology/pragmatics interface, since both phonological and discourse features are involved. Sessarego's and Rao's data may indicate that, at a certain point in the evolution of this dialect, Afro-Bolivians did not acquire a perfect command of such a linguistic interface and that the resulting intonational patterns were subsequently conventionalized and nativized by the following generations.

What is observed in ABS – and in all the AHLAs so far analyzed (see Sessarego & Rao 2016, 2018; Knaff, Rao, & Sessarego 2018; Butera, Sessarego, & Rao 2016) – is a lack of differentiation between prosodic patterns

124 Roots of Some Languages

Syllables	ca	yó	la	pri	mer	bom	ba	en	el	rí	o	Tám	bo	ra
Tones		L+H*		L+H*	H*	H-				L+H*		L+H*		L%

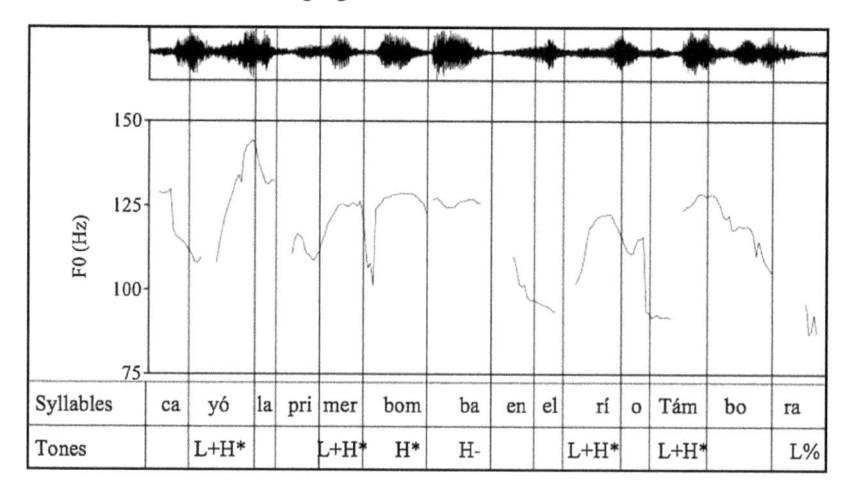

Figure 4.6 Sample F0 contours from Chocó Spanish data for *Cayó la primer bomba en el río Támbora* (The first bomb fell in the Támbora River)

that are usually employed in Spanish to indicate certain pragmatic contrasts. Indeed, our data point to a simplified set of intonational phonological targets in ABS: its pitch accent inventory is reduced, as L+H* is preferred in prenuclear context and not just in the prosodically salient nuclear phrase position; it appears that phonetic upstep, rather than phonological contrast through tonal alignment modifications, seems to be the main method of conveying increased emphasis; L+H* occurs at both terminal and non-terminal junctures, rather than distinguishing between L+H* at ip boundaries and final lowering to L* at IP boundaries, as many varieties of Spanish do in their declaratives; the L boundary tone is preferred in both phrase types (ip and IP), rather than clearly using H- at ip junctures to indicate the continuation of a thought; temporally speaking, the preference for L boundaries preceded by L+H* pitch accents suggests considerable preboundary lengthening effects that facilitate a rise-fall excursion; and, finally, these cumulative phonological results pragmatically translate to what speakers of many other varieties of Spanish could perceive as an overgeneralization of narrow focus or emphatic intonational strategies.

When we look at the CS data, we can observe some of the tendencies detected for ABS, but not all. Thus, in this respect, CS appears to lie somewhere in between ABS and standard Spanish. In fact, while at the lexical level we encounter earlier prenuclear peaks – corresponding with higher frequencies of the L+H* pitch accent – and a general lack of downstep across the utterance (Figure 4.2), at the iP boundaries it is possible to observe H- patterns, as

4.7 Interface Phenomena at the Root of Chocó Spanish's Origin

commonly encountered in other native varieties of Spanish to signal that the speaker has not finished speaking (Figure 4.6).

This suggests that, at least prosodically, CS is more similar to standard Spanish than ABS, a characteristic that further discourages a potential creole hypothesis for this dialect. The aforementioned tonal configurations are represented in examples (155–7), which schematically depict the prosodic patterns found in standard Spanish, CS, and ABS. These examples provide representations of the same generic, unmarked declarative utterance template for standard Spanish (in general) (155), CS (156), and ABS (157), respectively. In these examples, there are six content words, each containing a stressed syllable, spread across two ips, both of which belong to one IP. As can be observed, standard Spanish and ABS diverge at both the ip and PW levels, while CS behaves like ABS at the PW level – where it presents an L+H* pattern across the lexicon – and aligns with standard Spanish at the ip level, where it uses an H- tone on the first ip to signal the continuation of a thought.

(155) Standard Spanish
IP   [   ]L%
ip   [   ]H- [   ]L-
PW   PW   PW   PW   PW   PW   PW
           L+>H   *L+>H *L+H*   L+>H*L+>H* L*/L+H*
Syllable   σ   σ   σ   σ   σ   σ

(156) CS
IP   [   ]L%
Ip   [   ]H- [   ]L-
PW   PW   PW   PW   PW   PW   PW
           L+H*   L+H*   L+H*   L+H*   L+H*   L+H*
Syllable   σ   σ   σ σ   σ   σ

(157) ABS
IP   [   ]L%
ip   [   ]L- [   ]L-
PW   PW   PW   PW   PW   PW   PW
           L+H*   L+H*   L+H*   L+H*   L+H*   L+H*
Syllable   σ   σ   σ   σ   σ   σ

4.7 Interface Phenomena at the Root of Chocó Spanish's Origin

The linguistic interface model proposed in this chapter may help us better understand why a number of Afro-Hispanic dialects scattered across the Americas share similar linguistic phenomena, without necessarily recurring to a proto-creole explanation (Granda 1968; Schwegler 1991a). This account also partially deviates from Lipski's (1986) analysis, in which specific African substrate effects are taken as the possible reason behind the current data configuration encountered in these contact varieties. On the other hand, my hypothesis shifts the focus of the analysis to universal SLA processes. More specifically, features (a–f) in CS and in the rest of the AHLAs are seen as the byproduct of *advanced* SLA processes, which are hampered by processability and language interface constraints (e.g., syntax/pragmatics, syntax/morphology, syntax/semantics, pragmatics/phonology interfaces).

In line with recent minimalist models on the nature of second language development (Herschensohn 2000), the acquisition of the lexicon and of its formal features (Borer 1984) is supposed to develop gradually through a UG-driven path, and the differential specification of certain functional elements (T, Num, etc.) seems to play a pivotal role. In the specific case of CS and the other AHLAs, I hypothesize that this process generated several possible L2 grammars with different parametric configurations. The variable second language learners' output resulting from this acquisition process represented the PLD of the following generations of speakers, who nativized these second language varieties into new L1 grammars. Thus, the features reported for CS and for the other AHLAs may be seen as the result of a conventionalization process of advanced SLA strategies, which tend to occur every time an individual acquires Spanish as a second language and, for this reason, may be said to represent grammatical instantiations of a universal path of L2 development.

5 Black Slavery in the Pacific Lowlands of Colombia

5.1 Introduction

The colonial and postcolonial history of Chocó is strongly connected to the sociopolitical development of its surrounding regions. In fact, the powerful miners residing in Antioquia, Cali, and Popayán were those who originally pushed the Spanish colonial enterprise toward this remote frontier until conquering the region, one of the richest mineral areas of the Americas (Colmenares 1979). In particular, the principal actors in this colonial mission were the mining families from Popayán, who, after several attempts to penetrate the region, finally managed to defeat the native populations by the end of the seventeenth century (Hansen 1991). From that point until the abolition of slavery in 1851, several white entrepreneurs entered the region with their gangs of black slaves (*cuadrillas*) to exploit the rich gold mines of the province. In 1851, slavery was formally abolished in Colombia. This resulted in a shortage of labor force in the Chocó mines. Consequently, the majority of the white people residing in the region abandoned the area, leaving behind their former slaves, whose descendants form today more than 90 percent of the local population (Sharp 1976).

This chapter provides an overview of the aforementioned phases of Chocó history, a history made of conquest, mining enterprises, slavery, and resistance. The goal of this analysis is to cast light on the sociohistorical facts that characterized colonial and postcolonial Chocó to understand to what extent they may have shaped the genesis, evolution, and current nature of Chocó Spanish (CS). Thus, the following sections offer a sociohistorical account of this Colombian region to decide whether the scenarios envisioned by the Monogenesis-Decreolization Hypothesis (Granda 1976; Schwegler 1991a) and the Afrogenesis Hypothesis (McWhorter 2000) could really be applied to Chocó, or if a different model is needed to account for the data.

5.2 The Conquest of the Region (1500–1680)

The northern part of Chocó was one of the first mainland regions explored by the Spaniards. Since the first decades of the sixteenth century, the conquerors knew that this region was rich in mineral resources; nevertheless, for more than two centuries this area remained out of their colonial control (Sharp 1976: 15). Indeed, the presence of bellicose native populations, tropical diseases, and a hot climate discouraged Spanish establishment in the area. Even if they were not attracted by the option of living and residing in Chocó, the Spaniards tried to conquer the region on several occasions, but as it is well known, this did not turn out to be an easy task (Sharp 1976: ch.2) and according to Hansen (1991: i), it took them "nearly 300 years to bring Chocó under the Crown's control."

Attempts of Spanish expansion into the Chocó region took place throughout the sixteenth and seventeenth centuries and the conquering phases usually coincided with declining gold production in the surrounding regions of the colony (Hansen 1991: ch.1). Nevertheless, none of these expeditions resulted in any successful stable subjugation of the local populations. For this reason, in the mid-1660s the Spanish Crown decided to take a much more active role in the conquering mission. Following the advice of Diego de Egües, President of the Audiencia de Santa Fe, the Crown required the governors of Antioquia, Popayán, and Cartagena, and the President of the Audiencia of Panama to send their troops to the Chocó to conquer this area. Once the Chocó had been colonized, each provincial government would take control over the territories they had conquered (Hansen 1991: 65).

The advice of Diego de Egües was primarily based on logistic and financial calculations. Indeed, the President of the Audiencia de Santa Fe was concerned with providing Popayán and Antioquia with an overland route to Panama, and in particular, he wanted to increase the Royal Treasury's revenue by exploiting the mineral resources of the region (Hansen 1991: 63). In fact, Diego de Egües' recommendation came at a time of serious economic crisis, where the gold production of the colony had reached its lowest levels (Colmenares 1979: 316).

The royal call to join forces to undertake the Chocó mission was not followed by all the provinces invited by the King. Indeed, neither Panama nor Cartagena sent troops to Chocó. We still do not know exactly why Panama refused to participate in this enterprise; however, we have documentation indicating that the governor of Cartagena pointed out that the time for such a mission was not ripe and that he would not have sent his men to a certain death in a region populated by "wild Indians" (Hansen 1991: 67). Eventually, the main participation in this colonial enterprise came from Antioquia and Popayán.

During this phase, both *payaneses* and *antioquenos* penetrated the Chocó. The former entered from the southern part of the region, establishing a foothold

5.2 The Conquest of the Region (1500–1680)

among the Noanamá Indians and subsequently among the Tatamá and Chocó, while the latter advanced from the northern side, thus fighting against the Citará tribe. Soon after the first successful conquering attempts, the *gobernación* of Popayán and the *gobernación* of Antioquia began disputing the jurisdictional control over the areas recently colonized. The conflict over Chocó between these two *gobernaciones* lasted for several years and was eventually resolved by the end of the 1680s, when Popayán took effective administrative control over the region (Hansen 1991: 97).

At that point, given the advancing colonization of the region, several miners moved from surrounding areas – in particular from Popayán – to the Chocó, and took with them slave gangs to exploit the rich gold deposits of the area. Colmenares (1979: 169) states that:

It has been observed that between the end of the seventeenth century and the beginning of the eighteenth century some *Payanense* owners moved their slave gangs to Chocó from the mining districts of Popayán. (Author's translation)[1]

Colmenares' claims are further confirmed by Cantor (2000: 47), who not only suggests that the first slaves proceeded primarily from Popayán, he also adds that they were for the most part *mulatos* (mulattoes) and *criollos*. In fact, he indicates that:

... from the first years of the Spanish occupation (by the end of the seventeenth century), many *criollos* and mulattoes, who were sold by the residents of Popayán, entered the mines in the region of the Atrato river (Author's translation).[2]

Based on the historical data we have, it is not possible to exactly establish how many Spaniards moved in with their slaves to the region in those years. Nevertheless, Hansen (1991: 106) estimates that some 200 people may have entered the Chocó by 1673, a number that would grow even further by the arrival of a Franciscan mission in the following years (from 1673 to 1676). Additionally, she reports a piece of demographic information provided by the priest Antonio Marzal (Pacheco 1962: 495), who indicated that by 1678 there were at least 136 slaves and many free blacks across the Chocó (Hansen 1991: 106). We also know that the slave gangs introduced into the region had to be supplied with foodstuffs. For this reason, the Spaniards tried to establish Indian settlements close to the mining camps. The natives were forced to grow corn and bananas (among other crops) to feed the *cuadrillas* of black miners.

---

[1] Original Spanish version: *Se ha visto como a fines del siglo XVII y comienzos del XVIII algunos propietarios payaneses trasladaran sus cuadrillas al Chocó desde los distritos mineros de Popayán.*

[2] Original Spanish version: *... desde los primeros años de la ocupación española (finales del siglo XVII), ingresaron a las minas del Atrato muchos criollos y mulatos, quienes frecuentemente eran vendidos por los vecinos de Popayán.*

Table 5.1 *Composition of Don Antonio de Veroiz's* cuadrilla *in 1694 (Cantor 2000: 48)*

Number	Name	Origin	Age
1	Joseph	Mulato	26
2	Ventura	Mulato	24
3	Joseph	Arara	21
4	Francisco	Mina	50
5	Pedro	Arara	36
6	Antonio	Congo	38
7	Joseph	Congo	38
8	Simón	Mulato	22
9	Geromina	Mulata	25
10	Isabel	Mulata	Unknown
11	Domingo	Unknown	Unknown
12	María	Mulata	Unknown
13	María's daughter	Mulata	5 months

We do not possess a detailed demographic census for this early phase of the Chocó colonization. Nevertheless, from an analysis of the available documents concerning the composition of the first *cuadrillas*, it is possible to understand that the *criollo* and *mulato* presence in the region had always been significant, so that, from the very beginning of the Spanish occupation of Chocó, Latin American-born slaves have always been more numerous in this region than the African-born ones, called *bozales*. Cantor (2000: 47–8) offers data concerning the composition of the first slave gangs as a way of stressing the importance of the American-born captives in forming the local cultural identity of the first black inhabitants of the region. He exemplifies such a scenario by providing the following table, which indicates names, origins, and ages of the members of a slave gang belonging to the miner Antonio de Veroiz in 1694 (Table 5.1).

Data show that the *cuadrilla* consisted of seven mulattoes, two slaves proceeding from Congo, two Araras, one Mina, and one slave of unknown origin. Cantor (2000) highlights how the American-born slaves were key to implementing the acculturation process among the first Chocoan *cuadrillas*. He (2000: 48) states that:

It is notable that half of the slave gang consisted of mulattoes, who had experienced more contact with the colonial world; moreover, this information pertains to the year 1694, which highlights that the mulattoes (as well as the *criollos*) took part in the process of cultural construction from the very beginning of the Spanish occupation. (Author's translation)[3]

---

[3] Original Spanish version: *Es llamativo que la mitad de la cuadrilla estaba integrada por mulatos, quienes habían tenido mayor contacto con el mundo colonial; además, la*

Several Indian uprisings took place during the 1660s, 1670s, and 1680s. Some of them were so brutal that they resulted in the killing of many Spanish miners, their slaves, and some missionaries. In 1669 four Franciscan missionaries were killed by natives living in the Atrato region. Another big Indian revolt happened in 1684 in the Quibdó region. The natives joined forces with some black slaves and managed to take control over the area. Eventually, in 1685, the Spanish army, led by Governor Juan Bueso de Valdes, succeeded in defeating the enemies and put an end to the Indian uprising in 1686. This was the last big conflict that saw the Indians as protagonist of a successful revolt. From that point on, the Spaniards managed to systematically increase their control over Chocó and more and more entrepreneurs proceeding from Popayán entered the region with their slave gangs to carry out mining activities (Hansen 1991: 367).

Sharp (1976: 30) suggests that "by 1690 the Chocó was generally considered pacified" and "for the first time sizable numbers of Spaniards began to enter the area with their *cuadrillas.*" With the Indians of the central Chocó under control, the Spaniards faced the new threat of foreign invasion before finally securing the region. English pirates, allied with the Cuna Indians, attacked the Spaniards on several occasions. The first attack happened in 1679; the fights continued for several years until the beginning of the eighteenth century. A major battle took place in 1702, near the mouth of the Berbera River, where a troop of Spanish soldiers succeeded in killing 105 Englishmen. By that point, neither the Indians nor the English could dislodge the Spaniards. Sharp (1976: 33) indicates that by 1703 "more and more Spaniards were occupying the Chocó." He also states that "the conquest of the Chocó had ended, but the story of slavery, mining, food supply, and contraband trade had just begun" (1976: 33).

5.3   *Cuadrillas* in Popayán c. 1680s

Given that the first slaves introduced in the Chocó mainly came from *cuadrillas* previously working in the Popayán deposits, understanding the nature of slavery and of mining work in the province of Popayán up to that point may help us obtain a better idea of the first black workers who entered this more recently pacified region.

Colmenares (1972: ch.5) indicates that for several decades, after the conquest of Popayán (1536–1570), mining work was carried out by the native populations, who were forced to extract precious metals from the local deposits until their almost complete extinction; while, on the other hand, recurring to a black workforce had never been easy. He claims that (1972: 203) *"el empleo de*

información corresponde a 1694, lo cual evidencia que los mulatos (junto con los criollos) participaron en el proceso de construcción cultural desde los primeros años de la ocupación española.

esclavos negros planteó siempre problemas, que, sumados a otros, explican la decadencia de los centros mineros" (the use of black slaves always implied problems, which, in concomitance with other issues, explain the ruin of the mining centers).

Indeed, while forcing Indians in the mines did not imply any high cost to the Spaniards, the same cannot be said for the use of black slaves. During those years (1530–1580), the Crown conceded *licencias* to private entrepreneurs to introduce a certain number of Africans into the colony, but most of the miners could not afford to purchase them in big numbers. It is for this reason that Colmenares (1972: 205) states that:

it is not therefore likely that before 1580 slaves could be used massively in the mining districts ... Popayán always suffered from labor-force shortages. (Author's translation)[4]

Indeed, in 1592 the lawyer Auncibay wrote a letter to the King highlighting the high need for a black workforce in the area (1972: 205):

... about the blacks that should be taken to the Department of Popayán, to the cities of Cali, Popayán, Almaguer and Pasto, some two thousand blacks are needed. (Author's translation)[5]

A request for 800 slaves was made in 1598 by the *procurador de Popayán*; in 1603 the same appeal was reiterated by the governor Vasco de Mendoza y Silva, and in 1615 an identical application was sent by the treasury official, Jeronimo de Ubillus. Nevertheless, since in all these requests the assumption was that the Crown would have conceded the slaves to the miners as a credit and that they would have paid for them later, after using the captives in the extracting operations, the King never met such requests in full. Over the seventeenth century, the number of slaves in the province was augmented, but black introduction was never massive. In 1628, the total number of slaves found in Popayán mines and haciendas was 250, while in 1659 they were 313 (Marzahl 1978: 46). As far as the shift to black slave labor is concerned, we know that it was quite gradual during the seventeenth century in the city of Popayán. Indeed, Marzahl (1978: 45) points out that:

Christóbal de Mosquera was one of the town's first encomenderos to shift to slave labor in mining. In 1626 he bought thirteen slaves who were part of a larger consignment then

---

[4] Original Spanish version: *no es entonces probable que antes de 1580 se hayan empleado esclavos de manera masiva en los distritos mineros ... Popayán siempre sufrió penuria de mano de obra.*

[5] Original Spanish version: *... sobre los negros que convienen se lleven a la gobernación de Popayán, a las ciudades de Cali, Popayán, Almaguer y Pasto, que son necesarios hasta dos mil negros.*

being sold in Popayán. This was the largest number of slaves bought in the town until then.

Even the regions like Antioquia and Zaragoza, which during the previous century had benefited from the introduction of more consistent cargoes of black captives, in the 1670s were left with a much reduced number of slaves. Indeed, by 1675 the captain Juan Bueso de Valdes reported that the total number of slaves found in the Antioquia region was no more than 400, while Zaragoza had some 60 captives left (Colmenares 1972: 213).

Overall, the slave trade in the Popayán region was not huge by the end of the seventeenth century. The non-massive introduction of slaves in Popayán during the seventeenth century had to do with several factors. First, the slave trade was not based on a free market; rather, the Spanish Crown had the monopoly of this business: the King would concede only a certain number of *asientos* 'trading licenses,' and traders would have to pay *almorjarifazgor* 'import taxes' and *alcabalas* 'sales taxes' on each slave (Bryant 2005: 31). Such market constraints already limited the volume of slave introduction into Spanish America. Moreover, slave introduction to Popayán, on the western side of Colombia, implied additional obstacles. In fact, in order to be sold in this city, *bozales* had to be shipped from Africa to Cartagena (on the Atlantic coast of Colombia) and then, from there, they had to be sent through the Magdalena River and forced to walk over inland roads to Popayán (Map 5.1). The journey was extremely strenuous and many casualties tended to occur among the captives. It was not only the transatlantic crossing that implied inhumane travel conditions, Pickard (2010: 31–2) indicates that the Magdalena River navigation and the overland route were also extremely dangerous. He quotes a traveler of that time who described the roads around Popayán as "the worst in the world." All of these logistic barriers inevitably resulted in higher prices for the slaves sold in Popayán than those sold in Cartagena. Indeed, data show that while by the end of the seventeenth century the price for an adult male slave in Cartagena was around 350 pesos, in Popayán the average price reached 500 pesos (Colmenares 1979: 66–7). For these reasons, transactions concerning big cargoes of slaves at this time were not common. Rather, slave buyers tended to purchase one or two captives at a time (1979: 66).

Given the impediments related to taking *bozal* slaves to Popayán, a good percentage of the captives sold in this market by the end of the seventeenth century and beginning of the eighteenth century were *criollos*, primarily locally born, and in part also proceeding from already settled colonies (viz., Panama, the Caribbean). The shortage of *bozales* was particularly significant during this period due to problems with the supply of African captives related to the Nine Years' War (1688–1697) and the War of Spanish Succession (1701–1714) (Colmenares 1979: 55).

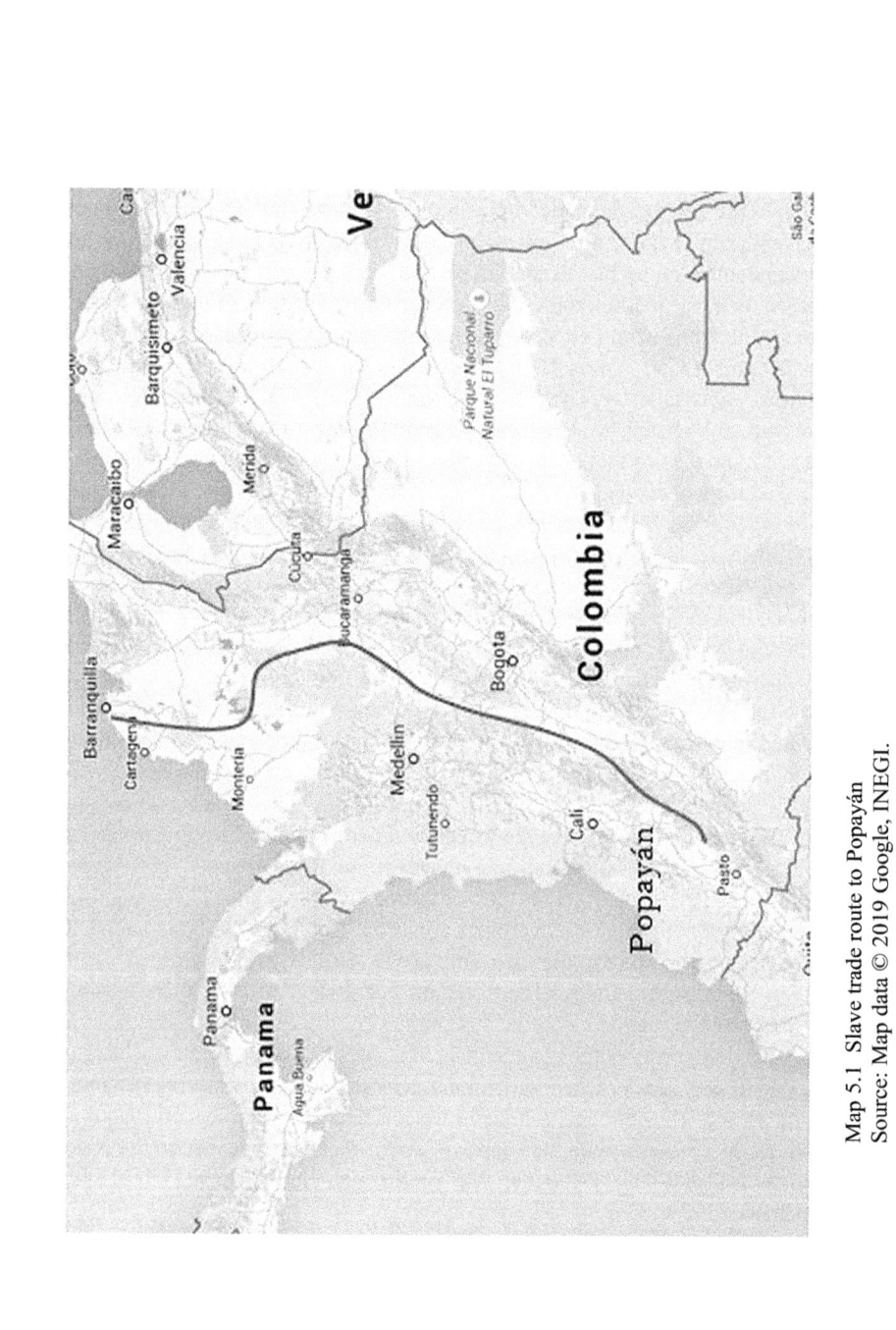

Map 5.1 Slave trade route to Popayán
Source: Map data © 2019 Google, INEGI.

5.3 *Cuadrillas* in Popayán c. 1680s

In relation to this issue, Robert West, an expert in the Spanish colonial mining enterprise, suggests that since Hispaniola was the first Spanish colony to develop mining activities, it soon became a sort of logistic hub, where captives would be bought, trained, and subsequently sold at a profit to be employed in other colonies (West 1949, 1953). This practice did not exclusively concern the labor force employed by the mining industry. Rather, Caribbean slaves, trained in a variety of jobs, could be encountered in a number of Latin American territories during the early colonial period. Evidence of this practice has been provided by a number of scholars working on colonial Latin American history. Restall (2000: 190–1), for example, reports the observations of one royal official from Hispaniola, Alonso López de Cerrato, who commented on how many Spaniards residing in the island "made a living by buying Africans [*bozales*], teaching them some trade [*alguna industria*] and then selling them at a profit on the mainland" (see also Aguirre Beltrán 1946: 20). In regards to the colonial mining industry, West (1953: 1) highlights the importance played by Hispaniola in the overall enterprise and begins his book, *Colonial placer mining in Colombia,* by stating that:

With the establishment of Santo Domingo as a supply base for the mining camps (1496), eastern Hispanola became a center from which Spanish conquest and culture spread to other parts of tropical America.

West's observation, if combined with the linguistic data presented in Chapter 3, may already explain why CS and several other AHLAs share so many features, which are also common to Caribbean Spanish dialects. Moreover, if we analyze this information in light of the Founder Principle, which suggests that a large proportion of the structure of today's contact languages was determined by the vernaculars of the founder populations (Mufwene 1996), we may begin to understand why CS looks more like a Spanish dialect than a Spanish creole.

Some readers may argue that a part of the slaves proceeding from already settled colonies may have spoken a creole language. Indeed, during the course of recent linguistic conferences, some colleagues have pointed out to me the importance of Panama as a potential source of creole speakers since in Lipski's (1989) book on *The Speech of the Negros Congos in Panama*, the possibility that the black dialect spoken by this community has a creole ancestor is not completely excluded. This is a valuable point, and it could be possible that some American-born slaves acquired a Spanish creole before entering the Chocó. In fact, since no written diachronic data of CS are available, we know virtually nothing about the earlier phases of this contact vernacular. However, I remain of the idea that clear sociohistorical and linguistic evidence should be provided in order to build a convincing theory of (de)creolization. Casting light on the past is always an approximation, so it will never be completely exact. The best we can do is to try to make sense of the available information we have.

For this reason, I do not claim that my reconstruction of colonial Chocó is perfect; rather, I try to build a story that appears to be the most likely one, based on the *available* data we have. As far as I can tell, the chance of a Spanish creole being introduced from Panama and used systematically by the majority of the blacks living in colonial Chocó is quite slim for at least two reasons. First of all, such a language has never been reported, not even for Panama, and a closer look at Lipski's study suggests that even the author of the book on the *Negros Congos* suggests that blacks in Panama largely "assimilated to the national standards ... from the early colonial periods" (1989: 68), so that the dialect spoken by the *Negros Congos* would find its root in a variety of colonial Afro-Hispanic speech, but this was in all likelihood nothing like a Spanish creole (1989: 75). Second, if that language in fact existed and was spoken in colonial Chocó, it is difficult to understand how it could disappear so completely in a remote region of this kind, where pressure from the standard norm has always been minimal and remains minimal even today (see Section 5.5 on this point).

Slave transactions became more significant after the conquest and pacification of Chocó. However, the captives involved in the mining exploitation of the newly conquered region were – for the most part – not arriving directly from Africa; rather, they proceeded from the recently dismissed mines of Popayán (Colmenares 1972: ch.5). Moreover, the cargoes of slaves introduced in the new mining sites were not huge, in contrast to McWhorter's (2000: 7) observation that "starting in the late seventeenth century, the Spanish began importing massive numbers of West Africans." On this point, Colmenares states (1972: 214) that:

The contribution of the slaves to the mineral exploitation of New Granada regained importance after the pacification of Chocó. For this reason, the slave trade becomes significant only at the end of the seventeenth century. The slaves working in Chocó came from dismissed mines in Popayán or from the agricultural sector. It is not likely, therefore, that large numbers of slaves had been used in the new mines by the beginning of the eighteenth century. (Author's translation)[6]

After an analysis of the historical information available for seventeenth-century Popayán, we may conclude that this region did not present the socio-historical conditions that have generally been held responsible for creole formation. A concomitance of trading restrictions, logistic limitations, and financial constraints prevented the massive introduction of an enslaved labor force. Moreover, the blacks sold in the market were not for the most part

---

[6] Original Spanish version: *El aporte de los esclavos en las explotaciones mineras de la Nueva Granada cobró importancia de nuevo a partir de la pacificación del Chocó. Con todo, el tráfico negrero sólo es perceptible a partir de fines del siglo XVII. Los esclavos que trabajaban entonces en el Chocó proveían de explotaciones abandonadas en Popayán o del sector agrícola. No es probable, pues, que a comienzos del siglo XVIII haya sido abundante el número de esclavos que trabajaban en los nuevos yacimientos.*

bozales speaking African languages; rather, the majority of them were locally born or proceeded from already settled colonies, thus they were *criollos* and could probably speak good approximations of Spanish.

5.4 The Mineral Exploitation (1680–1851)

5.4.1 Slave Market Transactions

Even after this initial colonial period, which was characterized by a reduced number of *bozales* and a more significant presence of Spanish-speaking captives, the importation of African-born slaves into western Colombia never achieved huge volumes. This was primarily due to the uncertainty with the *asientos* – conceded by the Spanish Crown to specialized trading companies – as well as to the financial constraints imposed by the high costs related to the introduction of *bozales* into this distant Andean region. West (1953: 84) states that:

Throughout the remainder of the colonial period the importation of Negros into western Colombia was sporadic. Although the supply of slaves from Africa to Cartagena was under government regulation, arrival of slave ships was uncertain. Moreover, the high cost of transport into the interior often made the price of slaves prohibitive to many miners.

During the last two decades of the seventeenth century, Spanish miners from the surrounding areas began to enter the Chocó with their slave gangs. As we saw, the main business actors in this mining enterprise were the rich and politically well-connected mining families of Popayán. As the conquest of Chocó proceeded, the demand for more enslaved workers increased. This trend is reflected in the slave transactions of Popayán's market at that time. Colmenares (1979: ch.3) provides an account of the Popayán slave market from 1680 to 1800. The historian indicates that this market received between 6 and 20 percent of all the slaves that were shipped to Cartagena. Besides the *bozales* proceeding from Cartagena, Colmenares' calculations include also the *criollo* captives, thereby reflecting the percentage of slaves who were born and sold in Colombia, as well as those who might have reached this colony from other Spanish territories (viz., Panama, the Caribbean, etc.). Since Popayán was the most important slave market in western Colombia, Colmenares (1979: 56) indicates that the transactions reported for this city may well reflect the slave trade trends for the captives taken to Chocó.

Table 5.2 shows the percentage of slaves sold in Popayán with respect to Cartagena's sales during the different *asientos* (1698–1757), while Table 5.3 reports the transactions of *criollos* and *bozales* according to their age during the period 1690–1780.

Table 5.2 *Percentage of slaves sold in Popayán with respect to Cartagena's sales (Colmenares 1979: 56)*

Year	Asiento	Cartagena's sales	Year	Popayán's sales	%
1688–1702	Cacheu	2,538	1699–1703	383	15.0
1703–1713	Guinea	4,251	1704–1715	320	7.5
1715–1718	South Sea Co. I	1,430	1716–1720	123	8.6
1722–1727	South Sea Co. II	3,949	1722–1728	248	6.3
1730–1736	South Sea Co. III	4,919	1730–1738	991	20.1
1746–1757	Moyort-Noriega	12,957	1746–1757	765	5.9
	Total	30,044		2,830	9.4

Table 5.3 *Slaves sold in Popayán 1690–1789 (% according to their age) (Colmenares 1979: 36)*

Ages	Criollos (1,074 cases)	Bozales (749 cases)
0–5	7.0	0.2
6–10	13.5	2.8
11–15	22.3	25.6
16–20	27.9	39.9
21–25	14.8	16.7
26–30	10	9.2
31–35	1.8	2.9
36–40	2.7	2.7
Total	100	100
%	58.9	41.1

As can be observed, Popayán represented a major center for slave commerce in colonial times since it received a significant percentage of the African captives sold in Cartagena. Indeed, in Bryant's (2005: 67) words, it was "*the slave market of North Andes.*" Nevertheless, even if between 6 and 20 percent of Cartagena's slaves were resold in Popayán (see Table 5.2), it is worth pointing out that – as indicated in Table 5.3 – during the period 1690–1789, a key phase for the Chocó mineral exploitation, almost 60% of all the slaves sold in Popayán were *criollos*, thus they were not directly proceeding from Africa. This factor indirectly suggests that a good part of the enslaved workers taken to this region probably introduced into the area either native varieties of Spanish or advanced interlanguages.

5.4 The Mineral Exploitation (1680–1851)   139

Transactions concerning *criollos* and *mulatos*, in fact, were significantly more frequent in Popayán than in Cartagena. This was particularly true when the supply of African-born slaves was low: for example, between 1690 and 1701, during the Succession War (1701–1714) and when there were interruptions with the trading licenses (1715–1720, 1740–1745, and 1753–1759) (Colmenares 1979: 57). Colmenares suggests that the most important period for slave transactions in Popayán's market goes from 1716 to 1738, during the South Sea's *asiento*, when the enslaved population of Chocó almost doubled from a few thousand (in 1711) to almost four thousand (1979: 57). As for the Monogenetic-Decreolization Hypothesis (Granda 1976; Schwegler 1991a), which would suggest that a Portuguese-based creole may once have been spoken in Chocó, it must be said that while until 1640 the royal *asientos* were conceded for the most part to Spanish and Portuguese traders, after that date the majority of the slave trade to Spanish America passed into the hands of English, French, and Dutch companies (Peralta Rivera 2005). Since by 1640 Chocó was not even completely conquered, the probabilities of a massive introduction into the region of Portuguese creole-speaking slaves are quite reduced.

Colmenares also states that the number of *bozales* decreased significantly from 1760 and that from 1780 only *criollos* were sold in this market. Indeed, he suggests that an analysis of the *cuadrillas* sold in Popayán shows how the number of *criollos* increased steadily during the eighteenth century until 1780, since "*a partir de 1780, el mercado podía alimentarse casi exclusivamente con esclavos nacidos aquí*" (beginning in 1780, the market could function almost exclusively by relying on locally-born slaves).

5.4.2 Cuadrillas' Dynamics

Additional data on early colonial demographics are provided by Cantor (2000: 49–50), who analyzes the composition of some Chocoan *cuadrillas* in 1718. In particular, he focuses on the slave gang belonging to the miner Luis de Acuña and concludes that:

in these records we can again see the important presence of the *criollo* and mulatto slaves living among people with different African backgrounds. According to this information, approximately 56% of the slave gang consisted of *criollos* and mulattoes; 24% were Asara; 15% were Congo and 6% were Popo. (Author's translation)[7]

---

[7] Original Spanish version: *en este registro nuevamente se encuentra una presencia importante de criollos y mulatos conviviendo con gente de diverso origen africano. De acuerdo con esta información, aproximadamente el 56% de la población de la cuadrilla estaba conformada por mulatos y criollos; el 24%, por gente de nación Asara; el 15%, por esclavizados de nación Congo y el 6%, eran de nación Popo.*

The author stresses (2000: 56) one more time how the vast presence of American-born slaves, combined with a high fragmentation of the other ethnic groups proceeding from Africa, favored the diffusion of the Spanish culture, the Spanish language, and the Christian faith among the blacks living in Chocó:

> Based on the available historical documentation, we may think that the aggregation of people proceeding from highly divergent backgrounds implied a linguistic and cultural fragmentation within the slave gang, a context in which the contact among blacks and whites developed. Such a fragmentation implies the absence of shared culture, language and beliefs ... The concept of fragmentation ... was, nevertheless, relative since there was a large number of mulattoes and *criollos*, who shared the Castilian language and eventually became familiarized with the Christian faith. (Author's translation)[8]

Given the aforementioned demographic accounts, it makes sense to believe that even though McWhorter (2000: 8) – reporting Sharp (1976: 21–2) – states that "there were 600 slaves in the Chocó in 1704, 2000 in 1724, and 7088 by 1782," such captives were for the most part not African-born, but rather *criollos*, thus, again, they may have spoken vernacular varieties of Spanish rather than African languages. Indeed, it is Sharp (1976: 21) who stresses the fact that when he uses the word "black," he does not necessarily mean African, but rather any person of African ancestry, including *mulattoes, criollos*, etc.:

> Doubtless many of the people listed as black were in fact *mulattoes* or *pardos* (black-white offspring), or *zambos* (black-Indian offspring). The census records simply employed the terms *blancos* (whites), *indios* (Indians), *esclavos de varios colores* (slaves of various colors) and *libres de varios colores* (freedmen of various colors). Hence the word *negro*, or black, as used in the Chocó, did not apply only to those of pure African descent.

This piece of information suggests that, even though in Chocó "there was no period of numerical parity between blacks and whites" (McWhorter 2000: 8), the principal language introduced into the region by the black population was Spanish and not a variety of African languages "ranging from Senegal down to Angola" (p. 7). In fact, it would be misleading to equal blacks to *bozal* speakers of African languages. Quite conversely, data suggest that the majority of the Afro-descendants introduced in Chocó were *criollos*, who probably spoke Spanish or close approximations to it. Thus, the sociohistorical information

---

[8] Original Spanish version: *Con base en la documentación histórica disponible se piensa que la agregación de gentes caracterizadas por la extraordinaria diversidad de procedencias determinó una situación de relativa fragmentación lingüística y cultural dentro de cada cuadrilla, contexto dentro del cual se desarrolló el contacto entre los diversos negros y de éstos con los blancos. Tal fragmentación implica la ausencia de una cultura, un idioma y un sistema de creencias comunes y compartidas por todos los miembros de la cuadrilla ... El concepto de fragmentación ... se plantea como un hecho relativo por cuanto existía un alto número de mulatos y criollos, quienes compartían como idioma común el castellano y eventualmente conocían el cristianismo.*

5.4 The Mineral Exploitation (1680–1851)

we find for this second colonial phase further provides explanations for why in Chocó a Spanish dialect is spoken today, rather than a Spanish creole.

Recent investigation on the evolution of sugarcane plantations in Chincha, Peru have shown how Spanish planters tried to make sure that a certain percentage of the slaves working on their haciendas were *criollos,* since growing sugarcane required complex skills that would be more easily learned by workers capable of understanding Spanish (Flores Galindo 1984: 28, 109; Sessarego 2015a: 102, 114). It is therefore feasible – and it makes perfect sense – that to carry out mining activities in a recently colonized area like Chocó, the *cuadrillas* proceeding from Popayán would be composed – for a good share – of experienced personnel, who could speak Spanish. They would have been in charge of supervising and teaching the unskilled workers and the *bozales*. On the other hand, it would have been very difficult to manage a slave gang where on average 97% of the captives were *bozales*, speaking a variety of African languages – as some may infer by reading that "whites were a mere 3 percent of the total population" (McWhorter 2000: 7). Common sense suggests that few miners would have liked to put themselves in such a context and tried to run their business under such conditions.

Cantor (2000) reconstructs the living and working dynamics of the Chocoan *cuadrillas* during the mineral exploitation phase of the region. He focuses on the slave gang as the basic social unit dictating the rhythm of work and life in colonial Chocó. Cantor (2000: 97) shows how the owners of the mine and slave gang (*dueños de mina y cuadrilla*) were usually absent and relied for the administration of the mine on local overseers (*capataces*). The slave gang was hierarchically organized. Each *cuadrilla* was formed by different groups of workers; each group depended on the orders given by a captain (*capitán*). Captains were workers the owner could trust. They had to be skilled in the mining job and tough enough to be respected by the rest of the gang. They were usually *criollos* and played a major role in the *proceso de aculturación* (acculturation process), which not only implied the diffusion of mining techniques among the slaves but also the transmission of the Spanish language and Christianity. In fact, Cantor (2000: 98, 160) states that:

> The mining work implied the acquisition of the techniques and the assimilation of the technology (production tools) by the slaves proceeding from different geographical and cultural backgrounds ... On the other hand, the daily routine was the proper scenario for the diffusion of Spanish and eventually of Christianity (Author's translation).[9]

---

[9] Original Spanish version: *El trabajo en las minas implicó el aprendizaje de las técnicas y la asimilación de la tecnología (instrumentos de producción) por parte de los esclavizados de diversa procedencia geográfica y cultural ... De otro lado, la rutina diaria fue el escenario propicio para la difusión del castellano y eventualmente del cristianismo.*

Moreover, in each working group, the slave-gang captains must have contributed to the diffusion of Spanish during the working days, since the majority were mulattoes and/ or *criollos* (Author's translation).[10]

As far as language diffusion is concerned, Cantor (2000: 161) also stresses how miners wanted their slaves to learn Spanish to facilitate the carrying out of the mining activities. For this reason, in some cases they even relied on Spanish-speaking captives to teach the language to the recently arrived *bozales* through Christian indoctrination:

... miners stimulated the diffusion of Spanish among the working groups to facilitate comprehension of the given orders and realization of the working activities. In addition, they assigned some *criollos* to the teaching of this language among the rest of the slaves through the repetition of prayers (Author's translation).[11]

As for the diffusion of the Christian faith, Cantor (2000: 162) admits that the presence of missionaries and clerics was quite reduced in the region and that, for this reason, the Church could not directly educate the black slaves as in other parts of the country. Nevertheless, the presence of *capillas* (chapels) in the mining centers was not rare and also quite diffuse was the practice of asking the captains to indoctrinate the captives so that "*algunos capitanes de cuadrilla participaron en la enseñanza del cristianismo*" (some slave-gang captains participated in the teaching of Christianity). Sharp (1976: ch.8) and Cantor (2000: ch.2) also analyze a variety of colonial documents concerning the mining enterprise in the region and discover that in the manuals provided by the owners to the "*adminstradores de minas*" (mine administrators) there were precise instructions stressing the importance of teaching the captives the principles of the Catholic faith to instill Christian obedience into them (1976: 139; 2000: 162), while marriage among slaves was encouraged and family units were preserved (1976: 140; 2000: 165). In fact, creating families was conceived as a way of building stronger bonds among the slaves, the rest of the gang, and the mine. Moreover, it had the function of reducing the probabilities of slave escape and rebellion, activities that were made more difficult if a captive had a family to support (1976: 141). These very pragmatic techniques used by the Chocoan miners appear to parallel those adopted by the Company of Jesus in the management of the slaves working on their Ecuadorean and Peruvian sugarcane plantations (Sessarego 2013b, 2015a). All these

---

[10] Original Spanish version: *Además, en cada grupo de trabajo, los capitanes de cuadrilla debieron contribuir a la difusión del castellano en las jornadas diarias de trabajo, puesto que la mayoría eran mulatos y/o criollos.*
[11] Original Spanish version: *... los mineros estimularon la difusión del castellano en el interior de los grupos de trabajo para facilitar la comprensión de las ordenes impartidas y la realización de las labores. Inclusive, destinaron algunos criollos a la enseñanza de este idioma entre los demás esclavizados a través de la repetición de las oraciones.*

managerial strategies, especially those related to the systematic religious indoctrination of the captives, may be seen as an additional factor favoring the acquisition of Spanish by the black miners.

The aforementioned data indicate that, when we zoom into the Chocoan *cuadrillas'* living dynamics, we find further evidence suggesting that the spread of the Spanish language among the captives was facilitated by demographic, working, and religious factors: the majority of the slaves were *criollos*, the fact of carrying out labor activities in Spanish optimized mining operations, and Christian education offered additional resources to learn the language.

5.4.3 Demographic Trends

Sharp (1976: 195) provides a table to show the evolution of Chocó racial groups from 1636 to 1856 (see Table 5.4). As he points out, the terrain, climate, and isolation that the Spanish encountered in the region made the Chocó a very unattractive region for settlement. These factors account for the fact that the whites always represented a small fraction of the entire population. When the first major census was completed in 1778, only 332 people out of a total population of 14,662 (2.3%) were classified as whites. Thirty years later, the number of white residents had increased to 400, but by this time the total population had also increased, to 25,000, which meant that the Spanish now represented an even smaller portion of the population (1.6%) than they had in 1778. On the other hand, Indians, who were the undiscussed majority by the beginning of the mid-seventeenth century, passed from 60,000 in 1660 to 4,732 in 1763, and slightly increased during the following years. Their demographic collapse has been explained as a result of war, diseases, harsh working conditions and – especially – fleeing. The only racial category that grew systematically over the entire period is the Afro-descendant one, which includes both slaves and freedmen. Data clearly indicate that by 1778 they were already the majority (5,756 slaves and 3,160 freedmen, out of a total of 14,662 people).

As far as the increase on the overall number of blacks is concerned, historians have suggested that besides a percentage of captives who were purchased outside of Chocó and consisted of both *bozales* and *criollos* (probably along the patterns reported in Table 5.3 for Popayán) (Colmenares 1979: 56–9; Bryant 2005: ch.4), a significant contribution to the numerical increase of the black sector of the population had to do with the relatively high levels of reproduction. Indeed, after analyzing a variety of inventories describing the composition of Chocoan *cuadrillas*, Sharp (1976) highlights that, given the extraordinary percentages of old slaves, black life expectancy must have been quite high, so that "blacks did survive the rigor of mining in the Chocó in surprising numbers" (1976: 125). Moreover, based on the significant number of children found in these communities and the overall increase in the Afro-descendant population,

Table 5.4 *Chocó population 1636–1856 (Sharp 1976: 199)*[13]

Year	White	Slaves	Freedmen	Indians	Total for Province of Atrato	Total for Province of Nóvita	Total for Chocó
1636	-	100	-	-	-	-	-
1660	-	-	-	60,000	-	-	-
1680	-	41	-	-	-	-	-
1688	-	100	-	-	-	-	-
1704	-	600	-	-	-	-	-
1724	-	2,000	-	-	-	-	-
1759	-	3,918	-	-	-	-	-
1763	-	4,231	-	4,732	-	-	13,963
1778	332	5,756	3,160	5,414	7,132	7,530	14,662
1779	335	5,916	3,348	5,693	7,482	7,804	15,286
1781	336	6,557	3,612	6,202	8,300	8,707	16,707
1782	359	7,088	3,899	6,552	8,442	9,456	17,898
1783	-	-	-	-	8,464	-	-
1808	400	4,968	15,184	4,450	-	-	25,000
1820	-	-	-	-	-	-	22,000
1825	-	4,843	-	-	-	-	17,250
1835	-	3,260	-	-	9,669	11,525	21,194
1843	-	2,496	-	-	13,409	13,951	27,360
1851	-	1,725	-	-	22,597	21,052	43,649
1856	-	-	-	-	23,752	22,110	45,862

he concludes that "birth rates exceeded the death rates" (1976: 126), especially during the last decades of the eighteenth century, when the slave importations were minimal and the total black population almost doubled from 10,987 in 1782 to 20,152[12] in 1808, thus augmenting at a rate of 2.45 percent annually.

It should also be highlighted that during the 1778–1782 phase freedmen represented 40 percent of the total Afro-descendant population, and that by 1808, this category became more than three-quarters of the entire group (15,184 out of a total of 20,152). The presence of such a significant number of freed blacks is consistent with the reports of several historians suggesting that manumission was common in Chocó, since slaves could work during their days off to accumulate gold and pay for their own freedom (Mosquera 2004; Colmenares 1979; Bryant 2005). Sharp, in fact, states that "manumission in Chocó was not only possible but actual" (1976: 22). Statements like this help us understand why by 1851, the year of the abolition of slavery, only 1,725 slaves

---

[12] Owing to an error of calculation, Sharp (1976: 126) reported a total of 19,968 blacks, rather than 20,152.
[13] Dash indicates information unavailable.

5.4 The Mineral Exploitation (1680–1851)

Table 5.5 *Black population in the Chocó, 1704–1843 (West 1957: 100)*

Year	Slaves	Freedmen	Total
1704	600	-	-
1759	3,915	-	-
1778	5,828	3,160	8,988
1789	5,916	3,342	9,258
1806	4,608	-	-
1843	2,505	18,000[14]	-

were found in the region, while the remaining Afro-descendant population consisted of free people.

The demographic information provided by Sharp (1976: 195) in Table 5.4 for the eighteenth and nineteenth centuries matches – to a good extent – the data collected by West (1957: 100), who twenty years earlier relied on a variety of colonial and postcolonial sources to provide a picture of the evolution of the enslaved and the free populations in the Chocó (Table 5.5). In fact, as can be observed in Table 5.5, during the 1770s and 1780s the freed group represented more than one-third of the entire population, which, by the 1840s, was estimated to represent some 80 percent of the total.

Data clearly show that slaves who achieved manumission were not exceptional in Chocó, rather, they were common. In the next chapter, we will examine the legal and economic reasons behind this fact and how such social dynamics may have played a significant role in shaping CS grammar.

In summary, given the available data on the period going from 1680 to 1851, it seems unlikely that a Spanish creole might have formed or have been preserved in the region during those years. This is not because this period represents a phase of Chocó history where blacks and whites were in equal numbers, so that the former group could learn Spanish from the latter; rather, the main point here for understanding why CS is not a Spanish creole is that the majority of the blacks who were taken to Chocó during the colonial era could – in all likelihood – speak Spanish before entering the region, while those who couldn't went through a *"proceso de aculturación"* (process of acculturation) (Cantor 2000), which made it possible for them to acquire this language.

---

[14] Given that there is no precise account concerning the freed population in 1843, West (1957: 100) indicates that this figure is an estimate. He assumed that by this time some 80% of the black population consisted of free people.

5.5 The End of Slavery and Underdevelopment in Present-day Chocó

With the end of slavery in 1851, the already few white residents that Chocó had until that point left the region, since they could no longer exploit the rich mineral resources of the Department by relying on slaves (Sharp 1976: 16). The departure of the ruling class resulted in an almost complete lack of interest in developing the department on the government side in the years to come.

During the last century private foreign companies have become interested in the exploitation of the mineral resources of the region. Oftentimes powerful transnational corporations, in agreement with the Colombian governments, have been granted permission to carry out mining operations on a large scale in order to extract mineral resources, in particular gold, silver, and platinum. This has caused considerable tensions with the local farmers, fishermen, and traditional miners, who have often been deprived of their lands and forced to accept "infamous compensations" in exchange (Escalante 1971: 105). The use of big excavators and dredges combined with the dumping of chemical products into the local rivers (especially mercury, related to the extraction of gold) have caused serious damage to the local environment and its inhabitants (1971: 113–26).

To worsen the already complex social context of Chocó, starting in the 1960s guerrilla warfare has spread throughout the region, so that the *Fuerzas Armadas Revolucionarias de Colombia* (Revolutionary Armed Forces of Colombia), and a number of other local militias, have been carrying out a variety of illegal activities, often related to extortions, kidnappings, and drug trafficking. After almost two centuries since the end of slavery in Colombia, Chocó remains one of the poorest regions in the country. With a big comparative deficit in terms of public infrastructures, schools, media communication, and basic services, the Department of Chocó is a region that remained – to a significant extent – isolated from the rest of the country.

Given these factors, contrary to what was originally suggested by some scholars (Granda 1978; Schwegler 1993), it does not seem likely that a once-spoken Pan-Hispanic creole could have dissolved so completely through a process of decreolization due to contact with standard Spanish. On the other hand, it appears more reasonable to postulate that CS – along with several other AHLAs (Sessarego 2013a) – was probably never a creole, but rather closely approximated to standard Spanish from its early stages of formation.

5.6 Remarks on the Nature of Chocó Spanish in Relation to Its History

Sociohistorical evidence has been provided here to cast light on the genesis and evolution of CS. In particular, this chapter has tested the feasibility of the

5.6 Remarks on the Nature of Chocó Spanish in Relation to Its History 147

Decreolization Hypothesis (Granda 1976; Schwegler 1991a) and the Afrogenesis Hypothesis (McWhorter 2000) for this vernacular.

An analysis of the most characteristic CS linguistic features (see chapters 3 and 4) has suggested that all the grammatical elements ascribed to a previous creole stage for this dialect can also be classified as the result of advanced SLA processes and/or Caribbean features, which do not necessarily imply any previous (de)creolization phase. This interpretation of the findings has been further supported by the historical data we presented in the current chapter, which link Chocó, as well as other Latin American mining departments, to the previously colonized Caribbean region (West 1953). Moreover, the sociohistorical information available for Chocó, from the beginning of the Spanish settlement of the region (1680s) to the abolition of slavery (1851), does not appear to indicate that the sociodemographic factors favoring the development and/or preservation of a creole language were in place.

We have observed that a concomitance of financial and logistic factors limited the introduction of African-born workers into the region, so that, even during the peak of the mineral exploitation, 60 percent of the slaves taken to Chocó were *criollos* (Colmenares 1979), who in all likelihood could speak vernacular varieties of Spanish. They were not *bozales* speaking only African languages. We also saw that the probability of a Portuguese-based creole being introduced into colonial Chocó was even more reduced. Indeed, by the time the Spaniards started using black workers in this region, Spanish America was no longer receiving the bulk of *bozal* captives from Portuguese trading companies (Peralta Rivera 2005).

An analysis of the living and working conditions of black miners in colonial Chocó revealed that slavery may not have been as harsh as in other colonies in the Americas (Sharp 1976). In particular, due to the pragmatic techniques implemented by the local *administradores de minas*, family units were preserved, manumission was common, and Christian education was systematically taught. All in all, these factors may have facilitated the acquisition of Spanish in the region and indirectly reduced the chances of creole formation. Finally, given the most recent history of Chocó, it does not appear that this region experienced such an intense linguistic pressure from standard Spanish after slavery abolition that it could have led to the radical decreolization of a pre-existing creole.

For all these reasons, CS should be seen neither as a decreolized language (Granda 1974; Schwegler 1993) nor as a missing Spanish creole (McWhorter 2000); rather, I would suggest that this contact variety approximated Spanish from the early stages of its formation and still preserves some of the typical SLA traces widely encountered in colonial texts describing *habla bozal*. Given that neither the Monogenesis-Decreolization Hypothesis nor the Afrogenesis Hypothesis appear to be able to provide a satisfactory account for the genesis and evolution of CS (and of many other AHLAs), the rest of this book will provide a new model to cast light on the Spanish creole puzzle and, in so doing, colonial Chocó will be used as a testing ground for the recently-proposed Legal Hypothesis of Creole Genesis (LHCG) (Sessarego 2015a, 2017a).

6 Testing the Legal Hypothesis of Creole Genesis on Colonial Chocó

6.1 Introduction

Slavery existed since antiquity and assumed, depending on the times and places, different forms and legitimations (Winks 1972). As far as black slavery in the colonial transatlantic context is concerned, different scholars have suggested divergent hypotheses on the nature of the Spanish system in relation to the systems implemented by the other European powers that took part in the colonization of the Americas. In particular, while certain researchers, such as Tannenbaum (1947), have claimed that Spanish slavery was less harsh in the treatment of slaves than the other systems (see also Freyre 1940), other authors, such as Boxer (1962), Davis (1966), and Genovese (1967), have objected that even though the Spanish written regulations might have appeared more humane and less strict, the actual praxis of slavery across Spanish colonies would contradict such an idealized vision, so that the life of a slave living in a Spanish colony would have essentially been like the life of a slave working across the territories belonging to other European colonial powers, especially if such a captive was living in plantations or mines far away from the urban centers, where it was materially impossible to resort to the law to protect one's legal rights.

In recent studies I have reexplored this well-known debate and reinterpreted it to understand the different evolutions of Afro-European contact languages in the Americas (Sessarego 2015a, 2017a). In particular, I have analyzed the legal development of slavery across times and places, from the ancient system contained in the Roman *Corpus Juris Civilis* (CJC) to the divergent legal systems implemented by a variety of European colonial powers in the territories they controlled in the Americas. This comparative analysis resulted in what I have called the "Legal Hypothesis of Creole Genesis" (LHCG), which suggests that Spanish slavery was indeed different – both in theory and in practice – from the other systems implemented in the "New World", and that such differences ultimately played an important role in shaping the Afro-European varieties that developed in the Americas. Indeed, findings indicate that the Spanish legal system in matters of slavery had one key peculiarity that differentiated it from the rest of the European legislations: it granted legal personality to the slaves. Having legal personality in a given legal system implies, among other things, being capable of acquiring a series of legal rights, such as taking part in civil lawsuits, entering into contracts, getting married, the possibility of receiving an education, owning property, etc. All of these rights, directly or indirectly derived from the concept of legal personality, were completely absent or highly restricted in the colonies outside the Spanish rule, since black captives in all these territories were not granted legal status; rather, for the most part, they were just considered to be human chattel.

The LHCG claims that the relative paucity of Spanish creoles in the Americas may be conceived – in part – as the byproduct of these divergent legal practices, which had a significant effect on the evolution of Afro-European social dynamics in the colonies and, consequently, on the contact varieties that developed from such different scenarios. In particular, I have suggested that the reason why European slave laws were so heterogeneous is partially due to their dissimilar degrees of reception of Roman law. Indeed, the LHCG argues that if certain colonies in the Americas were more or less conducive to language creolization than others, it is – to a good extent – due to the degree of legal Romanization their homeland countries went through in ancient times (Sessarego 2015a: 157).

The main aim of the current chapter is to show how the recently proposed LHCG may represent a valid alternative to the Monogenesis-Decreolization Hypothesis and the Afrogenesis Hypothesis to cast light on the genesis and evolution of CS and of many other AHLAs. In particular, this chapter will offer a comparative account of slavery in the Americas and take Chocó as a testing ground for the LHCG.

After summarizing the main points of the LHCG, I will provide a brief account of Roman slave law, the legal regulations that, in one way or another, provided the foundations for all the European slave systems that developed in the Americas. This will offer us a legal basis on which to compare and contrast Spanish slave law to the other types of slavery under analysis (English, French, Portuguese, and Dutch). In a second phase, we will inspect how these formal regulations (law in books) may have had a real effect – or not – on the lives of the black captives living and working in Spanish America (law in action) (Pound 1910), and especially in colonial Chocó, to understand to what extent the Spanish legal system may have played a role in the non-creolization of Spanish in the Pacific lowlands of Colombia and in the rest of the Americas.

6.2   Key Aspects of the Legal Hypothesis of Creole Genesis

The LHCG is rooted in the idea that law plays now – in the present – and played back then – in the past – a central role in the regulation of social dynamics. As a result of this belief, I assume that in order to understand certain aspects of a given colonial society, it is important, among other things, to get a good idea of the legal rules that regulated such ambits of colonial life. Since one of the main aims of this project is to get a better understanding of the genesis and evolution of the Afro-European languages of the Americas, I thought that something could be learned by inspecting the different legal systems regulating black slavery across the European colonies overseas, and how such regulations might have shaped the relations between blacks and whites in these territories, as well as the languages that developed out of such colonial scenarios.

After carrying out such a legal analysis, I am convinced that comparative slave law can be used as a powerful research tool to understand why in certain former colonies creole languages are spoken, while in others they are not. In particular, I think this type of investigation may help us cast light on the long-lasting Spanish creole debate concerning the paucity of Spanish-based creoles in the Americas. The LHCG, in fact, suggests that due to the presence of legal personality, Spanish slaves had a number of legal rights that significantly improved their standards of living and chances of acquiring Spanish and integrating into free society. This fact, I argue, is probably the most important "piece" to solve the Spanish creole "puzzle" and thus to understand the historical reasons behind such a "mysteriously absent creoles cluster under a single power" (McWhorter 2000: 39).

The LHCG does not deny that several other important factors, besides the legal one, might have had a major effect on the non-creolization of Spanish in the Americas (viz., the Spanish Crown's regulation of slave trading, logistic limitations on the introduction of *bozales* to the colonies, the economic structure of certain territories, etc.); nevertheless, the LHCG points out an aspect of colonial slavery, which is shared by all the Spanish colonies, in contrast to all the other European territories in the colonial Americas (i.e., presence vs. absence of slaves' legal personality), and which, therefore, can provide us with a reasonable generalization. Moreover, the LHCG also offers food for thought on why the only two existing Spanish creoles spoken in the Americas (Papiamentu and Palenquero) are actually found where Spanish law never applied: in the Netherland Antilles and in San Basilio de Palenque, a former maroon community of Colombia, where – by definition – the Spanish settlers could not impose their rule.

6.3 Slavery in Rome

What we know about Roman law is – for the most part – what we have learned from the *Corpus Juris Civilis* (CJC), the most influential Roman legal text, which was created from 529 AD to 534 AD under the administration of Emperor Justinian. The CJC had a deep impact on the legal history of Europe. In fact, it was received, to different degrees, by the legal systems that developed during the Middle Ages from the fall of the Roman Empire.

Roman slaves were not legal persons; they were legally conceived as cattle or human chattel, thus they were property and did not enjoy all the aforementioned rights that the acquisition of legal personality implies. Nevertheless, slaves were classified as a special type of property, thus, they could receive an education and, if it was for the economic benefit of their owners, they could be used to perform highly skilled jobs. Since slaves were not legal persons, they could not own property. However, if their master agreed, they could receive a compensation for their work, the *peculium*. The *peculium* represented an incentive to work harder; it consisted of a certain percentage of the profit the owner obtained thanks to the slave's work. Slaves could accumulate the *peculium* to eventually pay their price back to the master and become free people. For this reason, the *peculium* did not represent any additional cost to the master. On the contrary, it consisted of a big advantage, since the owner could receive back the sum he originally paid for the slave and use it again to purchase a younger captive, after having freed the older one (Marrone 2001).

Slavery was not based on race; rather, there were three main ways that could determine the enslaved status of a human being, independently of his/her racial characteristics or ethnic group: 1) war prisoner; 2) offspring of an enslaved woman; 3) somebody who sold himself/herself into slavery (usually to repay a debt).

Since slaves lacked legal personality, they could not appear in court as witnesses, and they could not either sue their masters or provide evidence against them. They did not have the right to marry, but they could have sexual partners. As a result, they did not have any sort of family rights, and could be separated from their lovers and children without any limitation.

It is important to highlight that Roman slave law was for the most part a matter of private law (between the slaves and their masters); it did not generally concern public law. For this reason, it was not the state's business to determine how a master should educate, feed, clothe, reward, or punish a slave. That was generally left to the owner to decide, as he wished, in his best interest.

6.4 A Comparative Analysis of Slave Law in the Americas

The thesis proposed by Tannenbaum (1947) on the supposedly more mild-mannered slavery under Spanish rule is rooted in the fact that the black slave in Latin America, unlike the captives living in other European colonies, was in a certain way "the beneficiary of an ancient legal heritage" (Tannenbaum 1947: 45). This means that the presence of a legal system that regulated slavery in the Iberian Peninsula since Roman times, well before the Americas were discovered, benefited the legal status of those who would become slaves several centuries later, in the "New World."

This being said, Tannenbaum's hypothesis is essentially based on two fundamental concepts: a) the Spanish system contemplated a series of norms concerning manumission, marriage, family, punishments, etc., that provided slaves with protection against potential abuses; b) the Catholic Church took an active role in regulating the relations between slaves and masters and, by doing so, it managed to improve captives' living conditions, since "masters were admonished to protect the moral welfare of their slaves and see to their spiritual instruction" (Sharp 1976: 139).

Through a comparative analysis of colonial slave laws, this section shows how Spanish formal regulations on black bondage significantly diverged from those of the other European powers involved in the colonization of the Americas. In fact, the legal concept of "slave/serf" was adopted by the Spanish system in ancient times, from the CJC; it was gradually revisited in the medieval code, called the *Siete Partidas*, and then subsequently modified through the promulgation of the *Leyes de Indias*, the regulations designed for colonial Americas. On the other hand, such a legal concept followed different evolutionary paths in the other European systems. This resulted in highly heterogeneous sets of rules that regulated black slavery across the different European colonies in the Americas. In particular, in contrast to the rest of the European legal systems, Spanish regulations on forced black labor were unique in acknowledging legal personality to the slave. This implied a series of rights for Spanish captives, which were completely absent or highly restricted in the other systems (Sessarego 2015a, in press a).

The following subsections will provide a comparative account of slavery legislations in the Americas. As we will see, all of them were inspired, in one way or another, by the Roman CJC. However, due to a concomitance of historical factors (most importantly, the different times in which Roman slave law influenced each specific system), the slave laws that emerged across the European colonies in the Americas ended up being quite divergent. Such heterogeneous systems regulated in different ways the roles that blacks and whites played in society, and, as a result, had a significant effect on the Afro-European contact varieties that formed in the New World.

6.4.1 The Spanish System

Slavery existed in Spain since antiquity, since the Roman colonization of the Iberian Peninsula. Indeed Spain, along with Portugal, was one of the few European countries that already had an established legal tradition on slavery before the "discovery" of the Americas. In fact, Spain received – with minimal modifications – the slave law contained in the CJC, and during the thirteenth century it codified such regulations in the *Siete Partidas*, created under the administration of King Alfonso X, el Sabio.

The *Siete Partidas* provided the foundations for the further evolution of the Spanish legal system in the Americas, which was adapted to the different colonial needs through the systematic promulgation of the *Leyes de Indias* (colonial laws). In the *Siete Partidas*, much like in the Roman CJC, a human being could be reduced into slavery for three main reasons: 1) war prisoner, 2) offspring of an enslaved woman, 3) somebody who had to sell themselves into slavery (usually to repay a debt). One important difference between the Spanish and the Roman systems in relation to the aforementioned points developed due to the influence of the Catholic Church: only non-Christian war prisoners could become Spanish slaves, Christians could not (Andrés-Gallego 2005: 58).

The most radical departure of the Spanish system from the Roman one, however, was that Spanish slaves acquired legal personality, which opened the door for the attainment of a number of rights completely unknown to the Roman slave. As a result, Spanish slaves could take part in civil lawsuits both as plaintiffs and defendants. They could even sue their masters if they were punished too harshly or mistreated. In order to make slaves' legal actions more effective, a royal law of 1528 established the figure of the *protector de esclavos* (slave protector), a state lawyer specialized in slave law, whose main assignment was to help captives in need of legal assistance (Andrés-Gallego 2005: 65).

Slaves could get married. As far as this and other family rights are concerned (viz., the right to not be separated from the married partner or from children), the Catholic Church played a major role. In fact, the Church insisted that blacks had a soul and that, therefore, they had to be educated not to sin. The institution of marriage was therefore conceded to slaves to protect them from the sin of fornication. As a result, their marriages had to be preserved, so that a married couple and their children could not be separated or sold as individual tokens to different masters living in different cities. Moreover, if two slaves belonging to two different masters got married, the owners could not move far away and bring the slaves with them, thus depriving husband and wife from seeing each other. In the case in which one of the masters decided to move, he had to either sell his slave to the other owner, or buy the other captive from him before moving, so that the marriage between the slaves could be preserved. Interracial marriages were not exceptional, and even more common were interracial sexual affairs. Masters often freed the children they had with their slaves; this phenomenon eventually led to a growing free mulatto sector of the population across Spanish America.

Slaves could accumulate capital to pay their price back to the master and, in this way, become free people. In the *Siete Partidas*, as in the Roman system, slaves could not own property, but could receive the *peculium*, if the master agreed to it. Nevertheless, a *Ley de Indias* promulgated in 1541 established that the *peculium* had to become compulsory, so that each master had to provide it to its captives. Such a *peculium* could be paid to the slaves in different ways. It could be provided in cash, or with extra goods, or with time off and production means (such as a piece of land on which to grow their own produce) (Andrés-Gallego 2005: 60).

The possibility of pocketing the *peculium* provided Spanish slaves with additional chances of accumulating capital to become free. Moreover, during the eighteenth century, a new and more sophisticated way of achieving manumission developed in the Spanish colonies: the *coartación*. The *coartación*, as we will see in Section 6.7, consisted of a mortgage mechanism the slaves could set up with their masters to obtain manumission. The captives would pay periodic installments to the owners, and the more they paid, the more time off they obtained to work on their own, accumulate capital, and pay off the rest of their debt. The *coartación*, therefore, implied a virtuous circle, which allowed thousands of slaves to become free people across Spanish America (Lucena Salmoral 1999a).

Given the early reception of Roman slave law by Spain, centuries before the colonization of the Americas, the Spanish system had time to evolve during the medieval period. Such rules were then automatically applied to Spanish America at the onset of colonization, even before the introduction of black captives into what eventually became the Spanish overseas colonies. Indeed, as Watson (1989: 47) points out, in Spanish America there was "law regulating slavery before there were slaves to be regulated." As we will see, such a statement did not apply to the other European territories in the "New World."

6.4.2 The English System

Watson (1989) stresses that Spanish and English slave laws differed drastically. The most important reason behind such a divergence had to do with the fact that England did not receive Roman law in ancient times and, as a result, slavery did not exist in England before the colonization of the Americas. The English, therefore, could not rely on a legal heritage like the Spanish did. Consequently, in order to fill such a legislative gap, "a law on slavery had to be made from scratch" (Watson 1989: 63). Moreover, the Spanish law-making machinery was highly centralized. For this reason, the law of the Spanish colonies was essentially the law made in Madrid, and could only be made in the colonies by local governors and viceroys with the permission of the King. On the contrary, the law of the English colonies was, for the most part, made locally, by the colonists. Thus, English slave law started being created overseas, over time, mainly by juridical court precedent and by statute.

English slave law, therefore, was not imposed by the motherland; rather, it was the result of local processes, involving colonial judges and local authorities. Colonial judges had to create a law on slavery in a context in which they could not rely on any established slave code. For this reason, it was common practice to refer to Roman law, and thus to a system that was comparatively harsher on slaves than the one the Spanish society was able to elaborate during the course of its medieval history. As for the law created outside the judicial courts, colonial authorities often approved statutes that established even stricter rules on slaves than those originally stated in the CJC. In particular, a key characteristic that differentiated English slave law from the Roman and the Spanish ones had to do with greater attention paid by the English legislators to the regulation of the public aspects of slaves' life. In fact, as we indicated in Section 6.3, Roman slave law was primarily a matter of private law. For this reason, it was up to the master in Rome to decide how to clothe, employ, educate, punish, etc., a slave. On the other hand, all those aspects of slaves' lives tended to be regulated by statute in the English territories, so that in many instances, a master was not even allowed to treat his slaves better than what had been established by law. Watson (1989: 66) exemplifies the difference between the Spanish system and the English one in matters of private versus public law by stating that in Spanish America a slave belonged to his owner, while in English America he belonged to "every citizen – at least he was subordinated to every white."

This stronger emphasis on public law is reflected in the fact that in most English colonies the local authorities established the types of clothes the slaves could wear, the types of punishments that had to be inflicted upon those who did not obey orders (even if the master decided to forgive them), the prohibition of formal education for blacks, etc. Moreover, since blacks did not have legal personality, they could not own anything. As a result, they were not allowed to either buy or sell anything and their masters could not even decide to donate them any goods. Slaves had to live with their masters, and could not live anywhere else, not even with their owners' permission.

Watson (1989) provides extracts from several US statutes on slavery, showing that, in many states, paying black captives for their work was absolutely forbidden; they could not receive any *peculium*, or work a parcel of land for their own benefit. Since slaves had no legal personality, they could not sue their masters or any other person. They could not take part in civil lawsuits, but could be prosecuted for criminal actions and there was a specific legal system that regulated criminal law for slaves. As far as manumission is concerned, Watson (1989) shows that becoming a freed black was far more difficult in English America than in the Spanish colonies. In fact, in some US statutes, manumission was not even an option. In other cases, it was conceded that a slave could become free, but that would usually happen only with the permission of the governor, given a good reason. The institution of marriage was not contemplated for slaves. Slave couples could be separated and their children sold to different masters. Interracial relations were usually prohibited.

When we compare English slave law to the Spanish one, we can immediately observe how the absence of legal personality in the former system deprived English slaves of a set of rights they had in the Spanish-ruled colonies. Such limitations inevitably affected both the private and the public spheres of slaves' life and, therefore, their possibilities of integration in colonial society. Such a systematic segregation, in my view, significantly contributed to the formation and/or preservation of contact varieties in English America, which diverged more substantially from their lexifier than the Afro-Hispanic dialects that formed in the territories under Spanish rule.

6.4.3 The French System

Researchers working on the legal history of France describe this region as a country where two different legal traditions coexisted in the medieval period until the advent of a progressive homogenization, which was started by King Charles VII in 1454 and subsequently carried out by the following governments (Hespanha 2003).

One legal tradition was based on customary law. It consisted of local customs and was not generally written. It applied in the northern parts of France (*pays de droit coutumier*). The other legal tradition was more significantly affected by Roman law, it was written, and applied in the southern territories (*pays de droit écrit*). In certain regions of southern France serfdom existed until 1798. It consisted of free services that local peons had to do for the landlord, but it was significantly different from Roman slavery. This type of serfdom, however, did not belong to the legal tradition of Paris (*coutume de Paris*), the system that was eventually exported to the French colonies in the Americas. For this reason, the French, like the English, had to create a legal system to regulate black slavery from scratch; thus, unlike Spain, France did not have a well-established slave law. Consequently, they borrowed massively from the CJC and tried, in this way, to fill such a legal gap (Watson 1989: 83–5).

Watson (1989) points out two main factors that differentiated French slave law from English slave law: 1) French slave law was for the most part created in Paris by the French legislators, and not in the colonies by judges and local authorities; 2) the French legislators were lawyers trained in Roman law, and the socioeconomic conditions in ancient Rome differed drastically from those found in the French Caribbean.

The French legal effort to provide the overseas colonies with a system to regulate black slavery resulted in the *Code Noir* (Black Code), which was passed by King Louis XIV in 1685. This code reproduced, to a good extent, the slavery rules found in the CJC, and, as a result, it diverged quite radically from the Spanish *Siete Partidas*, which had significantly evolved from the ancient Roman regulations.

Given the stronger ties between the *Code Noir* and the CJC, French slaves did not have legal personality. Slaves were classified as human chattel; they could not own any property, but, in line with Roman law, if their master agreed, they could receive a *peculium*. In the original *Code Noir*, few restrictions were imposed on manumission, which could be conceded by the master to the slave without any specific justification. Nevertheless, over time, slave manumission became more constrained. Indeed, a royal ordinance of 1713 established that manumission could be granted only if local authorities approved it (Watson 1989: 90).

As in the English system, French slave law was more concerned with the public sphere of slavery than the Spanish one. To a certain act of disobedience corresponded a specific punishment, preestablished by law, which could not be forgiven by the master. Overall, the set of punishments allowed by French law were more severe than those contemplated by the Spanish system (Watson 1989: 83–90). Moreover, since slaves had no legal personality, they could not take their masters to court if they had been punished too harshly, beyond what was established by law.

Slavery was based on race and race mixing was highly discouraged. A free person could not marry a slave. If a master had children with his slave, their offspring would be confiscated by the state and would automatically become slaves with no possibility of becoming free people in the future (Watson 1989: 88). Owing to the pressure exerted by the Church, slaves could get married – but only if their owners agreed. Married couples and their children could not be separated and sold as individual tokens, as in the Spanish system.

When we compare the French system to the Spanish one, we can observe how, overall, the former was stricter on black captives than the latter. Such regulations more significantly limited slaves' chances of becoming free people and their possibilities of integration in colonial society.

6.4.4 The Dutch System

Roman law was not homogeneously received by all the United Provinces of the Netherlands. As a result, certain regions, such as Friesland and Holland, underwent a more significant Romanization than other territories, such as Gelderland, Overijssel, and Drente. Nevertheless, a legal characteristic that all the Netherlands Provinces shared was the absence of the institution of slavery, which was not received from the Roman tradition. In addition, the Dutch colonies in the Americas were not directly controlled by the Dutch government; rather, a private company, the Dutch West India Company, was the organization ruling on those territories. Since neither the United Provinces of the Netherlands or the Dutch West India Company had a legal tradition regulating slavery, as in the case of France and England, the Dutch had to create a new system to regulate forced black labor in the overseas colonies. To do so, they also borrowed directly from the CJC. As a result, the bulk of Dutch slave law consisted of Roman slave law. The Dutch only introduced small modifications to it through the use of *placaaten* (local ordinances), which had the goal of addressing issues of administrative nature. To this point, Watson (1989: 110) states:

> The problem is that the rules of the Roman law, as they were set out in the *Corpus Juris Civilis* and as understood by later scholars, were so taken for granted that they were not restated. And little of this law was changed. The *placaaten* basically added only local police law.

Dutch slaves, therefore, did not have legal personality, they could not own property or take their masters to court, they could receive a *peculium* (if the owner agreed), they could not get married, etc. The *placaaten*, for the most part, introduced restrictions on their ability to sell and buy objects, celebrate ceremonies, wear certain clothes, etc.; thus, they regulated several aspects of their public life, about which Roman law did not have much to say. Moreover, Dutch law imposed more constraints on manumission than the CJC did. Indeed, the Edele Hove van Politie, the local Police Department, had to approve the master's application for slave manumission before the slave could be set free.

In summary, as can be observed, the direct borrowing of Roman law into the Dutch system implied that the Dutch slave had no legal personality. Consequently, black captives within the Dutch system did not enjoy most of the rights Spanish slaves had. Such a difference, in addition to the further restrictions introduced by the *placaaten*, significantly reduced the slaves' ability to become free people and the chances of improving their living conditions to better climb the social ladder.

6.4.5 The Portuguese System

The status of Portuguese slave law may be seen as a compromise between the Spanish system, which received Roman law in ancient times and evolved greatly from it, and the other European systems, which borrowed Roman law only during the colonial phase and did not achieve such a great degree of legal innovation from the Roman tradition. In fact, Portugal received the Visigothic Code (654 AD), which had inherited the Roman institution of slavery, but the system did not evolve to the extent the Spanish one did, so that Portuguese slaves did not have legal personality. Nevertheless, some similarities between the Portuguese and the Spanish colonial systems existed, in part because the law that was designed for the organization of the Portuguese colonies in the Americas (*Ordenações filipinas*) had been promulgated by Philip II, a Spanish king, who in the sixteenth century ruled over both Portugal and Spain.

According to the Portuguese system, slaves could not be treated cruelly; however, since they did not have legal personality, they could not sue their masters in cases of mistreatment. Moreover, as far as mistreatments are concerned, the *Ordenações filipinas* were somehow ambiguous. While, on the one hand, this legal text appeared to be gentler on captives than other European regulations, since it stated that "the owner could only punish a slave, as a father a son, or as master a servant" (Watson 1989: 100), in other parts it contradicted itself by indicating that owners were allowed to inflict cruel punishments, such as mutilations.

Owing to the pressure of the Catholic Church, slaves could get married. Marriage had to be preserved, so that husband, wife, and their offspring could not be separated and sold individually. Manumission appeared to be more in line with the Roman and Spanish laws. Consequently, it was not as strictly regulated as in the French, English, and Dutch systems and, in general, it only required the master's willingness to free his slaves. Watson (1989: 100) also points out the peculiar situation in which slaves could be directly manumitted by the Royal House if they denounced their masters to the justice in case of illegal trafficking (especially for trafficking concerning gold and expensive woods), or if they found a diamond of twenty or more carats.

The notion of *peculium* also existed in the Portuguese system, but it was not implemented as in the Spanish colonies. In fact, since 1541 the *peculium* was compulsory in Spanish America, and it led to the self-manumission of many thousands of blacks; in Brazil, however, it was not obligatory, and many masters did not provide it for their slaves in such a systematic way. As a result, becoming a freed slave in this Portuguese colony was significantly more challenging than across Spanish America (Watson 1989: 91–101).

The early reception of Roman law and the pressure exerted by the Catholic Church grouped Portuguese slave law with the Spanish one, so that in both systems marriage was conceded to slaves, the *peculium* existed, and manumission could be achieved. These common patterns may have had a significant influence on shaping the Afro-Portuguese contact varieties spoken in Brazil. In fact, a detailed sociohistorical and legal analysis of slavery in Brazil may be able to shed new light on the debate concerning the (non)creolization of Portuguese in this Latin American country, which, in line with the English and French Caribbean, experienced a massive introduction of enslaved Africans during the colonial period (Guy 1981, 2004; Holm 1992, 2004; Naro & Sherre 2000, 2007; Lipski 2006; Lucchesi, Baxter, & Riberio 2009). Nevertheless, the lack of legal personality for Portuguese black captives represents a key difference between the Spanish and the Portuguese systems.

6.5 Spanish Slave Law during the Eighteenth Century 161

As a result, the living and working conditions of Brazilian slaves were comparatively harsher and their chances of climbing the social ladder were significantly more reduced.

6.5 Spanish Slave Law during the Eighteenth Century

Having provided a general comparative overview of colonial slave laws in the Americas, I will now focus on a more specific context: the legal system characterizing Spanish black bondage during the eighteenth century, the century in which, as we saw in Section 5.4, Chocó experienced an intense phase of mineral exploitation. Before proceeding with this endeavor, it is crucial to understand the nature of Spanish policy on slave trafficking during this historical period. It must be said that such a policy formed in a socioeconomic context with peculiar characteristics, which, again, differentiated Spanish America from the rest of the European colonies overseas.

As Lucena Salmoral (2000a: 115) reminds us, slave trafficking had for a long time a secondary importance in the Spanish colonial enterprise. The author backs his claim by highlighting that "*Hispanoamérica recibió aproximadamente un millón y medio de esclavos durante el régimen conlonial, que representa apenas el 12% del total de la trata continental*" (Spanish America received approximately one and half million slaves during the colonial regime, which represents only 12% of the total continental traffic). This statement acquires particular value if we compare the forced-migration fluxes of Africans to Spanish America with those concerning other European colonies (see Table 6.1) (Lucena Salmoral 2000a: 115).

As Table 6.1 shows, the slave traffic toward Spanish America was the first to begin. It formally started on August 18th, 1518, when the King authorized

Table 6.1 *African slave importations to European colonies in the Americas*[1]

Colonies	XVI century	XVII century	XVIII century	XIX century	Total
Spanish	75,000	292,500	578,600	606,000	1,552,100
Portuguese	50,000	500,000	1,891,400	1,145,400	3,586,800
English	–	527,400	2,802,600	–	3,330,000
French	–	311,600	2,696,800	155,000	3,163,400
Dutch	–	44,000	484,000	–	528,000
Total	125,000	1,675,500	8,453,400	1,906,400	12,160,300

[1] An anonymous reviewer asks whether the Dutch slave importations reported in this table would contradict my argument about a comparatively limited use of enslaved workforce in Spanish America. They do not, since the Dutch only colonized a relatively small portion of the Americas

Lorenzo de Gouvenot to introduce 4,000 black slaves into the "New World" (Lucena Salmoral 2000a: 115). This business officially finished in 1820, but in practice the Crown only began to repress illegal trafficking and eventually also black bondage around 1845. For this reason, Spanish America was the second-last place in the Americas, before Brazil, to abolish slavery. If we consider that black slavery lasted in Spanish America for almost three and half centuries and that the territory controlled by the Spanish Crown was the largest among the European colonies, we can easily understand how the black population in Spanish America was less concentrated than in the settlements controlled by other European powers. This was the case, in part, because Spain, in contrast to France and England, did not develop plantation economies in the Americas early on; rather, at the beginning of its colonial enterprise, Spain was primarily concerned with the exploitation of mineral resources, so that the use of enslaved blacks to work in the fields did not attain for several centuries the economic importance it had in French- and English-controlled Caribbean islands.

The Spanish Caribbean, and particularly Cuba, turned into a plantation economy only in the second half of the eighteenth century (Lucena Salmoral 2000a: 216). Indeed, in order to implement such an economic system, the Spanish Crown decided to increase the flux of slaves to Spanish America. In 1789, with the objective of developing the local agricultural production, the King even removed the monopolistic regulations that restricted slave trafficking and opted for free trade. It is with such a goal in mind that the Spanish Crown tried to carry out several legal reforms during the eighteenth century. The King wanted to prepare the colonies for what was supposed to represent the beginning of a massive slave introduction to the Spanish territories overseas. The result of such a legal effort was the *"Instrucción sobre educación, trato y ocupaciones de los esclavos en todos los dominios de Indias e islas Filipinas"* (Instruction concerning slaves' education, treatment, and occupation across all the American colonies and the Philippine islands) (Figure 6.1), which succinctly summarizes the main slave regulations that applied in the Spanish Empire during the eighteenth century.[2]

From a legal point of view, New Granada's slave law during the eighteenth century was similar to the systems implemented in the rest of Spanish Americas. Therefore, besides a few bills (*cédulas*) and some specific regulations, most of the legislation directly derived from the *Siete Partidas* (written between 1256 and 1265) and from the *cédulas generales* (general bills), which were collected in the *Recopilación de Indias*, promulgated in 1680. As a result,

---

(Suriname and the Dutch Antilles). Thus, the slave density in these territories was quite high, especially if we compare the size of these colonies to the vastness of Spanish America.

[2] A copy of the *Instrucción* and its English translation can be consulted in the Appendix of this book.

6.5 Spanish Slave Law during the Eighteenth Century

New Granada and the rest of the eighteenth-century Spanish colonies, unlike the territories under French control, did not have a black code that regulated African slavery. To be precise, as Lucena Salmoral (1995: 34) points out, the only general code, which covered the topic of slavery and had homogeneous recognition across all Spanish America, was the *Siete Partidas*, created in Spain during the thirteenth century. Indeed, due to several historical reasons, all attempts to create a Pan-American colonial code failed.

Louisiana was the only Spanish colony with a slave code in the eighteenth century. In fact, on October 27th, 1769, Governor O'Reilly approved such a legal text, a few years after the passage of this territory from French to Spanish control (Lucena Salmoral 1999a: 360). For this reason, the Louisiana black code was strongly influenced by the French *Code Noir*, which, in several cases, was in sharp contrast to the system adopted in the rest of Spanish America (Sessarego 2015a: 129–31). During the eighteenth century, two attempts to create a black code for Hispaniola were put forward, the first one in 1768 and the second one in 1784, but neither of them was successful due to the pressure exerted by the Latin American slave owners (Lucena Salmoral 2000a: 35).

After the failure of these codes, given the urgency to provide the American colonies with an easily consultable text that summarized the basic legislation concerning black slavery soon after the free slave trade decreed on February 28th, 1789, the Crown decided to approve the aforementioned *Instrucción*. The *Instrucción* was published in Madrid on May 31st, 1789, and was immediately communicated to the colonies. Nevertheless, given the complaints put forward by the slave owners, its effects had to be suspended a few months later. This text, however, for the most part, just summarized the law already in force; it did not introduce any substantial modification to it; in fact, as Levaggi (1973: 91) highlights, the *Instrucción "no introdujo mayor novedad en el régimen de la esclavitud, ya que su expresa intención no fue otra que facilitar la observancia de normas que, si bien dispersas, estaban en vigor"* (did not introduce major changes to slave law, since its clear objective was to provide an easy consultation to the rules that – even a scattered across the legal system – were already in force) (Lucena Salmoral 1996a: 163). The study of such a legal text, therefore, will provide us with a synthetic and systematic analysis of eighteenth-century Spanish slave law, both in New Granada and in the rest of the Spanish colonies overseas.

When the Crown published the *Instrucción*, it wanted to transform the Spanish colonial economy into a system more similar to the ones implemented by the English and the French in the Caribbean. For this reason, as we will see, the *Instrucción* does not mention any regulation concerning slaves' manumission, which in the English and French colonies was not as common as in Spanish America (Lucena Salmoral 1994, 1996a, 1996b, 1999a, 1999b). Nevertheless, an analysis of Spanish slave law cannot overlook such a widespread practice. For this reason, after analyzing chapter by chapter the *Instrucción*, we will pay attention to this phenomenon; in particular, we will examine the development of a new type of manumission called *coartación*, a self-manumitting system characteristic of Spanish America, non-existent in the territories controlled by other European nations.

6.6 *Instrucción Sobre Educación, Trato, y Ocupaciones de los Esclavos*

Lucena Salmoral (1996a, 1996b) provides a historical account for the phases that led to the creation, publication, and subsequent repeal of the *Instrucción*, showing how in a tense preindependentist scenario, the Spanish Crown could not risk making enemies among the members of the Latin American ruling class.

The author offers a review of the main steps that led to the creation of such a regulation, which began with the entrusting of it on February 19th, 1789 to Don Antonio Porlier, a government official with significant legal and administrative experience in the Americas. At that time, Don Polier was the Minister of Justice and, within two months, thanks to the help provided by his collaborator Don Antonio Romero, completed the *Instrucción* and turned it into the *Junta de Estado* (State Assembly) on April 27th of the same year (Lucena Salmoral 1996a: 157–8).

6.6.1 The Cédula*'s Content*

The *Instrucción*'s content consists of a brief introductory note by the King, followed by fourteen chapters, for a total of eight pages (see Appendix; Lucena Salmoral 1966a, 1966b). The royal note explains the reasons and the objectives behind this regulation, which had the function of summarizing and organizing, in a systematic way, all of the previous legal norms concerning black slavery. The purpose was to offer an easily accessible text for all the slave owners in Spanish America, in line with the principles of the Catholic faith, humanity, the state's well-being, and in view of the demographic effects that would follow from the free slave trade to the Americas:

In the Decree of the *Leyes de Partida* and other Bodies of Legislation in these Kingdoms, in the laws of the *Recopilación de Indias* (Compilation of the Laws of the Indies), general and particular Decrees . . ., and in the Ordinances . . . in accordance with the principles and regulations dictated by Religion, Humanity, and the good of the State . . . the number of slaves in both Americas will be increased considerably. (Author's translation)[3]

---

[3] Original Spanish version: *En el Código de las Leyes de Partida y demás Cuerpos de la Legislación de estos Reinos, en el de las de la Recopilación de Indias, Cédulas generales*

6.6 *Instrucción Sobre Educación, Trato, y Ocupaciones de los Esclavos* 165

REAL CÉDULA
DE SU MAGESTAD
SOBRE
LA EDUCACION, TRATO Y OCUPACIONES
DE LOS ESCLAVOS
EN TODOS SUS DOMINIOS DE INDIAS,
É ISLAS FILIPINAS,
BAXO LAS REGLAS QUE SE EXPRESAN.

MADRID.
EN LA IMPRENTA DE LA VIUDA DE IBARRA,
AÑO DE MDCCLXXXIX.

Figure 6.1 Cover of *Instrucción sobre educación, trato y ocupaciones de los esclavos*

The first chapter refers to the Catholic education the slaves had to receive. It indicates that black captives had to be instructed into the religious principles every holy day, during which they could not be forced to work, except for during the harvest season. During those days off, the owner had to hire a priest to celebrate Mass and teach the slaves Christian doctrine. Moreover, the owner had to make sure that "*todos los días de la semana, después de concluido el trabajo, recen el Rosario . . . con la mayor compostura y devoción*" (every day of the week, after the work has been completed, they say the Rosary . . . with the utmost composure and devotion). This practice, as we can imagine, may have served as a key means of language teaching, and it is significant to notice the importance the Crown gave to such an educational point, which consists of the *Instrucción*'s very first chapter.

The second chapter concerns issues related to slaves' alimentation and clothing. It states that black servants had to be provided with food and clothes as needed, according to their age and gender, as established by the local authorities in "*acuerdo del Ayuntamiento y audiencia del Procurador Sindico, en calidad de Protector de los Esclavos*" (agreement with the Local Government and in the audience of the Court-Appointed Prosecutor, in the role of Protector of the Slaves).

The third chapter refers to the slaves' work, which, given that the *Instrucción*'s goal was to align Spanish colonies with their English and French counterparts, had to be primarily concerned with "*Agricultura y demás labores del campo*" (Agriculture and other labors of the field). It was established that the black captives would have two hours a day to work on their own, for their own benefit, a sort of *peculium*. Moreover, it stated that the working age was from seventeen to sixty-five, and that the slaves could not carry out activities for which they were not fit; for example, women could not do excessively heavy work.

The fourth chapter focuses on the celebrations and games that would have taken place during the days off, during which "*los dueños no pueden obligar, ni permitir, que trabajen los esclavos*" (the owners cannot force, nor allow, that the slaves work) after they "*hayan oido Misa y asistido a la explicación de la Doctrina Cristiana*" (have heard Mass and attended the explanation of the Christian Doctrine). Again, in this chapter it is possible to observe the emphasis placed by Spanish slave law on Catholic indoctrination, which must have favored language acquisition among the captives.

The fifth chapter dictates the rules concerning slaves' houses and sickbays, which were supposed to meet some simple comfort standards and had to be

y particulares . . ., y en las Ordenanzas . . . conforme a los principios y reglas que dictan la Religión, la Humanidad y el bien del Estado . . . se aumentará considerablemente el número de esclavos en ambas Américas.

6.6 Instrucción Sobre Educación, Trato, y Ocupaciones de los Esclavos

provided with basic drugs to prevent the spread of diseases among the black captives and offer them minimal health care.

The sixth chapter refers to the treatment that had to be provided to the elderly and chronically ill, who had to be supported by their owners "*sin que éstos puedan concederles la libertad por descargarse de ellos*" (without [the owners] being allowed to free them in order to get rid of them).

The seventh chapter focuses on slaves' marriage. Marriages had to be favored to avoid the sin of fornication, "*tratos ilícitos de los dos sexos*" (illicit behaviors between the two sexes). The owners could not hinder their captives' marriage. If two slaves belonging to different masters got married, the marriage had to be preserved. For this reason, if one of the owners decided to move to a different city, a solution had to be found, which usually consisted of the purchase of the wife by the master owning the husband, so that the couple could live together.

The eighth chapter has the following title: "*Obligaciones de los esclavos y penas correccionales*" (*Obligations of the slaves and correctional penalties*). This chapter establishes that, given the owners' obligations toward their slaves, the captives had to obey their orders or face some corrective punishments. Such punishments could consist of prison, handcuffs, grips, etc. or no more than 25 lashes "*con instrumento suave, que no cause contusión grave o efusión de sangre*" (with a soft instrument, that does not cause serious bruising or bloodshed).

The ninth chapter deals with harsher punishments, which concerned particularly serious crimes, and could only be applied by the *Audiencia* tribunal in the presence of a *protector de esclavos*. These punishments, in certain particular cases, could even consist of body mutilations and death. However, they could not be inflicted on any captive by anybody, not even their masters, unless the tribunal had established it after a fair trial.

The tenth chapter mentions the punishments to be inflicted on the owners who do not respect the regulations established by the *Instrucción*: a fee of 50 pesos for the first infraction, 100 hundred pesos for the second one, 200 hundred pesos for the third time. In case the master keeps breaking the rules, "*se procederá contra el culpado a la imposición de otras penas mayores*" (it will proceed to impose other harsher penalties against the person found guilty). If the owner perpetrates a major infringement against the slave, maybe due to the infliction of an excessively harsh punishment, "*se procederá contra el dueño o el mayordomo criminalmente*" (criminal procedures will be undertaken against the owner or overseer) and the captive will be confiscated and sold to a new master.

The eleventh chapter indicates that the only people who had the right to punish a slave were his owners and overseers; nobody else could do so, and if somebody did, they would have to face legal consequences as if they had harmed a free person.

The twelfth chapter states that the owners had to present to the local authorities a complete list of their slaves on an annual basis. If one such captive escaped or died, the owner had to report the fact within three days. This was established to prevent the owners from inflicting violent death upon their slaves.

The thirteenth chapter points out ways of discovering potential cases of slave mistreatment. Each village had to nominate a *visitador* (administrative official), who would pay visits to the *haciendas* three times a year to make sure that the rules established by the *Instrucción* would be respected. Moreover, it was indicated that the Church could carry out further inspections. In fact, the members of religious orders, after having questioned the slaves, could file a complaint against the owners. Such a complaint was considered enough to start an investigation against the master. Therefore, Polier's *Instrucción* implied quite serious control over the slave owners, whose *haciendas* not only were periodically inspected by the *visitadores*, but also, and foremost, by religious authorities.

Finally, the fourteenth chapter established the creation of a fund consisting of the fines applied to the slave owners. That money would have been used to pay the *visitadores* and, therefore, to enforce the *Instrucción*.

6.6.2 Reactions to the Cédula

As we have mentioned in Section 6.5, the Latin American ruling class did not like the regulations imposed by the *Instrucción*. Even though this legal text for the most part just reorganized norms that were already in force, without introducing new ones, it made, nevertheless, some small changes to the system, which were perceived by the owners as a serious threat to their property rights. Lucena Salmoral (1996a: 165) points out that chapters eight and thirteen, which referred to a maximum limit of twenty-five lashes (rather than two hundred, as previously indicated in the *Recopilación de Leyes de Indias*) and to the introduction of a stricter controlling system, were "*los dos dentonatores principales que despertaron la indignación de los proprietarios de esclavos*" (the two main detonators that woke up slave owners' indignation).

The news concerning the publication of the *Instrucción* generated several complaints among the slave owners, who put pressure on several colonial authorities to suspend its effects. The first Latin American reaction to these regulations came from Caracas, Venezuela, where the mayor, Juan José Enchenique, without even having personally read the *Cédula*, under the pressure of the slave owners, declared to the *Audiencia* that in Venezuela slaves were treated very well and that the level of control and punishment exerted on the local black captives was needed to make sure revolts would not take place. Moreover, he complained about the fact that, unlike the French masters, the

6.6 Instrucción Sobre Educación, Trato, y Ocupaciones de los Esclavos 169

Spanish owners were not allowed to inflict harsher penalties upon their slaves; rather, they always had to recur to tribunals, even though cases of black violence against masters and overseers were not exceptional. The mayor foresaw that the instruction, if implemented, would have caused a black revolution and that *"no tardará mucho tiempo, [para que] se alcen [los negros] con la Provincia, acaben con todos los blancos Españoles y se hagan señores del país"* (it won't take a long time before black people will revolt in the Province, they will kill all the white Spaniards and become the owners of this country) (Lucena Salmoral 1996a: 167).

Similar issues were also raised in Cuba, where the Governor, Don Domingo Caballero, on December 14th, 1789 directly addressed Polier to express the slave owners' concerns. The colonial authority requested the suspension of the *Instrucción*'s effects, since – in his view – it would have led to the ruin of agriculture and to potential rebellions among the slaves. A few weeks later, in a letter dated February 19th, 1790, the *Comisarios de la Havana* (Havana commissars) directly asked the King to suspend the *Instrucción* effects by virtue of Law 24, title 1, book 2 of the *Recopilación de Indias*, which provided local authorities with the legal powers to suspend the effects of any royal *cédula* in case it was clear that *"de su cumplimento se seguirá escandalo conocido o daño irreparable"* (by applying it a sure disaster and irreparable damage would follow) (Lucena Salmoral 1996a: 168).

One of the points that worried the Cuban authorities the most had to do with the limit of twenty-five lashes, as indicated in the *Instrucción*'s 8th chapter. Lucena Salmoral (1996a: 171) points out that the *Comisarios* claimed that:

the promulgation of this law and the idea that slaves will get from it, that we will never be able to inflict upon them a stronger punishment, will make them feel fearless, and they will no longer feel subordinated to their masters and overseers. (Author's translation)[4]

Similar complaints were sent to Madrid by colonial authorities in New Spain, Santo Domingo, Louisiana, and New Granada, where the masters systematically indicated that these modifications to the legal system, even if minimal, could have resulted in a state of chaos, in which the blacks would end up subjugating the whites, since they would no longer be afraid of serious corporal punishment.

As far as New Granada is concerned, and in particular the southern and the Pacific zones, Lucena Salmoral (1996a: 172) reported the complaints by the Governor of Popayán, Don Diego Antonio Nieto, who, on February 16th, 1792, wrote a letter to the Viceroy of Santa Fe, where he highlighted the risks that the

---

[4] Original Spanish version: *la promulgación de esta ley y el fijo concepto en que quedarán los esclavos de que jamás les podemos imponer mayor castigo, les hará perder absolutamente el temor, se desentenderán de la subordinación a sus amos y mayorales.*

application of *Instrucción*'s chapters 8 and 13 would have implied. In fact, the main problem was to do with the limit to twenty-five lashes and having to resort to a tribunal if a more serious punishment had to be inflicted. Moreover, the stricter controls on the masters carried out by the *visitadores* and by church members were perceived as inappropriate, since they would have implied additional costs for the slave owners. Soon afterwards, the miners operating in the Barbacoa area put together a document elucidating the reasons why they opposed such chapters; moreover, they underlined how slaves' well-being was in their own interest, so that they would never punish a captive unless strictly necessary. Nevertheless, they wanted to be free to inflict exemplary punishments, if necessary, since "*en gente tan inmadura vale mucho más la amenaza que la ejecución [de la pena]*" (with such immature people the threat of a punishment is more powerful than its actual execution).

Similar reactions to the *Instrucción* also took place in other parts of Colombia, as well as in Chocó, where we know of a letter written by the slave owner Don Bernardo Cabezas to the King, in which the master is – one more time – pointing out "*los inconvenientes que se seguirían si el castigo se limitase a veinte y cinco azotes*" (the problems that would follow if the punishment were limited to twenty-five lashes) (Lucena Salmoral 1996a: 176).

Given the different complaints proceeding from a variety of Latin American regions, the *Instrucción* had to be put aside. The *Consejo de Indias*, responsible for such a decision, in fact, tried to find a solution that could be satisfactory for the members of the colonial elite, who were the real owners of Spanish America, as well as for the Spanish Crown, which was afraid of potential antimonarchic revolts in those territories. For this reason, on March 31st, 1794, the *Consejo* provided a peculiar decree, which stated what follows:

the Royal Law's effects should be suspended and, without the need to revoke it . . ., it must be told to the tribunals and other American courts that, without publishing it . . ., if the situation requires it, they should follow the spirit of its articles. (Author's translation)[5]

Therefore, as the Cuban authorities had originally requested, Law 24, title 1, book 2 of the *Leyes de Indias* was applied to suspend the effects of the *Instrucción*, since "*de su cumplimiento se seguiría escándalo conocido o daño irreparable*" (by enforcing it a sure disaster and irreparable damage would follow) (Lucena Slamoral 1996a: 176). With a bit of irony, Lucena Slamoral (1999a: 178) highlights how, paradoxically, colonial Spanish settlers had to "*obedecer el «espíritu» de una Cédula no publicada, o publicada pero*

---

[5] Original Spanish version: *que se suspendan los efectos de la Real Cédula y que, sin necesidad de revocarla . . ., bastará que por ahora se encargue reservadamente a los Tribunales y Jefes de América que, sin publicarla, . . . procuren en los casos y ocurrencias particulares que se ofrezcan, ir conformes al espíritu de sus artículos.*

suspendida" (obey the "spirit" of a Law that was not published, or published but suspended).

All of these legal issues, recently brought to the attention of the readers by the historian Lucena Salmoral, have oftentimes led other researchers to believe that the *Instrucción* was a Pan-American black code. Actually, the *Cédula* was shorter than a typical code and, given the strong reactions that it generated among the colonial elite, it never really became part of the established legal system, even though a close analysis of several colonial trials shows how judges might have referred to the "spirit" of such a work when it came to decide on a number of cases (King 1939; Sharp 1976; Meiklejohn 1981).

6.7 The Development of the *Coartación* Institute

Even though the *Instrucción* did not mention manumission, it is crucial to explain how slaves could obtain freedom in Spanish America, since it would be misleading to analyze the colonial dynamics of black slavery in these territories without paying attention to such a widespread practice. As we will see, in fact, slaves' manumission was so common that over time, through a consuetudinary process, it turned into an even more effective means of obtaining freedom, the *coartación*.

The *coartación* was a means of slave liberation that developed during the eighteenth century in Spanish America (Lucena Salmoral 1999a). This system represented an evolution of the traditional manumission mechanism, which was originally based on a single payment for the total slaves' market value, after the captives had accumulated enough funds, proceeding from their *peculium*. The *coartación*, on the other hand, allowed the slaves to obtain freedom by depositing periodical installments: the more the slaves paid, the more free time they obtained to work on their own and accumulate more capital. In certain cases, as Lucena Salmoral (1999a: 347) points out, "*la coartación . . . incidió en rebajar los salarios que los amos cobraban a sus esclavos jornaleros, lo que les permitía aumentar el peculio y la posibilidad de ahorrarse más pronto*" (the *coartación* . . . had an effect on reducing the daily sums the slaves had to pay [to their masters], this resulted in an increase of their *peculium* and of their chances of becoming free more quickly).

It was therefore a mechanism that implemented a virtuous circle to obtain freedom, and it was based on a legal instrument without peers in the Americas. Lucena Salmoral highlights that slaves could also resort to other means to achieve freedom; for example, they could try to escape (even though this was certainly a risky strategy), or they could obtain manumission as a gift from their master (often conceded to the most trustworthy servants in the owner's last will). Nevertheless, the author points out that the most common way of becoming free was the *coartación*, which "*generó el mayor número de manumisiones, permitiendo la aparición de una población negra libre que fue característica de estas colonias*" (generated the highest number of manumissions, resulting in a freed black population, which was very common in the colonies).

Lucena Salmoral (1999a: 359) shows how the periodic installments paid by slaves to their masters were systematically written down in a title of trade. Once the total amount was paid, the slave automatically obtained his freedom and received a *carta de ahorro* (document of freedom) attesting so. This mechanism developed through a consuetudinary process. During the eighteenth century, the *coartación* became quite common across Spanish America, so that at that point it had to be incorporated and further regulated by the legal system. Lucena Salmoral (1999a: 362) reports Watson's (1989: 51) words on this issue: "*coartación resulted from practice, not from official intervention of royal legislation*" (the *coartación* was the result of praxis, it was due to neither an official intervention nor the royal legislation). He also shows that the first time such a mechanism was mentioned and recognized by the legal system was on June 21st, 1768, when the *Gobernador de La Havana* summarized its function in a *Real Cédula*, in which he related *coartación* to the *alcabala* (the royal tax on slave transactions). The abovementioned document, in fact, discussed the problems related to the liberation of slaves and its taxation, and discoursed on whether the tax (4 percent of the slave's value) had to be paid by the master or by the freed servant.

By analyzing the letters exchanged between the *Consejo de Indias* (Indian Council) and the *Contaduría General* (General Accounting Department) concerning *coartación*, Lucena Salmoral (1999a: 363–4) casts light on a series of consuetudinary customs, which were deeply rooted in colonial Spanish America. The main characteristics of such a legal phenomenon may be summarized as follow:

1) Slaves had the right of *coartación* even against the will of their owners.
2) The slave's value at the time of manumission had to be the same as that of the original purchase. The owner could not claim that the value had increased because the slave had learned a profession during the time spent in servitude.
3) Once the total amount was paid, the slave automatically became free.
4) If the manumission was freely conceded by the master to the slave, the *alcabala* did not have to be paid to the state; it was forgiven.
5) The *alcabala* also did not have to be paid when it was the slave who paid for the manumission.
6) The *alcabala* had to be paid by the new buyer, if the owner sold the slave willingly (it was included in the price).

6.7 The Development of the *Coartación* Institute

7) The *alcabala* was paid by the owner, if he was forced by the tribunal to sell the slave (for example, in case of mistreatment).
8) If the slave misbehaved, and therefore put pressure on the owner to sell him, his price could be increased by the *alcabala* value (this practice was seen as a punishment for the slave; it limited his ability to obtain freedom in the future).
9) When a slave, who had already paid part of his value – through the *coartación* process – was sold to a new master, the installments the captive had paid up to that point had to be taken into account, and had to be subtracted from his sale price. In this way, as soon as he paid the remaining part to the new owner, he would become free.

As Lucena Salmoral (1999a: 136) reminds us, during the eighteenth century, several attempts were made to modify the abovementioned norms. In particular, the slave owners on quite a few occasions tried to pressure the King to increase the value of the slaves who had learned a profession during the time spent in servitude; nevertheless, the Crown systematically rejected such proposals.

As far as New Granada is concerned, Lucena Salmoral tells us the anecdotal case that sees as protagonist the mayor of Lorica, Colombia, who in 1789 was not sure about whether or not the *alcabala* had to be paid when the owner decided to manumit his slave for free. To solve this dilemma, the mayor asked the Gobernador of Cartagena, who consulted the Viceroy, who directly reported to the King. The Crown's answer materialized in the *Real Cédula* of October 17th, 1790, when the King highlighted that "*no debe exigirse el referido derecho de alcabala del contrato que se celebra entre el señor y el esclavo, cuando éste se redime por precio adquirido lícitamente, y lo mismo cuando por pura liberalidad de su dueño obtiene la libertad*" (the *alcabala* is not due in the case of a contract between a master and a slave, when the captive becomes free by paying a sum he accumulated licitly, and when the owner concedes freedom to the slave for free) (Lucena Salmoral 1999: 371). As far as the Chocó is concerned, Sharp (1974: 92) indicates that *coartación* was highly common and that it represented a real "safety valve." In fact, it reduced the chances of revolt since slaves knew that, if they worked hard, they could obtain freedom relatively easily.

The data reported by Lucena Salmoral (1999a) show that, in Colombia and in the rest of Spanish America, the *coartación* was a widespread legal instrument during the eighteenth century. To conclude this session and summarize it with the Lucena Salmoral's words we may say that "*la coartación fue sin duda el mejor y mayor mecanismo de liberación de los esclavos en la América española y permitió la aparición de una importante población libre, que la diferenció de otras colonias americanas*" (the *coartación* was without any doubt the best and most powerful way of obtaining freedom in Spanish America and it allowed the formation of a significant free population, which differentiated Spanish America from the rest of the European colonies) (Lucena Salmoral 1999: 374).

In summary, the information presented in this section, concerning eighteenth-century Spanish America, also suggests that Spanish slave law (in books) appeared to be less harsh on black captives and to provide them with more rights than any other European system. Moreover, the fact that the *coartación* originated as a consuetudinary phenomenon, rather than as the result of a conscious act by the legislator (Watson 1989: 51), indicates that it was the byproduct of social praxis, and thus a concrete instance of "law in action."

6.8 Law in Books versus Law in Action

Until this point, the current chapter has been principally concerned with providing a comparative formal account of slave regulations across the Americas (law in books). Data have shown that, at least on paper, Spanish slavery significantly diverged from the other slave systems analyzed, especially because it was the only law that granted legal personality to slaves. Nevertheless, since a legal tradition is effective only if reality conforms to it, in this section I will try to bridge the gap between the idealized legal status of Spanish slaves and their social reality (law in action).

This effort will, in the best-case scenario, only consist of an approximation to reality, since it is materially impossible to provide a perfect picture of the past (Crespo 1995; Sessarego 2013c). Therefore, we will try to reconstruct the reality of colonial Spanish slavery by recurring to the pieces of evidence we have available today. By acknowledging the inherent limitations that such a task implies, this study does not pretend to offer all the answers to the many questions surrounding the Spanish creole debate; rather, what the LHCG means to do is to point out that a number of social, demographic, and historical processes participated in the non-creolization of Spanish in colonial Latin America and that the legal regulation of black captivity represents a key factor in the genesis and evolution of the Afro-Hispanic dialects that developed at that time.

This section is composed of three subparts. The first one consists of a collection of statements proceeding from a variety of colonial clerics, travelers, and diplomats, who made comparisons between the reality of Spanish slavery and the other European systems implemented in the Americas. This will offer an impressionistic analysis of how "law in books" might have been reflected in "law in action" (Pound 1910), or at least, of how such a reality might have been perceived by these observers in colonial times. The second subsection provides an account of how historical data offer evidence of the actual presence in Spanish America of the most important slaves' rights – derived from the concept of legal personality – which may be seen as key indicators of a process of gradual integration into colonial society (especially: property, family, access to juridical means, manumission, the right not to be abused). The third and last part focuses specifically on the Colombian context, and in particular, on colonial Chocó, a department that, given its cultural and geographic isolation, may have presented a bigger gap between "law in books" and "law in action" than other, more urbanized, regions of Spanish America. Such a scenario will, therefore, serve as the perfect testing ground for the LHCG.

The LHCG suggests that Spanish slave law, which included norms concerning property rights (fundamental to obtain manumission, especially via *coartación*), family preservation, Catholic education, rules against mistreatments, access to courts (i.e., the *protector de esclavos*), etc. placed the Spanish slaves in a better position than any other European captives; it favored their integration in society and their acquisition of the colonial language, thus significantly reducing the chances of Spanish creolization in the Americas. Obviously, we should not forget that such a formal legislation may not have been perfectly reflected in real life (Pound 1910), especially in rural areas far away from legal courts. The following sessions will focus on such a debate to see to what extent the legal praxis of Spanish slavery (law in action) corresponded to the formal regulations written "in books." Thus, colonial Chocó, a region often described as "on the frontier" for its isolation from the rest of Colombia (Whitten 1974; Sharp 1976) will be used here to test the LHCG.

6.8.1 Some Comments on Black Slavery in Spanish America

Reconstructing how Spanish slave law may actually have had a real effect on society is a difficult task. In previous studies (Sessarego 2015a, 2017a), I have tried to cast light on this issue by relying on different pieces of colonial evidence. One of such sources of historical information consists of the remarks provided by a variety of colonial observers, who commented on the nature of Spanish slavery and compared it to the other European systems. Here I will reproduce such comments, which will provide us with an impressionistic analysis of how these people perceived the social reality of slavery at that time.

Andrés-Gallego (2005: ch.6), in his book *"La esclavitud en la América española"* (Slavery in Spanish America), offers a variety of statements that highlight how the Spanish system appeared to be comparatively less harsh on the slaves than the institutions designed by the other European colonial powers (see also Sessarego 2015a: ch.6). He reports a remark by the scientist Don Felix de Azara, who pointed out how black captives working in Paraguay during the eighteenth century were benefiting from better living and working conditions than those residing in other European territories overseas:

> Those laws and those cruel punishments that some people want to justify as needed to keep the slaves under control are unknown in this region. (Author's translation)[6]

The Prussian geographer Alexander de Humboldt, when visiting Mexico, at the beginning of the eighteenth century, also commented on the more protective nature of Spanish slave law in comparison with the other European regulations (2005: 242):

> As in all Spanish colonies slaves are more protected by the law than in other European territories. These laws are always interpreted in favor of freedom; the government wants the number of free blacks to increase. (Author's translation)[7]

Along the same lines is the statement of an anonymous Venezuelan observer of the nineteenth century, whose claims are as follows (Andrés-Gallego 2005: 243):

> The black slave in Venezuela is not an isolated individual, without resources, without protection, without goods, without hope: from our point of view, he is not a being perpetually condemned to hardship. If in some countries slaves are subject to such harsh conditions, in Venezuela the laws, the judges, and the smartly calculated individual and community interests provide slaves with rest from hardship and better chances of becoming part of society so that they are happy in their condition. (Author's translation)[8]

Of a similar opinion was Jeronimo José Salguero, consultant of the Audiencia de Buenos Aires, who, in 1807, elaborated on the great departure of Spanish slave law from Roman law by stating:

> A slave is entitled to receive a softer and more sympathetic treatment among us than among the Romans; this is an effect of the difference between our law on serfdom, and its motives, and the Roman one. (Author's translation)[9]

---

[6] Original Spanish version: *No se conocen esas leyes y esos castigos atroces que se quieren disculpar como necesarios para mantener a los esclavos dentro de los límites de sus deberes.*

[7] Original Spanish version: *Se hallan como en todas las posesiones españolas, algo más protegidos por las leyes que los negros que habitan las colonias de las demás naciones europeas. Estas leyes se interpretan siempre a favor de la libertad, pues el gobierno desea que se aumente el número de negros libres.*

[8] Original Spanish version: *El negro esclavo en Venezuela no es un ente aislado en medio del género humano, sin recursos, sin protección, sin bienes, sin esperanzas: no es en nuestra consideración un ser condenado perpetuamente a la fatiga y a las privaciones. Si en otros países los esclavos pueden existir en tan duras situaciones, en Venezuela las leyes, los magistrados y los intereses personales y comunes de los amos, más sabiamente calculados, les proporcionan para su conservación descanso en la fatiga, vínculos en la sociedad y contento en su condición.*

[9] Original Spanish version: *Tanto más acreedor es un esclavo entre nosotros a un tratamiento suave y piadoso, cuanta es la diferencia de servidumbre, y sus motivos, entre los que conoce nuestro derecho y la que usaron los romanos.*

6.8 Law in Books Versus Law in Action 177

Again in the nineteenth century, we can find similar remarks concerning slavery in Peru. This time the British traveler Stevenson (1828: 42–3; in Andrés-Gallego 2005: 273), after traveling across the Americas, indicated that the living conditions of black slaves in Peru were better than those found in other European colonies and – in some cases – they were even better than those of some white peons working in Europe:

> If the slaves in all the countries could be treated the way I saw people treat them in Peru, they would be, without any doubt, better off than many farmers working in the Old World. (Author's translation)[10]

For obvious reasons, Stevenson's comments should be taken with a grain of salt since, given the well-known cases of mistreatment (Andrés-Gallego 2005: 176–85), it is difficult to think that black captives in Peru would live in such an ideal environment. However, if we take these remarks as representative of the view of a European traveler who lived for some twenty years across the Americas and was familiar with English and French plantation societies, we may infer that Spanish slaves were comparatively better off than English and French captives.

Another quote reported by Andrés-Gallego (2005: 243) is the one taken from historian Núñez Ponte, who, in his book *Estudio histórico acerca de la esclavitud y de su abolición en Venezuela* (Historical study on slavery and abolition in Venezuela), published in 1911, highlights how slaves were protected by the law against mistreatments and assisted by state lawyers (*procurador de pobres*, also known as *procurador de negros*):

> The Spaniards did not abuse their slaves too much; ... there were highly philanthropic laws that ... softened blacks' living conditions, and prescribed punishments for the masters who excessively mistreated them; and a *procurador de pobres* defended them freely whenever it was needed. (Author's translation)[11]

A few years later, in 1916, historian Fernando Ortiz also commented on the milder treatments reserved for Spanish slaves, when compared with English and French ones:

> Many of the tortures described by travelers who visited the French and English colonies ... show that their anti-slavery or narrative zeal brought them to claim either that they were common there, and not here, or that slavery in those little Antillean colonies was much crueler than among the Spaniards; this is quite realistic and

---
[10] Original French version: *Si les esclaves de tous les pays pouvaient être traités de la même manière que ceux que j'ai été a portee de voir au Pérou, pendant le séjour que j'y ai fait, leur sort serait, sans contredit, plus heureux que celui de beaucoup de paysans de l'ancient monde.*
[11] Original Spanish version: *Ni tampoco usaron los españoles con sus esclavos de demasiada sevicia; ... Había leyes altamente filantrópicas que ... en algo suavizaban el rigoroso destino de los negros, y señalaban penas a los señores que en demasía les torturaban; y un procurador de pobres ejercía gratuitamente la función de defenderles cuando se hubiese menester.*

believable given the abundance of supporting documents showing the sophisticated cruelty of those Caribbean planters. (Author's translation)[12]

All of these remarks, which highlight how Spanish slaves' living and working conditions were generally better than those reserved for other European captives, suggest that Spanish "law in books," indeed, had a significant effect on "law in action," or at least this was the impression that all of these colonial observers had.

The investigations by Lucena Salmoral (1994, 1999a, 1999b, 2000a, 2000b, 2005), one of the leading scholars in Spanish colonial slavery, further support the idea that slavery in the Americas was a highly heterogeneous phenomenon and that being a slave in, say, an English or French colony implied significantly worse standards of living than being a slave in Spanish America. Lucena Salmoral's (1994: 63) position on this issue may be exemplified by a quote he reported from a letter of the *Consejo de Indias* (colonial Council), in which the members of this institution depicted how the legal and economic structure of English, French, and Spanish colonies influenced the actual reality of slavery in those territories. The *Consejo* commented on the fact that English and French colonies had to import on average some 50,000 *bozales* yearly in order to keep up with the agricultural production, since many slaves would die due to the extreme living and working conditions on the plantations. On the contrary, black communities in Spanish America experienced relatively high birth rates and captives had a longer life expectancy. For these reasons, production could rely more substantially on *criollo* captives rather than *bozales*. According to the *Consejo*, the reason why the number of slaves tended to decrease in Spanish colonies was not usually related to slave deaths, but rather to higher rates of manumission. In addition, interracial marriages and sexual affairs were not sanctioned by the law; so that a group of mixed-race people (*castas*) rapidly emerged in Spanish America, a good part of whom were set free at birth:

Among the Spaniards the number of slaves tends to decrease because it was easier to achieve manumission, but not because slaves would die due to inhumane working conditions, this gave birth to a variety of mixed races, called people of color, who originated from slavery. (Author's translation)[13]

---

[12] Original Spanish version: *Muchos suplicios descriptos por viajeros de las colonias francesas e inglesas ... demuestran o que su celo antiesclavista o narrativo les hizo presentar como frecuentes, hecho del todo desusados, o que la esclavitud en aquellas pequeñas colonias antillanas era mucho más cruel que entre los españoles, circunstancia está muy verosímil y creíble dada la gran abundancia de documentos justificativos de la refinada crueldad de los plantadores de las otras colonias de las indias.*

[13] Original Spanish version: *Entre los españoles se disminuye el número de esclavos por la facilidad con que se libertan, pero no porque perecen entre los rigores de un trato inhumano, pues en el fondo las varias castas, llamadas gentes de color, que deben su origen a la esclavitud.*

These remarks on manumission, stated by the *Consejo de Indias* for the overall trends across Spanish America, seem to closely match the situation we observed in colonial Chocó (see Chapter 5), where we saw that by 1778 the vast majority of the blacks living in the department were already free (Sharp 1976: 141–2).

6.8.2 An Analysis of Legal Praxis in Spanish America

As I have indicated in previous investigations (Sessarego 2015a, 2017a), the Spanish Crown – influenced by the Catholic church – acknowledged that black slaves were human beings with souls (Watson 1989). In fact, as we observed in the *Instrucciones*, slaves had to receive Christian education. They had to attend Mass and were not allowed to work during Christian festivities and had to pray on regular basis. Moreover, language teaching was often seen as fundamental to the correct reception of the Christian religion, a fact that has been highlighted by different scholars working on the management of slaves by religious orders (Cushner 1980; Macera 1966; Bouisson 1977) and, as we saw in Chapter 5, also by historians focusing on colonial Chocó (Sharp 1976; Cantor 2000).

In the following paragraphs, I wish to reproduce a few legal quotes taken from an ordinance of 1545 (Konetzke 1953: 237–8; Sessarego 2015a: 139–45), which may help us obtain a better understanding of the importance given by the Crown to the treatments and education provided to the slaves, which indirectly must also have had a significant impact on the acquisition of Spanish among the black captives. The first quote indicates that the owners could not punish black captives too harshly or for no reason:

First of all, we order ... that all the slaveholders take good care of their black slaves because they are related to us as Christians; masters should feed them and clothe them, they should not punish them cruelly, nor hurt them without a good reason; they are not allowed to amputate any parts of their bodies nor cause them any permanent damage, since it is forbidden by both divine and human laws. If they do so, the slave will be taken away from them, and they will have to pay a fee of twenty pesos, which will be given to the denouncer (Author's translation)[14]

The second extract highlights the fact that Christian education had to be systematically taught to the slaves. Captives, in fact, had to pray every day and, on each Sunday, they would also receive Christian indoctrination and attend Mass:

---

[14] Original Spanish version: *Primeramente se ... ordena que todos los señores de negros tengan cuidado de hacer buen tratamiento a sus esclavos, teniendo consideración que son próximos y cristianos, dándoles de comer y vestir conforme a razón, y no castigalles con crueldades, ni ponelles las manos, sin evidente razón, y que no puedan cortalles miembro ni lisiallos, pues por ley divina y humana, es prohibido, a pena que pierdan el tal esclavo para S.M. y veinte pesos para el denunciador.*

On every plantation ... there must be a white supervisor, who has to make sure that on the plantation there is a house or a hut functioning as a church with an altar, a cross and holy images, and in that place every morning, before going to work, blacks and natives must pray ..., and every Sunday and celebration day, after lunch and after having attended mass and having received the holy sacraments, workers have to get together and pray, they have to receive Christian education, so that they will be able to understand the faith; ... if the governor while visiting the plantation should realize that this regulation is not systematically respected, the owners will have to pay a fee of 30 pesos. (Author's translation)[15]

The third quote is of great interest from a linguistic perspective, since it reveals that Spanish language teaching was, in fact, compulsory, given that it represented a fundamental means to achieve the aforementioned indoctrination goals. In fact, according to this ordinance, Spanish had to be taught to the *bozales* within six months from the time of their purchase or the master would have incurred problems with the law:

It ... is mandatory for all slave owners to teach our common language to the slave within six months from the time of purchase; they also have to explain the meaning of the sacrament of baptism, they have to baptize them and instruct them in the Christian Faith; indeed all the blacks are friends with the Christians, they are easy to convert and happy to become Christian ... and if there were evidence that after such a period of time the slave owner did not meet the aforementioned requirements, then he would lose one fourth of the slave value the first time; for the second time, he would lose half of the value; and for the third time, the whole value ... and nobody in possession of a black *bozal* can sell him, or exchange him, or cede him after those six months without having brought him into the Christian faith; if this were to happen both the seller and the buyer would be guilty and would have to pay the consequences for their actions. (Author's translation)[16]

---

[15] Original Spanish version: *Item que todos los señores de haciendas ... tengan en ella un hombre blanco como mayordomo o mandador, el cual tenga cuidado que en dicha hacienda esté una casa o bohío como iglesia con su altar, con la señal de la cruz e imagines, y allí cada día por la mañana, antes que vayan los tales negros e indios a trabajar al campo, vengan a hacer oración ..., y todos los domingos y fiestas, después de comer, habiendo aquella mañana tenido misa con el santísimo sacramento de la eucaristías, se junten en la dicha iglesia o casa de oración y allí les enseñen la doctrina Cristiana, de manera que estén instruidos en la fe; ... a los tales amos y señores de los dichos negros e indios, demás de que se les pone de treinta pesos, por cada vez que dicho señor Gobernador fuere a visitar la gobernación y no hallare que se cumple esta orden y que está en su costumbre cotidiana.*

[16] Original Spanish version: *Item ... se les manda a cualquier señor de negro o negros, que como compren un negro esclavo, dentro de seis meses tengan cuidado como entrare en su poder, de hacelles aprender nuestra lengua vulgar y dalles a entender el sacramento del agua del santo bautismo y hacerlos bautizar y cristianar; pues todos los negros de su inclinación son amigos de los cristianos y fáciles de convertir a ello y lo tienen por presunción y valor ser cristianos como nosotros ... y si se le probare haber tenido descuido en esto y que se le ha pasado el dicho término y no ha procurado hacer lo que ansi arriba se declara, incurra en pena del valor de la cuarta parte del negro la primera vez, y por el Gobernador que fuere, le sea puesto otro término, cual le pareciere, para que lo haga; y si la segunda vez fuera remiso, pierda la mitad del valor*

6.8 Law in Books versus Law in Action

Analysis of the aforementioned extracts therefore indicates – one more time – that both the Spanish Crown and the Catholic church designed policies with the goal of Christianizing the black slaves, and that such policies probably had a significant effect on the acquisition of Spanish among the black captives. Such a political goal was therefore clearly reflected in the formal legislation regulating forced black labor in Spanish America. Nevertheless, what we want to understand now is to what extent such theoretical rules were actually enforced in practice. In other words, were these rules "in books" only describing a highly idealized slave status that did not represent at all what happened in practice? Or did they have some effect on "law in action"?

As we saw before, several colonial observers pointed out that the Spanish legal heritage on slavery – indeed – made a big difference and that had a significant effect on improving slaves' living and working conditions. Further evidence of this emerges from an analysis of colonial court trials. In fact, a number of scholars in the field of colonial history have systematically reported how Spanish slaves managed to rely on the legal system to fight for their rights (see, for example, Bryant 2004, 2005). In particular, black captives relied on juridical courts to protect the rights they were entitled to in the *Siete Partidas* and in the *Leyes de India*. Thus, there are various historical records documenting Spanish slaves fighting to not be mistreated, for the right to own property, for manumission, for family preservation, etc.

There are several cases in which slaves sued their masters for poor treatments. One example is the trial of Claudio and Bonifacio, two black captives from Barbacoa (in present-day Colombia) complaining in front of the High Court of Quito (Ecuador) in 1798 about the mistreatments received from their overseer (Bryant 2004: 330–40). In this specific case, the judge found the overseer guilty and offered protection to the two slaves. He also informed the juridical authorities in Barbacoa, so that they could further investigate the issue. Another case is the one of the slave Ignacio, from Córdoba (Argentina), who accused his master in 1764, Marcos Infante, of punishing him too harshly. Ignacio's accusation turned out to be successful, Mr. Infante was sent to jail, and the slave was sold to a different owner (Andrés-Gallego 2005: 199).

As far as family rights are concerned, it is again possible to find a vast literature. In 1768, for example, we see in San Miguel de Tucumán (Argentina) the local tribunal condemning a master to pay a fee and forcing him to sell his mistress, an enslaved woman, who was married to another slave (Andrés-Gallego 2005: 214–15). Another case related to slave marriage is the

del negro; y por la tercera todo el negro ... y si alguno que ansi comprare o hubiere en su poder el tal negro bozal y lo quisiere vender o trocar o enajenar antes de cumplidos los dichos seis meses, y no lo hubiere fecho cristianar, no lo pueda enajenar, sino fuere con el aditamento susodicho, y que el tal cargo tome sobre sí el que ansi después lo hubiere, so la dicha pena al uno y otro, vendedor y comprador.

one reported by Andrés-Gallego (2005: 194), in which the slave Pedro Pablo from Lima (Peru) forced his master to let him spend Saturdays and Sundays with his wife, and eventually succeeded in being sold to a different owner in 1770, so that this marriage could be preserved.

Cases concerning property rights were often related to the possibility of obtaining manumission. One such case is the one in which the slave Juana María Artaza, who in 1763 – again in San Miguel Tucumán – sued his master for not setting her free after he had promised her so in exchange for sexual favors. The court assigned a *protector de esclavos* to the black captive and this state lawyer managed to negotiate her freedom in exchange for the modest sum of 200 pesos (2005: 197). Another example in which a slave fought for his property rights in relation to manumission is the one of Joaquín, who in 1768 in Guadalajara (Mexico) managed to get back a sum of money he had accumulated to obtain freedom, which his master had unjustifiably taken away from him (Andrés-Gallego 2005: 199–200).

Andrés-Gallego (2005: 108) further suggests that in urban centers it was relatively easy for black captives to recur to the *protector de esclavos*, and that the vast majority of the legal trials he examined during the eighteenth century see slaves as winners. Nevertheless, it must be acknowledged that not all Spanish slaves in the Americas had the same degree of access to legal means to fight for their rights. Slaves living in big urban centers could resort more easily to the law than those residing in more rural areas (Andrés-Gallego 2005: 202, 221–3). However, even assuming that some masters would manage to violate slaves' rights with impunity, the number of captives who were capable of obtaining justice was arguably high, in particular if we compare Spanish America with the situations encountered in the rest of the European colonies, where slaves – deprived of legal personality – could not usually even fight in legal courts. Andrés-Gallego (2005: 217) exemplifies this situation by reporting Meiklejohn's (1981: 192) analysis:

Even if we suppose that – as it was probably the case – there were slave owners who mistreated their captives and managed to prevent them from filing a lawsuit, and lawyers who did not want to help them, the number of slaves who received justice and the number of lawyers who did their job in Santa Fe de Bogotá during the eighteenth century is just *"impressive."* (Author's translation)[17]

It is a sure fact that access to legal means in urban centers must have been higher than in rural regions. Nevertheless, it is also worth remembering that

---

[17] Original Spanish version: *Aun suponiendo que – como es verosímil – hubiera amos que maltrataran a sus esclavos y consiguieran impedirles que los denunciasen, y procuradores que no se quisieran malquistar con aquellos, el número de esclavos a quienes se hizo justicia y el número de procuradores que cumplieron con su deber defendiéndolos, concretamente en Santa Fe de Bogotá durante el siglo XVIII, es simplemente "impressive."*

a good part of the captives used in rural areas belonged to the Catholic Church. Indeed, the Company of Jesus alone was the biggest slave owner in Latin America, and in certain Spanish colonies it possessed more than one-fourth of the total number of black captives (Andrés-Gallego 2005: 188). As is well known, the Company of Jesus adopted a highly pragmatic management strategy, which aimed to maximize slaves' productivity and loyalty while minimizing risks of revolts. They did so by not violating slaves' rights and by treating them according to religious principles, which have been systematically reported as less brutal and more humane (see Macera 1966; Buisson 1997; Andrés-Gallego 2005). Moreover, they placed a strong emphasis on Christian education, which also indirectly implies Spanish language acquisition among the enslaved captives.

It would be naïve to think that Spanish slaves could always resort to the law to protect their rights. In fact, even though we found a variety of colonial observations commenting on the better living conditions of Spanish captives and vast juridical evidence suggesting that they had access – to a good extent – to legal means, we also have to realize that in some cases some formal rules "in books" may not have been systematically followed in practice, so that some slaves might have been mistreated; some may have not been given the *peculium* and some may have been deprived of their family rights, etc. However, besides these infractions, which may occur in all societies and that are quite difficult to quantify at this point, we must consider that such actions were classified as *illegal* according to the Spanish system, and therefore they were punishable by law. On the contrary, in the rest of the European colonies, such actions were often not even systematically seen as infractions; rather, in many cases they were the norm; they were legally backed by the legislators, and in many cases masters could not even treat their slaves better than what the legal system had established.

These sharp contrasts among legal systems must have had a significant effect on shaping the white-black social dynamics across colonial Americas and eventually the languages that developed out of such heterogeneous scenarios. Assuming that such a high degree of legal divergence had no real effect on regulating colonial societies is, in my view, a big historical fallacy. Linguistic studies would benefit immensely by integrating comparative slave law and colonial history into evolutionary models of creole language formations. Thus, any analysis of the development of Afro-European contact varieties in the Americas would gain much from paying closer attention to the social contexts in which such languages emerged.

6.9 The Colombian Case

In the case of Colombia, it is also possible to find a series of remarks highlighting the divergence of Spanish slavery from the other European systems.

For example, besides the aforementioned quote by historian Meiklejohn (1981: 192) (see Section 6.8) on the key role played by the *procuradores de negros* in assisting black slaves during trials in Santa Fe de Bogotá, it is worth pointing out the words of the Colombian writer Sergio Arboleda (1951: 84–5), quoted by historian Jaramillo Uribe (1963: 28–9), who described the living conditions of black slaves in the Cauca Department during the nineteenth century:

> The black slaves in colonial times are better off than many so-called free Indians. Their master's interest, and the fact that he knows that he will also own their offspring, implies that they live well and reproduce themselves. On the other hand, the white's vanity helps the black: the master wants his slaves to be noticed for their morality, for their good health, and for their proper behaviors; even the masters with a tough and cruel character give in to the pressure imposed by public opinion, public judgement. The slave is proud of his master's last name, he feels almost like a member of the family, and tries to accumulate his *peculium*. (Author's translation)[18]

Obviously, Sergio Arboleda's comments should not be taken literally, since, given the attested cases of mistreatment (Jaramillo Uribe 1963: 28–9), it would be unrealistic to think that Cauca slaves had such a happy life. Nevertheless, if we consider these words from the perspective of a scholar who analyzed forced labor exploitation from a comparative point of view (he was professor of Roman and Spanish law), and especially if we pay attention to his remarks on the existence of the *peculium*, we may infer that Colombian slavery might not have been as harsh as the systems implemented by other European powers, and we find additional evidence indicating that Spanish slaves received some sort of compensation for their work.

Moreover, if we analyze the historical reports emerging from the Colombian judicial trials, we can again detect all the types of legal actions related to the presence of legal personality (viz., cases concerning property, marriage, family, manumission, etc.), as in the rest of the Spanish colonies. One such case is a litigation that took place in Bogotá in 1708 between the slave Juan Ramos and the *Colegio de Noviciados de la Compañía de Jesús* (the Jesuit College of Novitiates). The litigation had to do with a house, which Juan claimed as his own, but which had been built on a piece of land that was subsequently donated to the *Colegio* (Díaz-Díaz 2001: 165). Also very common were cases concerning manumission, as the notarial deeds signed by Catharina Castro de Bolaños,

---

[18] Original Spanish version: *Los negros en su esclavitud son bajo la colonia menos desgraciados que muchos de los indios que se llaman libres. El interés de su señor, que los considera capital suyo y sabe que su descendencia le pertenecerá, procura su conservación y aumento. Por otra parte, la vanidad del blanco viene en auxilio de la suerte del negro: los amos quieren que sus esclavos se hagan notar por su moralidad, por su buena salud, y aun por sus modales y buen porte; hasta los de carácter áspero y cruel tienen que ceder en este punto al imperio de la opinión, al imperio de la sanción pública. El esclavo, por su parte, se enorgullece de llevar el apellido de su señor, se considera casi un miembro de la familia, y aprovecha las facilidades que se le brindan para crearse un peculio.*

who, in 1741, in Cauca, granted freedom to two slaves, María and Juan Simón, for having been trustworthy servants (Jaramillo Uribe 1963: 30). These are only some of the many legal records that could be mentioned here; for a more detailed list, see the collection of Colombian documents recently published by Jiménez Meneses & Pérez Morales (2013).

The data analyzed for Colombia in relation to black slavery align this colony with the rest of Spanish America. However, such a system, which was quite homogeneous across the territories ruled by the Spanish Crown, diverged in significant ways from the realities encountered in the other European colonies overseas. Such a legal diversity, which is essentially rooted in the dichotomy of presence versus absence of legal personality for slaves, must have played a major role in the evolution of black-white relations in the Americas and, eventually, on the development of the Afro-European contact varieties that formed across such heterogeneous societies.

Even though the comments provided by colonial observers and the juridical evidence emerging from legal trials appear to indicate that, in Colombia – and across the rest of Spanish America – "law in books" had a significant impact on "law in action," some skeptical readers may find it difficult to accept the LHCG and to believe that the Spanish legal system and the Catholic church could really improve slaves' living conditions in remote plantations and mines, far away from urban centers, where the law could not be systematically enforced and the church's presence was minimal. The Colombian Chocó perfectly matches such a scenario. In fact, it has often been described as a remote and isolated region, on the frontier of the Spanish Empire (Whitten 1974; Sharp 1976). Thus it represents the perfect "testing ground" for the LHCG.

6.10 Focus on Colonial Chocó

The fact that slavery cannot be taken as a uniform phenomenon across space and time is well known, and a variety of studies in the field of legal history have been dedicated to this topic (Winks 1972). One of the first authors to stress the marked differences between Spanish American slavery and other European colonial slave laws was Tannenbaum (1947), who claimed that slavery in Spanish America was generally a milder institution than under other colonial powers. Tannenbaum's proposal generated much debate in the field of colonial studies, and – inevitably – received some criticism. One of the weaknesses identified by his opponents was that his thesis was exclusively based on a legalistic approach, quite disconnected from the archival work, which would have permitted a more solid analysis of the reality of slavery in the Americas (Elkins 1959). Indeed, what Tannenbaum's model failed to explain was how "law in books" was actually reflected in the "law in action" (Pound 1910).

Historian William Sharp (1976) decided to contribute to this much-debated issue by testing Tannenbaum's proposal exactly on colonial Chocó, a remote region, where colonial law was not enforced. Actually, this is one of the main reasons why he decided to write his 1976 book, *Slavery on the Spanish Frontier: The Colombian Chocó 1680–1810*. Indeed, he dedicated an entire chapter to this issue: *"Slavery in Chocó: Law and Reality."* The chapter begins by identifying the two main claims on which Tannenbaum's proposal was based: (a) Spanish slaves were protected by potential abuses due to a series of regulations that provided them with a variety of rights concerning manumission, marriage, family issues, punishments, law suits against the masters, etc.; (b) the Catholic church had an active role in taking away some of masters' power over their captives so that slaves' living conditions improved (Sharp 1976: 130).

Sharp highlighted that neither (a) nor (b) were present in Chocó; in fact, on the one hand, legal protection could not be enforced since the reduced number of white settlers in the department could not justify the financial efforts that would have been required to establish a legal court in the region; for this reason, tribunals were not present in the province (Sharp 1976: 128, see also McWhorter 2000: 37). On the other hand, the number of clerics was so reduced (only eighteen priests in a total population of 17,898 in 1789) that they could not possibly be held responsible for significantly affecting slaves' living conditions (Sharp 1976: 131, see also McWhorter 2000: 37).

Given this scenario, Sharp proceeded to a close analysis of the archival documentation available from the mining operations carried out in colonial Chocó, including the local registers for manumission, marriages, etc., as well as the manuals provided by the owners to the administrators to maintain order in the *cuadrillas*. He discovered that – even though conditions (a) and (b) were not met – all the basic rights derived from the notion of legal personality were substantially found in colonial Chocó. In fact, slaves worked on average 260 days a year, since during the remaining time they were off (a sort of *peculium*) to provide for themselves and their families (1976: 134); they could accumulate goods, gold, and other properties to pay for their manumission (p. 135). Abuse of slaves was remarkably rare (p. 136). They were instructed in the precepts of the Catholic religion daily (p. 139). Marriage was supported, as well as the preservation of family units (p. 140).

Sharp's conclusions are further backed by Cantor's observations concerning punishments (2000: 101–8), manumissions (pp. 158, 170), family formation (pp. 165, 169–73), Spanish language diffusion, and Christian education (p. 159–62). In particular, he further stresses the presence of Spanish acculturation implemented by the *criollos* and mulattoes among the *bozales*. This process was facilitated not only by the fact that the *criollos* were the majority, but also by having a highly heterogeneous group of *bozales*, who did not identify with a single African group but rather had very diverged cultural and linguistic backgrounds, so that, as indicated in Chapter 5, the Spanish language served as a means of interethnic communication and "*la rutina diaria fue el escenario propicio para la difusión del castellano y eventualmente del cristianismo*" (the daily routine was the perfect situation for the spread of the Castilian language and eventually of Christianity) (p. 98).

Sharp (1976) clearly shows that all the aforementioned rights were not conceded to slaves because the Spanish miners were either nicer or kinder to their captives; rather, these more humane treatments were driven by a very pragmatic understanding of the fact that to better living/working conditions corresponded higher profits and less risk of revolts (p. 140). Indeed, giving slaves the basic tools to provide for themselves and their families was a basic requirement for having a healthy and productive workforce; religion was conceived as a means to teach the captives Christian obedience; marriage and family preservation were used to create stronger ties among the slaves, the rest of the gang, and the mine, since running away or rebelling would have been more difficult if a slave had a wife and children (p. 141). Such a pragmatic policy is what Cantor (2000: 102) also detects when he states that "*para ellos [los mineros], el esclavo era un factor de producción sobre el cual basaban su riqueza: por lo tanto no tenían intereses filantrópicos ni perversos, sino económicos*" (for the miners, the slave was a production factor on which they based their wealth: for this reason, they did not either have philanthropic interests or perverse ones; rather, they had economic ones).

The aforementioned factors, combined with the possibility of accumulating the *peculium* in a region extremely rich in gold resources, implied that captives had incentives and opportunities to work hard and achieve freedom. Sharp (1976: 141–2) stresses that:

Manumission in Chocó was not only possible but occurred. In 1778, 35.44 per cent of the black population was free (3,160 of 8,916) ... During the next thirty years the free black population increased by a remarkable 5.7 per cent a year. By 1808, 75.34 per cent of the black population in the Chocó was free.

All in all, this implies that certain social norms concerning slaves' living and working conditions were so rooted in the Spanish colonial society that even though no formal legal enforcement was present in Chocó, social praxis and entrepreneurial pragmatism encouraged their respect. In fact, what would have been the advantage for a rational slave owner to go against such social customs, which had developed within Spanish culture over centuries?

Sharp (1976: 142, 147) closes his investigation on Tannenbaum's proposal by saying:

It may be argued that the treatment designed for slaves in Chocó followed the pattern described by Tannenbaum ..., even though the Spanish legal system and the church were not directly involved ...
Slaveholders in Chocó understood the formula that better physical treatment resulted in healthier workers and greater productivity. Mistreatment led to dissatisfaction and possible rebellion. Profit motives helped determine slave treatment but ironically, behavior was in general accord with the Spanish conduct Tannenbaum ... described.

The aforementioned scenario does not appear to be an exception to the rule; rather, the living and working conditions in colonial Chocó parallel those reported for a number of other Spanish colonies that have been analyzed by combining sociohistorical and linguistic information (see Sessarego 2013b for Ecuador, Sessarego 2011a, 2014a for Bolivia, and Sessarego 2014c, 2015a for Peru). In particular, the pragmatic management implemented by the Chocoan miners closely resembles the working strategies adopted by the Company of Jesus in its Andean plantations, where Jesuits focused on maximizing production while minimizing risks of revolts and, in so doing, adopted educational techniques that favored Spanish language acquisition among the black captives.

The LHCG provides a new perspective for looking at the genesis and evolution of the AHLAs. This hypothesis does not pretend to be the answer to all the questions that gravitate around the Spanish creole debate. In fact, a variety of social, political, economic, and demographic factors had an effect on shaping these Afro-Hispanic contact varieties. Nevertheless, the LHCG identifies a key element that clearly differentiated Spanish slavery from the rest of the European systems (i.e., presence vs. absence of slaves' legal personality) and that resulted in a number of rights for the Spanish slave that were highly restricted or non-existent for the rest of the captives under other European administration in the Americas. Findings appear to indicate that this legal and cultural heritage, which developed in Spain over several centuries, had a significant effect on the praxis of Spanish slavery (law in action). It significantly influenced the white-black social dynamics of colonial Spanish America, even in regions like Colombian Chocó, where legal courts and the Catholic church were not necessarily present during the colonial phase. The LHCG, therefore, offers a reasonable generalization that addresses the problem of such a "mysteriously absent creole cluster under a single power" (McWhorter 2000: 39).

The study of CS grammar, as well as the linguistic analysis of the rest of the AHLAs, cannot be divorced from a sociohistorical investigation of their genesis and evolution. After analyzing colonial Chocó by evaluating the linguistic, legal, social, and demographic information available for this region, we may now better understand why contemporary CS is classified more as a Spanish dialect than a Spanish creole. This interdisciplinary approach, I believe, could easily be applied not only to the study of any other AHLAs, but also, more broadly, to the entire field of creole studies. It will help us – as an academic community – to extend both our linguistic and sociohistorical knowledge of these contact varieties and provide a look ahead to a truly fascinating period in the history of contact linguistics.

7 Final Considerations

Of all the Afro-Hispanic languages of the Americas (AHLAs), Chocó Spanish (CS) represents one of the most enigmatic varieties. In fact, CS is spoken in a region that has always been considered as an ideal place for creole formation and/or preservation but, from a linguistic point of view, this contact vernacular classifies more as a "Spanish dialect" than a "Spanish creole."

Two different hypotheses have been provided in the literature to account for this situation. On the one hand, the Monogenesis-Decreolization Hypothesis (Granda 1968 *et seq.*; Schwegler 1991a, 2014; etc.) has proposed that CS, along with the rest of the AHLAs, used to be a creole that decreolized due to more recent contact with standard Spanish, so that certain grammatical features found in this variety (viz., variable gender agreement across the DP, lack of subject-verb inversion in questions, etc.) would be seen as the remaining traces of a previous creole stage, while Papiamentu and Palenquero would represent the only Spanish creoles that survived such a decreolizing process. On the other hand, the Afrogenesis Hypothesis (McWhorter 2000) has claimed that Spanish never creolized in the Americas because a Spanish pidgin never formed in Africa and, therefore, a Spanish creole could not possibly develop in the New World. Consequently, according to this view, Papiamentu and Palenquero should be seen as Portuguese-based creoles, which only in a second phase of their evolution were relexified with Spanish lexicon.

The present book has challenged both hypotheses and has suggested that CS and the rest of the AHLAs may be better analyzed as the byproduct of advanced universal SLA strategies, which do not imply any previous (de)creolization phase for these varieties (Sessarego 2013a). Moreover, this study has built on the recently proposed Legal Hypothesis of Creole Genesis (LHCG) (Sessarego 2015a, 2017a) to account for the paucity of Spanish creoles in the Americas. In particular, without denying the importance of a concomitance of demographic, social, political, and economic factors that conspired against the creolization of Spanish in the New World, this work has pointed out a common element, which was shared by all the Spanish colonies, and that was absent in the rest of the European territories overseas: the presence of legal personality for black slaves – and the corollary of

Final Considerations 191

rights that this implied (viz., right not to be abused, owing property, family preservation, Christian education, etc.). In so doing, this book has provided a plausible generalization, which, among other things, explains why the only true Spanish creoles in the Americas are actually spoken where Spanish law never applied: in the Netherlands Antilles (Papiamentu) and in the former maroon community of San Basilio de Palenque, Colombia (Palenquero).

This study has offered a general sketch of CS grammar showing how it diverges – to a certain extent – from standard Spanish and how it aligns with the features found across a number of other AHLAs, Caribbean Spanish varieties, and vernacular dialects in general. Specifically, this work has identified the most salient grammatical phenomena, which have traditionally been ascribed to a previous decreolization phase for the AHLAs, and it has shown that all those linguistic elements can actually be explained as the instantiations of advanced SLA strategies related to processability constraints at the core of linguistic interface processes. Thus, I adopted Jackendoff's (1997, 2002) framework of linguistic interface architecture to account for the following AHLA features: (a) presence of bare nouns in subject position; (b) variable number and gender agreement across the DP; (c) invariant verb forms for person and number; (d) use of non-emphatic, non-contrastive overt subjects; (e) lack of subject-verb inversion in questions; (f) earlier prenuclear peaks – corresponding with higher frequencies of the L+H* pitch accent.

The patterns reported in (a–f) have been explained as the byproduct of phenomena involving high processing demands on the interface between different linguistic modules, which have been shown in a variety of language development studies to be challenging to master in SLA (Sorace 2003 *et seq.*). Along these lines, I analyzed them as *advanced, conventionalized L2 features,* which may be better conceived as the result of *L1 acquisition (nativization) of advanced L2 grammars.*

An investigation on the genesis and evolution of any AHLAs, I believe, should never divorce the linguistic analysis from the sociodemographic one. For this reason, I not only tried to document and explain the nature of CS grammar; rather, I also explored the historical facts that led to its formation. That research indicated that the scenario depicted by McWhorter (2000: ch.2) for Spanish Chocó does not match with its colonial reality. In fact, differently from what McWhorter claimed, this region never received massive importation of African-born slaves. On the other hand, the majority of the blacks who were used in the mining activities of colonial Chocó were *criollo* captives, who, in all likelihood, could already speak vernacular varieties of Spanish before entering the region (Colmenares 1979). Moreover, an analysis of *cuadrilla* dynamics cast light on the living and working conditions of the black miners used in the region. In particular, due to the pragmatic management implemented by the local *administradores de minas*, manumission became common practice, marriage was encouraged, family units preserved, and systematic Christian indoctrination was present. All of these factors favored, in one way or another, the acquisition of Spanish among the *bozales* and the conventionalization of a vernacular form of the language at the community level (Sharp 1976; Cantor 2000).

Particular attention has here been paid to an aspect of European colonization that so far has not received much attention in relation to the development of the Afro-European languages of the Americas: the legal regulation of slavery (law in books) and its actual implementation in colonial society (law in action) (Pound 1910). The potential divergence between legal theory and social practice, in fact, has also been one of the main criticisms of Tannenbaum's (1947) well-known proposal on the supposedly less harsh form of slavery under the Spanish rule. Thus, after summarizing the main points of the LHCG and providing a comparative analysis of colonial slave laws, this work has presented different pieces of historical evidence suggesting that Spanish slavery was not only different in theory from the rest of the forced labor systems implemented by the other European powers; rather, in practice it also appeared to significantly favor the assimilation of black captives into colonial society, and to provide them with incentives to acquire the colonial language.

In resonance with such a debate, colonial Chocó, a region often mentioned in relation to its isolation from the rest of Colombia and its lack of legal courts and clerics during the colonial period (Whitten 1974), has here been selected as a "testing ground" for the LHCG. After an analysis of the available information concerning the aforementioned dichotomy between "law in books" and "law in action" (Sharp 1976; Cantor 2000), in line with Tannenbaum's proposal, it has been suggested that Spanish slaves in this colony – and probably also in many other regions of Latin America – benefited from a cultural and legal heritage of slavery, which was missing in other European territories overseas, and which further favored the diffusion of the Spanish language in the region.

To understand how certain linguistic structures came into place, it is of fundamental importance to cast light on the historical contexts in which the languages presenting them developed. For this reason, this study has offered an analysis of CS that is rooted in both linguistic and sociohistorical research. Moreover, it has provided a new perspective for looking at the AHLAs in a broader sense, since it added a legal dimension to the Spanish creole debate. This book represents, therefore, an initial step in the integration of creole studies to other humanities disciplines, in this particular case, to legal history.

This project combines comparative colonial slave law and linguistics to explain why certain colonial societies might have been more conducive to creole formation and/or preservation than others (Sessarego 2017a, 2018a, 2018c). Moreover, an in-depth analysis of certain AHLA structures helped determine whether such phenomena should be characterized as the remaining

Final Considerations

traces of an earlier creole stage, or as the results of advanced second language acquisition strategies, which do not necessarily imply any previous (de)creolization phase (Sessarego 2013a, 2015a; Rao & Sessarego 2016, 2018). The historical information collected by means of interdisciplinary research was key to corroborate the linguistic findings and thus provide a better picture on the origin and evolution of CS.

This research points to a cohesiveness in the humanities that lies in the integration of up-to-date empirically based linguistic research with current legal and historical inquiries on the role played by slaves in colonial societies. The results proceeding from this investigation, as well as the multidisciplinary approach that produced them, can now be applied and tested on other creoles and Afro-European contact varieties. The next step is to compare how different legal systems and sociohistorical conditions may have shaped the languages spoken by other black communities in the Americas; this, in turn, will help us better understand both specific and universal patterns of contact-driven language restructuring.

Appendix

SPANISH VERSION[1]

Real Cédula sobre educación, trato y ocupaciones de los esclavos
Aranjuez, 31 de mayo de 1789
«Real Cédula de Su Majestad sobre la educación, trato y ocupaciones de los esclavos en todos sus dominios de Indias e islas Filipinas, bajo las reglas que se expresan, Madrid, En la Imprenta de la Viuda de Ibarra, año de MDCCLXXXIX.

El Rey. En el Código de las Leyes de Partida y demás Cuerpos de la Legislación de estos Reinos, en el de las de la Recopilación de Indias, Cédulas generales y particulares comunicadas a mis Dominios de América desde su descubrimiento, y en las Ordenanzas, que examinadas por mi Consejo de las Indias, han merecido mi Real aprobación, se halla establecido, observado y seguido constantemente el sistema de hacer útiles a los esclavos, y proveído lo conveniente a su educación, trato, y a la ocupación que deben darles sus Dueños, conforme a los principios y reglas que dictan la Religión, la Humanidad y el bien del Estado, compatibles con la esclavitud y tranquilidad pública; sin embargo, como no sea fácil a todos mis vasallos de América que poseen esclavos Instruirse suficientemente en todas las disposiciones de las Leyes insertas en dichas colecciones, y mucho menos en las Cédulas generales y particulares, y Ordenanzas municipales aprobadas para diversas Provincias; teniendo presente que por esta causa, no obstante lo mandado por mis Augustos Predecesores sobre la educación, trato y ocupación de los esclavos, se han introducido por sus dueños y mayordomos algunos abusos poco conformes, y aún opuestos al sistema de la Legislación, y demás providencias generales y particulares tomadas en el asunto. Con el fin de remediar semejantes desórdenes, y teniendo en consideración, que con la libertad, que para el comercio de negros he concedido a mis vasallos por el artículo primero de la

---

[1] This text has been adapted by Lucena Salmoral (1996b) to align with the current Spanish orthographic system. A digitalized version of the text with original orthographic convention is available here: www.afehc-historia-centroamericana.org/index.php?action=fi_aff&id=1109 (AFEHC 2006).

Real Cédula de veinte y ocho de febrero próximo pasado se aumentará considerablemente el número de esclavos en ambas Américas, mereciéndome la debida atención esta clase de individuos del género humano, en el ínterin que en el Código General que se está formando para los dominios de Indias, se establecen y promulgan las leyes correspondientes a este importante objeto: He resuelto que por ahora se observe puntualmente por todos los dueños y poseedores de esclavos de aquellos dominios la Instrucción siguiente.

CAPÍTULO PRIMERO

Educación

Todo poseedor de esclavos, de cualquier clase y condición que sea, deberá instruirlos en los principios de la Religión Católica, y en las verdades necesarias para que puedan ser bautizados dentro del año de su residencia en mis dominios, cuidando que se les explique la Doctrina Cristiana todos los días de fiesta de precepto, en que no se les obligará, ni permitirá trabajar para sí, ni para sus dueños, excepto en los tiempos de la recolección de frutos, en que se acostumbra conceder licencia para trabajar en los días festivos. En éstos y en los demás en' que obliga el precepto de oír Misa, deberán los dueños de haciendas costear sacerdote que en unos y en otros les diga Misa, y en los primeros les explique la Doctrina Cristiana, y administre los Santos Sacramentos, así en tiempo del cumplimiento de la Iglesia, como en los demás que los pidan o necesiten; cuidando así mismo de que todos los días de la semana, después de concluido el trabajo, recen el Rosario a su presencia, o la de su mayordomo, con la mayor compostura y devoción.

CAPÍTULO II

De los alimentos y vestuario

Siendo constante la obligación en que se constituyen los dueños de esclavos de alimentarlos y vestirlos, y a sus mujeres e hijos, ya sean éstos' de la misma condición, o ya libres, hasta que puedan ganar por si con qué mantenerse, que se presume poderlo hacer en llegando a la edad de doce años en las mujeres, y catorce en los varones; y no pudiéndose dar regla fija sobre la cuantidad y cualidad de los alimentos, y clase de ropas que les deben suministrar, por la diversidad de Provincias, climas, temperamentos y otras causas particulares; se previene, que en cuanto a estos puntos, las Justicias del distrito de las haciendas, con acuerdo del Ayuntamiento, y audiencia del Procurador Síndico, en calidad de Protector de los Esclavos, señalen y determinen la cuantidad y cualidad de alimentos y vestuario, que proporcionalmente, según sus edades y sexos, deban suministrarse a los esclavos por sus dueños diariamente, conforme a la costumbre del País, y a los que comúnmente se dan a los jornaleros, y ropas de que usan los trabajadores libres, cuyo reglamento, después de aprobado por la Audiencia del distrito, se fijará mensualmente en las puertas del Ayuntamiento de las Iglesias de cada pueblo, y en las de los oratorios o ermitas de las haciendas, para que llegue a noticia de todos, y nadie pueda alegar ignorancia.

CAPÍTULO III

Ocupación de los esclavos

La primera y principal ocupación de los Esclavos debe ser la Agricultura y demás labores del campo, y no los oficios de la vida sedentaria; y así, para que los dueños y el Estado consigan la debida utilidad de sus trabajos, y aquellos los desempeñen como corresponde, las Justicias de las ciudades y villas, en la misma forma que en el capítulo antecedente, arreglarán las tareas del trabajo diario de los esclavos proporcionadas a sus edades, fuerzas y robustez: de forma que debiendo principiar y concluir el trabajo de sol a sol, les queden en este mismo tiempo dos floras en el día para que las empleen en manufacturas u ocupaciones que cedan en su personal beneficio y utilidad; sin que puedan los dueños o mayordomos obligar a trabajar por tareas a los mayores de sesenta años, ni menores de diez y siete, como tampoco a las esclavas, ni emplear a éstas en trabajos no conformes con su sexo o en los que tengan que mezclarse con los varones, ni destinar a aquellas a jornaleras; y por los que apliquen al servicio doméstico contribuirán con los dos pesos anuales, prevenidos en el capítulo octavo de la Real Cédula de veinte y ocho de febrero último, que queda citada.

CAPÍTULO IV

Diversiones

En los días de fiesta de precepto, en que los dueños no pueden obligar, ni permitir, que trabajen los esclavos, después que éstos hayan oído Misa y asistido a la explicación de la Doctrina Cristiana, procurarán los amos, y en su defecto los mayordomos, que los esclavos de sus haciendas, sin que se junten con los de las otras, y con separación de los dos sexos, se ocupen en diversiones simples y sencillas, que deberán presenciar los mismos dueños o mayordomos, evitando que se excedan en beber, y haciendo que estas diversiones se concluyan antes del toque de oraciones.

CAPÍTULO V

De las habitaciones y enfermería

Todos los dueños de esclavos deberán darles habitaciones distintas para los dos sexos, no siendo casados, y que sean cómodas y suficientes para que se liberten de las intemperies, con camas en alto, mantas, o ropa necesaria, y con separación para cada uno, y cuando más dos en un cuarto, y destinarán otra pieza o habitación separada, abrigada y cómoda, para los enfermos, que deberán ser asistidos de todo lo necesario por sus dueños; y en caso que éstos, por no haber proporción en las haciendas, o por estar éstas inmediatas a las poblaciones, quieran pasarlos al hospital, deberá contribuir el dueño para su asistencia con la cuota diaria que señale la Justicia, en el modo y forma prevenido en el capítulo segundo; siendo así mismo de obligación del dueño costear el entierro del que falleciere.

CAPÍTULO VI

De los viejos y enfermos habituales

Los esclavos que por su mucha edad o por enfermedad no se hallen en estado de trabajar, y lo mismo los niños y menores de cualquiera de los dos sexos, deberán ser alimentados por los dueños, sin que éstos puedan concederles la libertad por descargarse de ellos, a no ser proveyéndoles del peculio suficiente a satisfacción de la Justicia, con audiencia del Procurador Síndico, para que puedan mantenerse sin necesidad de otro auxilio.

CAPÍTULO VII

Matrimonio de esclavos

Los dueños de esclavos deberán evitar los tratos ilícitos de los dos sexos, fomentando los matrimonios, sin impedir el que se casen con los de otros dueños; en cuyo caso, si las haciendas estuviesen distantes, de modo que no puedan cumplir los consortes con el fin del matrimonio, seguirá la mujer al marido, comprándola el dueño de éste a justa tasación de peritos nombrados por las partes, y por el tercero, que en caso de discordia, nombrará la Justicia; y si el dueño del marido no se conviene en la compra, tendrá la misma acción el que lo fuere de la mujer.

CAPÍTULO VIII

Obligaciones de los esclavos y penas correccionales

Debiendo los dueños de esclavos sustentarlos, educarlos y emplearlos en los trabajos útiles y proporcionados a sus fuerzas, edades y sexos, sin desamparar a los menores, viejos o enfermos, se sigue también la obligación en que por lo mismo se hallan constituidos los esclavos de obedecer y respetar a sus dueños y mayordomos, desempeñar las tareas y trabajos que les señalen, conforme a sus fuerzas, y venerarlos como a Padres de familia, y así el que faltare a alguna de estas obligaciones podrá y deberá ser castigado correccionalmente por los excesos que cometa, ya por el dueño de la hacienda o ya por su mayordomo, según la cualidad del defecto o exceso, con prisión, grillete, cadena, maza o cepo, con que no sea poniéndolo en éste de cabeza, o con azotes que no puedan pasar de veinte y cinco, y con instrumento suave, que no les cause contusión grave o efusión de sangre, cuyas penas correccionales no podrán imponerse a los esclavos por otras personas que por sus dueños o mayordomos.

CAPÍTULO IX

De la imposición de penas mayores

Cuando los esclavos cometieren excesos, defectos o delitos contra sus amos, mujer o hijos, mayordomos u otra cualquiera persona para cuyo castigo y escarmiento no sean suficientes las penas correccionales de que trata el capítulo antecedente, asegurado el delincuente por el dueño o mayordomo de la hacienda, o por quién se halle presente a la comisión del delito, deberá el injuriado o persona que lo represente dar parte a la Justicia, para que con audiencia del dueño del esclavo, si no lo desampara antes de contestar la demanda y no es interesado en la acusación, y en todos casos con el Procurador Síndico, en calidad de Protector de los Esclavos, se proceda con arreglo a lo determinado por las leyes a la formación y determinación del proceso e imposición de la pena correspondiente, según la gravedad y circunstancias del delito; observándose en todo lo que las mismas leyes disponen sobre las causas de los delincuentes de estado libre. Y cuando el dueño no desampare al esclavo y sea éste condenado a la satisfacción de daños y perjuicios en favor de un tercero deberá responder de ellos el dueño, además de la pena corporal, que según la gravedad del delito sufrirá el esclavo delincuente, después de aprobada por la Audiencia del distrito, si fuere de muerte o mutilación de miembro.

CAPÍTULO X

Defectos o excesos de los dueños o mayordomos

El dueño de esclavos o mayordomo de hacienda que no cumpla con lo prevenido en los capítulos de esta Instrucción sobre la educación de los esclavos, alimentos, vestuario, moderación de trabajos y tareas, asistencia a las diversiones honestas, señalamiento de habitaciones y enfermería, o que desampare a los menores, viejos o impedidos; por la primera vez incurrirá en la multa de cincuenta pesos, por la segunda de ciento, y por la tercera de doscientos, cuyas multas deberá satisfacer el dueño aún en el caso de que sólo sea culpado el mayordomo, si este no tuviese de qué pagar, distribuyéndose su importe por terceras partes, denunciador, juez y caja de multas, de que después se tratará. Y en caso de que las multas antecedentes no produzcan el debido efecto y se verificase reincidencia, se procederá contra el culpado a la imposición de otras penas mayores, como inobedientes a mis reales órdenes, y se me dará cuenta con justificación, para que tome la consigna providencia.

Cuando los defectos de los dueños o mayordomos fuesen por exceso en las penas correccionales, causando a los esclavos contusión grave, efusión de sangre, o mutilación de miembro, además de sufrir las mismas multas pecuniarias citadas, se procederá contra el dueño o mayordomo criminalmente, a instancia del Procurador Síndico, substanciando la causa conforme a derecho, y se le impondrá la pena correspondiente al delito cometido, como sí fuese libre el injuriado, confiscándose además el esclavo para que se venda a otro dueño si quedare hábil para trabajar, aplicando su importe a la Caja de multas; y cuando el esclavo quedase inhábil para ser vendido, sin volvérselo al dueño, ni mayordomo que se excedió con el castigo, deberá contribuir el primero con la cuota diaria que se señalase por la Justicia para su manutención y vestuario por todo el tiempo de la vida del esclavo, pagándola por tercios adelantados.

CAPÍTULO XI

De los que injurian a los esclavos

Como sólo los dueños y mayordomos pueden castigar correccionalmente a los esclavos con la moderación que queda prevenida, cualquiera otra persona que no sea su dueño o mayordomo no les podrá injuriar, castigar, herir, ni matar, sin incurrir en las penas establecidas por las leyes para los que cometen semejantes excesos o delitos contra las personas de estado libre, siguiéndose substanciándose y determinándose la causa a instancia del dueño del esclavo que hubiese sido injuriado, castigado o muerto; en su defecto, de oficio, por el Procurador Síndico, en calidad de Protector de los Esclavos, que como tal Protector, tendrá también intervención en el primer caso, aunque haya acusador.

CAPÍTULO XII

Lista de esclavos

Los dueños de esclavos anualmente deberán presentar lista firmada y jurada a la Justicia de la ciudad o villa en cuya jurisdicción se hallen situadas sus haciendas, de los esclavos que tengan en ellas, con distinción de sexos y edades, para que se tome razón por el Escribano de Ayuntamiento en un libro particular que se formará para este fin, y que se conservará en el mismo Ayuntamiento con la lista presentada por el dueño, y éste, luego que se muera o ausente alguno de la hacienda, y dentro del término de tres días, deberá dar parte a la Justicia para que con citación del Procurador Síndico se anote en el libro, a fin de evitar toda sospecha de haberle dado muerte violenta; y cuando el dueño faltare a este requisito, será de su obligación justificar plenamente o la ausencia del esclavo o su muerte natural, pues de lo contrario se procederá a instancia del Procurador Síndico a formarle la causa correspondiente.

CAPÍTULO XIII

Modo de averiguar los excesos de los dueños o mayordomos

Las distancias que median de las haciendas a las poblaciones; los Inconvenientes que se seguirían de que con el pretexto de quejarse se permitiese a los esclavos que saliesen de aquellas sin cédula del dueño o mayordomo, con expresión del fin de su salida, y las justas disposiciones de las Leyes para que no se auxilie, proteja y oculte a los esclavos fugitivos, precisa a facilitar los medios más proporcionados a todas estas circunstancias para que se puedan adquirir noticias del modo con que se les trata en las haciendas, siendo uno de éstos, que los eclesiásticos que pasen a ellas a explicarles la Doctrina y decirles Misa se puedan instruir por sí y por los mismos esclavos del modo de proceder de los dueños o mayordomos, y de cómo se observa lo prevenido en esta Instrucción, para que dando noticia secreta y reservada al Procurador Síndico de la Ciudad o Villa respectiva, promueva el que se indague si los amos o mayordomos faltan en todo, o en parte, a sus respectivas obligaciones, sin que por defecto de justificación de la noticia o denuncia reservada dada por el eclesiástico, por razón de su ministerio o por queja de los esclavos, quede responsable aquel a cosa alguna, pues su noticia sólo debe servir de fundamento para que el Procurador Síndico promueva y pida ante la Justicia que se nombre un individuo del Ayuntamiento u otra persona de arreglada conducta que pase a la averiguación, formando la competente sumaria y, entregándola a la misma Justicia, substancie y determine la causa, conforme a derecho, oyendo al Procurador Síndico, y dando cuenta en los casos prevenidos por las Leyes, y esta Instrucción a la Audiencia del distrito, y admitiendo los recursos de apelación en los que haya lugar de derecho. Además de este medio convendrá que por la Justicia, con acuerdo del Ayuntamiento y asistencia del Procurador Síndico, se nombre una persona o personas de carácter y conducta, que tres veces en el año visiten y reconozcan las haciendas, y se informen de si se observa lo prevenido en esta instrucción, dando parte de lo que noten, para que actuada la competente justificación, se ponga remedio con audiencia del Procurador Sindico, declarándose también por acción popular la de denunciar los defectos o falta de cumplimiento de todos o cada uno de los capítulos anteriores, y en el concepto de que se reservará siempre el nombre del denunciador, y se le aplicará la parte de multa que se deja señalada, sin responsabilidad en otro caso, que en el de justificarse notoria y plenísimamente que la delación o denuncia fue calumniosa. Y últimamente se declara también que en los juicios de residencia se hará cargo a las Justicias y a los Procuradores Síndicos, en calidad de Protectores de los Esclavos, de los defectos de omisión o comisión en que hayan incurrido por no haber puesto los medios necesarios para que tengan el debido efecto mis reales intenciones, explicadas en esta Instrucción.

CAPÍTULO XIV

Caja de multas

En las ciudades y Villas, que es donde deben formarse los reglamentos citados, y cuyas Justicias y Cabildos se componen de individuos españoles, se hará y tendrá en el Ayuntamiento una arca de tres llaves, de las que se encargarán el Alcalde de primer voto, el Regidor decano y el Procurador Síndico, para custodiar en ella el producto de las multas, penas y condenaciones, que se deben aplicar en toda las clases de causas que procedan de esta Instrucción, invirtiéndose precisamente su producto en los medios necesarios para su observancia en todas sus partes, no pudiéndose sacar de ella maravedíes algunos para otro fin, y con libramiento firmado de los tres claveros, con expresión del destino e inversión, quedando responsables y obligados a reintegrar lo gastado o distribuido en otros fines, para en el caso de que por alguna de estas causas o por otras no se aprueben las cuentas de este ramo por el Intendente de la Provincia, a quién anualmente se le deberán remitir, acompañándole testimonio del producto de las multas y de su inversión, con los documentos justificativos de cargo y data.

Para que tengan el debido y puntual cumplimiento todas las reglas prescritas en esta Instrucción derogo cualesquiera leyes, cédulas, reales órdenes, usos y costumbres que se opongan a ellas; y mando a mi Consejo Supremo de las Indias, Virreyes, Presidentes, Audiencias, Gobernadores, Intendentes, Justicias, Ministros de mi Real Hacienda y a cualquiera otros tribunales a quienes corresponda o puedan corresponder, que guarden, cumplan, hagan guardar, cumplir y ejecutar cuanto en esta mi Real Cédula se previene, que así es mi voluntad. Dada en Aranjuez a treinta y uno de mayo de mil setecientos ochenta y nueve. Yo El Rey»

ENGLISH VERSION

Royal Decree on the education, treatment, and occupations of slaves

Aranjuez, May 31st, 1789

≪Royal Decree of His Majesty on the education, treatment, and occupations of the slaves in all of his dominions of the Indies and Philippine Islands, and their stated regulations, Madrid, In the Printing House of the Widow of Ibarra, in the year 1789.

The King. In the Decree of the *Leyes de Partida* and other Bodies of Legislation in these Kingdoms, in the laws of the *Recopilación de Indias* (Compilation of the Laws of the Indies), general and particular Decrees circulated among my Dominions of America since its discovery, and in the Ordinances, which, having been examined by my Advisor in the Indies, have merited my Royal approval, finds it to be established, observed, and consistently followed that the system of making slaves useful, and to be well-provided for their education, treatment, and occupation that their Owners should give them in accordance with the principles and regulations dictated by Religion, Humanity, and the good of the State, is compatible with slavery and public tranquility; nevertheless, as it is not likely to be easy for all of my vassals in America who possess slaves to be sufficiently Instructed in all of the regulations of the Laws included in said collections, and much less in the general and particular Decrees, and municipal Ordinances approved for various Provinces; keeping in mind that for this reason, in spite of the mandates of my August Predecessors regarding the education, treatment, and occupation of slaves, some abuses in little agreement with, and even in opposition to, the system of Legislation and other general and particular rulings on the matter have been introduced by their owners and overseers. Taking into consideration that, with the liberty I have granted to my vassals for the trade of blacks in the first article of the Royal Decree of the past 20th of February, the number of slaves in both Americas will soon increase considerably, which warranted my attention to this class of individuals of the human race, in the interim, in the General Code (*Código General*) that is being created for the dominion of the Indies. With the intention of resolving such inconsistencies, laws corresponding to this important object have been established and promulgated: I have determined that for the moment the following Instructions be punctually observed by all owners and possessors of slaves in those dominions.

Chapter One

Education

All owners of slaves, of whatever class and condition, will instruct them in the principles of the Catholic Religion, and in the truths necessary for their baptisms within the first year of their residence in my dominions, being careful to explain to them the Christian Doctrine on all holy days of obligation, during which time they will not be obligated, nor permitted, to work for themselves nor for their masters, except during the fruit harvest, when it is customary to grant a license to work on holidays. On those days and others in which they are obligated to hear Mass, the owners of *haciendas* should employ a priest who will say Mass on these days and others and that on the first days teach them the Christian Doctrine, and administer the Holy Sacraments, both during times required by the Church and during times in which they request or need them; and being careful that every day of the week, after the work has been completed, they say the Rosary in their presence, or that of their overseer, with the utmost composure and devotion.

Chapter Two

On food and clothing

Being constant the obligation that the owners of slaves have regarding dressing and feeding them and their wives and children, being the wives and children of the same condition or now free, until they can earn enough to support themselves, which is presumed to be possible at twelve years of age for the women and fourteen for males; and not being able to give a fixed rule on the quantity and quality of the food and types of clothes that must be provided, given the diversity of Provinces, climates, temperatures and other particular causes; it is anticipated that regarding those items, the district Justices in the *haciendas*, in agreement with the Local Government (*Ayuntamiento*) and in the audience of the Court-Appointed Prosecutor (*Procurador Síndico*), in the role of Protector of the Slaves, will determine and decide the quantity and quality of food and clothing, which in proportion to their ages and sexes, must be given to the slaves by their owners daily, in agreement with that which is given to day laborers (*jornaleros*) and clothing used by free workers, those rules, after being approved by the district's Audience, will be placed on the Announcement doors of the Churches of each town and in the chapels and shrines of the *haciendas*, so that all take notice of this and no one can claim ignorance.

Chapter Three

Occupation of the slaves

The first and principal occupation of the Slaves must be Agriculture and other labors of the field, and not the trades of sedentary life; and so, in order that the owners and the State obtain the owed usefulness of their work, and that they perform their work as they should, the Justices of cities and villas, in the same manner as in the previous chapter, will arrange the tasks of daily work of the slaves in regards to their ages, strength and complexion: in such a way that starting and concluding their work from sunrise to sunset, they have in this same time two hours during the day to employ them in manufacture or occupations that aid them in their own personal benefit and usefulness; without allowing owners or overseers to force work on people older than sixty years of age nor younger than seventeen, as well as the female slaves, nor employ them in jobs not in accordance to their sex or where they have to mix with the males, nor destine them as daily laborers; and for those used in domestic service, the owners will contribute with two pesos a year, as provided in the eighth chapter of the Royal Decree of the past 28th of February, which has been stated.

Chapter Four

Entertainment

On holy days of obligation – when the owners cannot force, nor allow, that the slaves work, after they have heard Mass and attended the explanation of the Christian Doctrine – the owners will make sure, and the overseers in their absence, that the slaves of their *haciendas* – without them mingling with the slaves of other *haciendas*, and with separation of the sexes – occupy themselves in simple and plain entertainments, which the owners or overseers must witness, preventing them from excessive drinking, and allowing these entertainments to be concluded before the call to prayers.

Chapter Five

On shelter and healthcare

All the owners of slaves must give them separate rooms for the two sexes, when not married, and that these be comfortable and sufficiently safe from the elements, with high beds, covers, or enough clothing, and with separation for each one when there are more than two per room, and another room or shelter separated, protected and comfortable, for the sick, who must be assisted in all that is required by their owners; and in case that the owners, for not having space, or for being the *haciendas* near settlements, want to transfer them to the hospital, the owner must contribute with the daily stipend stated by the Justice for their living expenses, in the form and manner stated in the second chapter; being inasmuch the owner's obligation to pay for the burial in case the slave dies.

Chapter Six

On the old and constantly sick

The slaves who because of their old age or sickness are not in a state for working, likewise for children and minors of either of the two sexes, must be fed by the owners, without the owners being allowed to free them in order to get rid of them, unless they provide them with their own private purse which should be satisfactory to the Justice, with the audience with the Court-Appointed Prosecutor, so that they can support themselves without other assistance.

Chapter Seven

Marriage of slaves

The owners of slaves will prevent illicit behaviors between the two sexes, encouraging marriages, without preventing that they marry slaves from other owners; in such case, if the *haciendas* were far from each other, so that the spouses could not fulfill the objective of marriage, the woman would follow the husband, the owner buying her at just appraisal by experts named by both parties, and a third one in case of disagreement, named by the Justice; and if the owner of the husband does not agree on the purchase, the same action will be taken by the owner of the wife.

Chapter Eight

Obligations of the slaves and correctional penalties

Having the owners the obligation to the slaves of supporting them, educate them and employ them in labors useful and proportionate to their strengths, ages and sexes, without abandoning minors, the old or sick, it is followed by the obligation of the slaves to obey and respect their owners and overseers, to carry out tasks and labors that are indicated to them, in accordance to their strengths, and revere them as their Parents, and he who fails in any of these obligations can and must be punished correctionally for the excesses committed, either by the owner of the *hacienda* or their overseer, according to the nature of the offense or excess, with prisons, shackles, chains, clubs, or stocks, as long as it does not mean to put him upside down, or with more than twenty-five lashes, and with a soft instrument, that does not cause serious contusion or bloodshed, and such correctional penalties will not be imposed on slaves by people other than their owners or overseers.

Chapter Nine

On the imposition of harsher punishment

When the slaves commit excesses, offenses or crimes against their owners, wife or children, overseers or against another person for which punishment and chastisement were not enough with the correctional penalties that the previous chapter states, once the delinquent is secured by the owner or the *hacienda*'s overseer, or by whom was present during the commission of the crime, the affected or the person who represents them shall report it to Justice, so that with audience with the owner of the slave, if the owner does not abandon him before answering the claim and is not interested in the accusation, and in all cases with the Court-Appointed Prosecutor, in the role of Protector of the Slaves, proceedings are in accordance with what is stated by the laws in the formation and determination of the process and imposition of the corresponding sentence, in accordance with the crime's seriousness and circumstance; observing all in what the same laws decree about the cases of the free delinquents. And, when the owner does not abandon the slave and the slave is condemned to the satisfaction of damage and detriment in favor of a third party the owner must respond to the third party, in addition to the corporal punishment, that according to the crime's gravity the delinquent will suffer, after it being approved by the district's Audience, if it were death or amputation of a limb.

Chapter Ten

Offenses or excesses of the owners and overseers

The owner of slaves or the *hacienda*'s overseer who does not obey what is stated in the chapters of this decree about the education of the slaves, food, clothing, labor and task distribution, help to provide honest entertainment, provide room and healthcare, or who abandons minors, the old or sick; for the first time the owner will be fined fifty pesos, for the second time one hundred, and for the third two hundred, fines that the owner must pay even in the case that the overseer is the only one to blame, if he the overseer did not have the funds, distributing the amount in three parts, to the accuser, judge and Bank of Fines (*Caja de multas*) which will be explained later. In the case that the previous fines do not produce the expected result and reoccurrence is verified, it will be proceeded to impose other harsher penalties against the person found guilty, as disobedience to my royal orders, and an account will be given to me with justification, so that appropriate measures are taken.

When the defects of the owners or overseers were in excess of the correctional penalties, causing the slaves serious contusion, bloodshed, or mutilation of a limb, in addition to suffering the stated pecuniary fines, criminal procedures will be undertaken against the owner or overseer, at the request of the Court-Appointed Prosecutor, stating the case in agreement to law, the sentence corresponding to the crime committed will be imposed, as if the injured was free, in addition to confiscating the slave in order to be sold to another owner if he the slave were able to work, giving his cost to the Bank of Fines; and when the slave was unable to be sold, without returning him to the owner or the overseer that exceeded the punishment, the former should contribute a daily allowance as stated by the Justice for living expenses and clothing for the rest of the life of the slave, paying it in advance in thirds.

Chapter Eleven

On those who injure slaves

Since only the owners and overseers are allowed to correctionally punish the slaves with the moderation that has been stated, any other person who is not their owner or overseer will not injure, punish, hurt, or kill, without incurring in the sentences established by the laws for those who commit such excesses or crimes against free people, by following, substantializing and determining the case upon request of the owner of the slave who had been injured, punished or killed; in its defect, *ex officio*, by the Court-Appointed Prosecutor, in the role of Protector of the Slaves, and that said Protector, will also have intervention in the first case, even if there is an accuser.

Chapter Twelve

List of slaves

Annually, the owners of slaves will present a list, signed and sworn to the Justice of the city or villa in the jurisdiction where the *hacienda* is situated, of the slaves therein, with distinction of sex and age, so that the Scribe of the Local Government (*Ayuntamiento*) in a particular book that will be created for this matter, and that will be kept in the same Local Government with the list presented by the owner, and the owner, after anyone dies or is absent from the *hacienda*, and within three days, must report it to the Justice, so that with the official summons of the Court-Appointed Prosecutor it is written in the book, so that any suspicion of having violently killed the slave is avoided; and when the owner does not comply with this requirement, it is his obligation to completely justify either the absence of the slave or his natural death, or on the contrary upon request of the Court-Appointed Prosecutor procedure will follow the corresponding legal case.

Chapter Thirteen

A way to discover the excesses of the owners and overseers

The distances between the *haciendas* and the settlements; the inconveniences that would follow that, with the pretext of complaining, the slaves were permitted to leave the *haciendas* without a letter from the owner or overseer with the express permission of their exit, and the fair dispositions of the Laws so that escaped slaves are not helped, protected or hidden, require facilitation of a means more proportioned to all these circumstances so that news about how the slaves are treated in the *haciendas* can be acquired.

One of these being that the priests who go to the *haciendas* to explain the Doctrine and celebrate Mass can instruct themselves and through the slaves on the way the owners and overseers proceed, and how the rules of this Instruction are kept, so that giving secret and reserved notice to the Court-Appointed Prosecutor of the respective City or Villa, they promote inquiries with respect to whether the owners and overseers fail to uphold, in totality or in part, their respective obligations, without lack of justification of the notice or report given by the priest, by cause of his ministry or by complaints of the slaves, the priest to be responsible to any, since his notice should only be a foundation in order that the Court-Appointed Prosecutor promotes and asks the Justice that an individual from the Local Government (*Ayuntamiento*) or another person of proven conduct be named to conduct investigation, forming the competent summary and, giving it to the Justice, so it substantiates and determines the hearing, in conformity to the law, and abiding to the Court-Appointed Prosecutor, and taking notice in the cases stated by the Laws, and this Instruction to the district's Audience, and admitting the appellation resources in existence by Law.

In addition to these means, it will be established that, in agreement with the Local Government and assistance of the Court-Appointed Prosecutor, a person or persons of good character and conduct be named by the Justice, who will visit and examine the *haciendas* three times a year, and inform themselves if they can observe what is stated in this Instruction, reporting what they note, so that using competent justification, remedies are sought with an audience with the Court-Appointed Prosecutor, being declared by popular action [i.e., *ex officio*] to denounce the offenses or lack of obedience to each and every one of the previous chapters, and in the concept that the name of the accuser will always be reserved, and that the stated fine will be applied, without any other responsibility, in being proven notoriously and thoroughly that the accusation or denunciation was libelous.

And finally it is also declared that in their residency judgments the Justices and Court-Appointed Prosecutors will be in charge, in the role of Protector of the Slaves, of the errors of omission or commission in which they have incurred for not having taken the means necessary so that my Royal intentions have the proper effect, as explained in this Instruction.

Chapter Fourteen

The bank of fines

In the cities and towns, where the stated regulations are to be formed, and which Justices and Courts are composed of Spanish individuals, there will be made and held in the Local Government a chest with three keys, of which will be in charge the *Alcalde* of the first vote (Magistrate), the eldest *Regidor* (Alderman) and the Court-Appointed Prosecutor, to guard in it the product of the fines, penalties and sentences, that must be applied in all manner of cases that follow this Instruction, investing the product of the fines precisely in the means for the observance in all of its parts of the laws in the Instruction, not being allowed to extract from it any *maravedies*[2] at all for another purpose, and with deliverance signed by the three key-holders, with expressed use and investment, being held responsible and obligated to repay what is spent or distributed for other purposes, in case that for any of these or other causes the calculations of this branch are not approved by the *Intendente de Provincia* (Governor of the Province), to whom the fines will be remitted annually, accompanied by testimony of the product of the fines and their investment, with the document justifying roles and data.

In order that all the rules prescribed in this Instruction have the proper and accurate compliance, I revoke any laws, bonds, royal orders, customs and traditions that oppose them; and I order my Supreme Council of the Indies, Viceroys, Presidents, Audiences, Governors, Mayors, Justices, [and] Ministers of my Royal Hacienda and any other courts which correspond or can correspond, that they observe, obey, make observe, make obey and execute what this Royal Decree states, that that is my will. In Aranjuez, May 31st, 1789. I, the King≫.

---

[2] Spanish currency used during colonial times.

References

Adger, D. (2006). Combinatorial variability. *Journal of Linguistics*, 42: 503–30.
Adger, D. & J. Smith (2005). Variation and the minimalist program. In Cornips, L. & K. P. Corrigan (eds.), *Syntax and Variation. Reconciling the Biological and the Social*, 149–78. Amsterdam: John Benjamins.
AFEHC (2006). Asociación para el Fomento de los Estudios Históricos en Centroamérica. Available online at www.afehc-historia-centroamericana.org/index.php?action=fi_aff&id=1109
Aguilar, L., De la Mota, C. & P. Prieto (2009). Sp_ToBI training materials. Available online at http://prosodia.upf.edu/sp_tobi
Aguirre Beltrán, G. (1958). *Cuijla: esbozo etnográfico de un pueblo negro*. México, D. F.: Fondo de Cultura Económica.
Albor, H. (1984). Observaciones sobre la fonología del español hablado en Nariño. *El castellano de Nariño*, 33–52. Pasto: Tipografía y Fotograbado «Javier».
Alexiadou, A. (2001). Adjective syntax and noun raising: word order asymmetries in the DP as the result of adjective distribution. *Studia Lingüística*, 55, 3: 217–48.
Alvar, M. (1977). *Leticia: estudios lingüísticos sobre la Amazonia colombiana*. Bogotá: Instituto Caro y Cuervo.
Álvarez Nazario, M. (1974). *El elemento afronegroide en el español de Puerto Rico*. San Juan: Instituto de Cultura Puertorriqueña.
Álvarez, A. & E. Obediente. (1998). El español caribeño: antecedentes sociohistóricos y lingüísticos. In Pearl, M. & A. Schwegler (eds.), *América negra: panorámica actual de los estudios lingüísticos sobre variedades hispanas, portuguesas y criollas*, 40–61. Madrid/Frankfurt: Iberoamericana/Vervuert.
Amastae, J. (1986). A syllable-based analysis of Spanish spirantization. In Jaeggli, O. & C. Silva-Corvalán (eds.), *Studies in Romance Linguistics*, 3–21. Dordrecht: Foris.
Andrés-Gallego, J. (2005). *La esclavitud en la América española*. Madrid: Ediciones Encuentro.
Androutsopoulou, A., Español-Echevarría, M. & P. Prévost (2010). The syntax/morphology interface in Spanish L2 acquisition: focus on quantified DPs. *The Canadian Journal of Linguistics*, 55, 2: 149–80.
Aranovich, R. (2003). The semantics of auxiliary selection in Old Spanish. *Studies in Language* 27, 1: 1–37.
Arboleda, S. (1951). *La república en la América española*. Bogotá: Editorial A.B.C.
Arche, M. & L. Domínguez (2011). Morphology and syntax dissociation in SLA: evidence from L2 clitic acquisition in Spanish. In Galani, A., Tsoulas, G. &

G. Hicks (eds.), *Morphology and its Interfaces*. 291–320. Amsterdam: John Benjamins.
Bailey, B. (1965). Toward a new perspective in Negro English dialectology. *American Speech*, 40: 171–7.
Baker, M. (2008). *The Syntax of Agreement and Concord*. Cambridge: Cambridge University Press.
Bal, W. (1979). *Afro-Romanica Studia*. Albufeira: Poseidon.
Barbosa, P., Kato, M. & M. E. Duarte (2005). Null subjects in European and Brazilian Portuguese. *Journal of Portuguese Linguistics*, 4: 11–52.
Barnes, H. & J. Michnowicz (2013). Peak alignment in semi-spontaneous bilingual Chipilo Spanish. In Carvalho, A. & S. Beaudrie (eds.), *Selected Proceedings of the 6th Workshop on Spanish Sociolinguistics*, 109–22. Somerville, MA: Cascadilla.
Benítez del Cristo, I. (1930). Los novios catedráticos. *Archivo de Folklore Cubano*, 5, 2: 119–46.
Berlin, I. (1997). *Many thousands gone: the first two centuries of slavery in North America*. Cambridge, MA: Harvard University Press.
Bernini, G. (1987a). Le negazioni in arabo dialettale. In Bernini, G. & V. Brugnatelli (eds.), *Atti delta 4a giornata di studi camitosemitici e indeuropei*, 41–52. Milan: Unicopli.
Bernini, G. (1987b). Germanic and (Gallo)Romance negation: an area typology. In Ramat, P. (ed.). *Linguistic Typology*, 172–8. Berlin: Mouton de Gruyter.
Biberauer, Th. (2009). Jespersen off course? The case of contemporary Afrikaans negation. In van Gelderen, E. (ed.), *Cyclical Change*, 91–132. Amsterdam: John Benjamins.
Birdsong, D. (1992). Ultimate attainment in second language acquisition. *Language* 68, 706–55.
Boeckx, C. (2011). Approaching parameters from below. In Di Sciullo, M. & C. Boeckx (eds.), *The Biolinguistics Enterprise: New Perspectives on the Evolution of the Human Language Faculty*, 205–21. Oxford: Oxford University Press.
Borer, H. (1984). *Parametric Syntax. Case Studies in Semitic and Romance Languages*. Dordrecht: Foris.
Boretzky, N. (1983). *Kreolsprachen, Substrate und Sprachwandel*. Wiesbaden: Harrasowitz.
Bouisson, E. (1997). Esclavos de la tierra: los campesinos negros del Chota-Mira, siglos XVII–XX. *Procesos, Revista Ecuatoriana de Historia*, 11: 45–67.
Boxer, C. R. (1962). *The Golden Age of Brazil, 1695–1750: Growing Pains of a Colonial Society*. Berkeley: University of California Press.
Bruhn de Garavito, J. & L. White. (2000). L2 acquisition of Spanish DPs: the status of grammatical features. In Howell, S., Fish, S. & T. Keith-Lucas (eds.), *Proceedings of the 24th Annual Boston University Conference on Language Development*, 164–75. Somerville, MA: Cascadilla.
Bryant, S. (2004). Enslaved rebels, fugitives, and litigants: the resistance continuum in colonial Quito. *Colonial Latin American Review*, 13, 1: 7–46.
Bryant, S. (2005). *Slavery and the context of ethnogenesis: African, Afro-Creoles, and the realities of bondage in the Kingdom of Quito, 1600–1800*. Ph.D. Dissertation. Columbus, OH: The Ohio State University.

References

Bulk, C. van (1952). Languae bantoues. In Meillet A. & M. Cohen (eds.), *Les langues du monde par un groupe de linguistes sous la direction de édition*, 847–904. Paris: Centre National de la Recherche Scientifique.

Burkhardt, P. (2005). *The syntax-discourse interface: representing and interpreting dependency*. Amsterdam: John Benjamins.

Butera, B., Sessarego, S. & R. Rao (2016). Aspects of Afro-Peruvian Spanish prosody. Paper presented at the *Hispanic Linguistic Symposium*. Georgetown University, Washington DC, October 2016.

Cabrera, L. (1976). *Francisco y Francisca: chascarrillos de los negros viejos*. Miami: Editorial C. R.

Camacho, J. (2006). In situ focus in Caribbean Spanish. In Sagarra, N. & A. J. Toribio (eds.), *Selected Proceedings of the 9th Hispanic Linguistics Symposium*, 13–23. Somerville, MA: Cascadilla.

Camacho, J. (2008). Syntactic variation: the case of Spanish and Portuguese subjects. *Studies in Hispanic and Lusophone Linguistics*, 1, 2: 415–33.

Camacho, J. (2013). *Null subjects*. Cambridge: Cambridge University Press.

Cameron, R. (1996). A community-based test of a linguistic hypothesis. *Language in Society*, 25: 61–111.

Camus Bergareche, B. (2006). La expressión de la negación. In Company Company, C. (ed.), *Sintaxis histórica de la lengua española. Parte I: la frase verbal*, 1165–1252. México: FCE, UNAM.

Canfield, L. (1981). *Spanish pronunciation in the Americas*. Chicago: University of Chicago Press.

Cantor, E. (2000). *Ni aniquilados, ni vencidos: los Emberá y la gente negra del Atrato bajo el dominio español*. Bogotá: Instituto Colombiano de Antropología e Historia.

Carstens, V. (2001). Multiple agreement and case-deletion: against Φ-in completeness. *Syntax* 4: 147–63.

Chatelain, H. (1888). *Grammatica elementar do kimbundu ou lingua de Angola*. Genebra: Typ. de C. Schuchardt.

Chaudenson, R. (1992). *Des îles, des hommes, des langues*. Paris: L'Harmattan.

Chaudenson, R. (2001). *Creolization of language and culture*. London: Routledge.

Chela Flores, G. (1986). Las teorias fonologicas y los dialectos del Caribe hispánico. In Núñez Cedeno, R., Paez, I. & J. Guitar (eds.), *Estudios sobre la fonología del español del Caribe*. 21–30. Caracas: Ediciones La Casa Bello.

Chierchia, G. (1998). Reference to kinds across languages. *Natural Language Semantics* 6: 339–405.

Chomsky, N. (1981). *Lectures on Government and Binding*. Dordrecht: Foris.

Chomsky, N. (1995). *The Minimalist Program*. Cambridge, MA: MIT Press.

Chomsky, N. (2000). Minimalist inquiries: the framework. In Roger M., Michaels, D. & J. Uriagereka (eds.), *Step by step: essays on minimalist syntax in honor of Howard Lasnik*. Cambridge, MA: MIT Press.

Chomsky, N. (2001). Derivation by phase. In Kenstowicz, M. (ed.), *Ken Hale: a life in linguistics*, 1–52. Cambridge, MA: MIT Press.

Chomsky, N. & H. Lasnik (1993). The theory of principles and parameters. In Jacobs, J., von Stechow, A., Sternefeld, W. & T. Vennemann (eds.), *Syntax: An International Handbook of Contemporary Research, Vol. 1*, 506–69. Berlin: Walter de Gruyter.

Clements, C. (2009). *The Linguistic Legacy of Spanish and Portuguese*. Cambridge: Cambridge University Press.
Clements, C. & A. Koontz-Garboden (2002). Two Indo-Portuguese creoles in contrast. *Journal of Pidgin and Creole Languages*, 17: 191–236.
Cohen, M. & E. Nagel (1934). *An introduction to logic and scientific method*. London: Routledge.
Colantoni, L. (2011). Broad-focus declaratives in Argentine Spanish contact and non-contact varieties. In Gabriel, C., & C. Lleó (eds.), *Intonational Phrasing in Romance and Germanic: Cross-linguistic and Bilingual Studies*, 183–212. Amsterdam: John Benjamins.
Colantoni, L. & J. Gurlekian (2004). Convergence and intonation: historical evidence from Buenos Aires Spanish. *Bilingualism, Language and Cognition*, 7, 2: 107–19.
Colmenares, G., (1972). *Historia económica y social de Colombia 1.537–1.719*. Ediciones Culturales, Bogotá.
Colmenares, G., (1979). *Historia económica y social de Colombia: Popayán una sociedad esclavista 1680–1800*. Bogotá: La Carreta.
Contreras, H. (1986). Spanish bare NPs and the ECP. In Bordelois, I., Contreras, H. & K. Zagona (eds.), *Generative Studies in Spanish Syntax*, 25–49. Dordrecht: Foris.
Córdova Álvarez, P. (1995). *El habla del Azuay*. Cuenca: Núcleo del Azuay de la Casa de la Cultura Ecuatoriana "Benjamin Carrión."
Coronel Feijóo, R. (1991). *El valle sangriento de los indígenas de la coca y el algodón a la hacienda cañera jesuita, 1580–1700*. Quito: ABYA-YALA.
Correa, A. (2012). *El español hablado en el pacífico de Colombia: dos rasgos fonéticos de presunto sustrato africano*. In Orozco, R. (ed.). *Colombian Varieties of Spanish*. Madrid/Frankfurt: Iberoamericana/Vervuert.
Cowper, E. (2005). The geometry of interpretable features: infl in English and Spanish. *Language*, 81: 10–46.
Crespo, A. (1995). *Esclavos negros en Bolivia*. La Paz: Librería Editorial Juventud.
Cuba, M. (2002). *El castellano hablado en Chincha*. Lima: Talleres Gráficos de Angélica Tapia.
Cuervo, R. J. (1955). *Apuntaciones críticas sobre el lenguaje bogotano con frecuente referencia al de los países de Hispano-América*. Bogotá: Instituto Caro y Cuervo.
Cushner, N. (1980). *Lords of the land: sugar, wine, and the Jesuit estates of coastal Peru*. Albany: State University of New York Press.
Cuza, A., (2013). Crosslinguistic influence at the syntax proper: interrogative subject-verb inversion in heritage Spanish. *International Journal of Bilingualism*, 17: 71–96.
DANE (2005). *Libro Censo Nacional 2005*. Bogotá: Departamento Administrativo Nacional de Estadística.
Davies, M. (2002) *Corpus del Español: 100 million words, 1200s–1900s*. Available online at www.corpusdelespanol.org.
Davis, D. (1966). *The Problem of Slavery in Western Culture*. Ithaca, NY: Cornell University Press.
Delafosse, M. (1931). Afrique occidentale française. In Honotaux, G. & A. Martineau (eds.), *Historie des colonies francaises et de l'expansion de la France dans le monde*, T. IV, 1–365. Paris: Société de l'Historie/Librarie Plon.

Delicado-Cantero, M. & S. Sessarego (2011). Variation and syntax in number expression in Afro-Bolivian Spanish. In Ortiz-López L. (ed.), *Proceedings of the 13th Hispanic Linguistic Symposium*, 42–53. Somerville, MA: Cascadilla.

Díaz-Campos, M. & C. Clements (2005). Mainland Spanish colonies and Creole genesis: the Afro-Venezuelan area revisited. In Sayahi L. & M. Westmoreland (eds.), *Proceedings of the Second Workshop on Spanish Sociolinguistics*, 41–53. Someville, MA: Cascadilla.

Díaz-Campos, M. & C. Clements (2008). A Creole origin for Barlovento Spanish? A linguistic and socio-historical inquiry. *Language in Society*, 37: 351–83.

Díaz Díaz, R. A. (2001). *Esclavitud, región y ciudad*. Bogotá: CEJA.

Dieck, M. (1993). Notas breves sobre el español de Bahía Solano (choco). *Colombia país plurilingüe*, 21–3.

Dilley, L., Shattuck-Hufnagel, S. & M. Ostendorf (1995). Glottalization of Word-Initial Vowels as a function of prosodic structure. *Journal of Phonetics*, 24: 423–44.

Domínguez, L. (2013). *Understanding Interfaces*. Amsterdam: John Benjamins.

Duarte, M. E. (2000). The loss of the "avoid pronoun" principle in Brazilian Portuguese. In Kato, M. & E. Negrão (eds.), *Brazilian Portuguese and the null subject parameter*, 17–36. Madrid/Frankfurt: Iberoamericana/Vervuert.

Eguren, L., Fernández Soriano, O. & A. Mendikoetxea (eds.) (2016). *Rethinking Parameters*. Oxford: Oxford University Press.

Elkins, S. (1959). *Slavery: A Problem in American Institutional and Intellectual Life*. Chicago: University of Chicago Press.

Elordieta, G. (2003). The Spanish intonation of speakers of a Basque pitch-accent dialect. *Catalan Journal of Linguistics*, 2: 67–95.

Escalante, A. (1971). *La minería del hambre: Condoto y la Chocó Pacífico*. Medellín: Ediciones Universidades.

Esling, J., Fraser, K. & J. Harris (2005). Glottal stop, glottalized resonants, and pharyngeals: a reinterpretation with evidence from a laryngoscopic study of Nuuchahnulth (Nootka). *Journal of Phonetics*, 33: 383–410.

Fernández, Francisco. 1987. El negro cheche. In Montes Huidobro (1987). In *Teoría y práctica del catedratismo en los negros catedráticos de Francisco Fernández*, ed. Matías Montes Huidobro. Miami, FL: Miami Editorial Persona.

Ferraz, L. (1978). The creole of São Tomé. *African Studies*, 37: 3–68/235–88.

Flórez, L. (1950). El habla del Chocó. *Thesaurus*, 6: 110–16.

Flórez, L. (1951). *La pronunciación del español en Bogotá*. Bogotá: Instituto Caro y Cuervo.

Flórez, L. (1964). El español hablado en Colombia y su atlas lingüístico: presente y futuro de la lengua española. *Thesaurus*, 27: 268–56.

Flórez, L. (1973). *Las apuntaciones críticas de Cuervo y el español bogotano cien años después*. Bogotá: Instituto Caro y Cuervo.

Flores Galindo, A. (1984). *Aristocracia y plebe: Lima 1760–1830 (Estructura de clases y sociedad colonial)*. Lima: Mosca Azul.

Frampton, J. & S. Gutmann (2000). Agreement is feature sharing. Available online at www.math.neu.edu/ling/pdffiles/agrisfs.pdf.

Franceschina, F. (2002). Case and phi-feature agreement in advanced L2 Spanish grammars. In Foster-Cohen, S., Ruthenberg, T. & M. L. Poschen (eds.), *EUROSLA Yearbook*, 71–86.

References

Franceschina, F. (2005). *Fossilized Second Language Grammars*. Amsterdam: John Benjamins.
Furtado da Cunha, M. A. (2007). Grammaticalization of the strategies of negation in Brazilian Portuguese. *Journal of Pragmatics*, 39: 1638–53.
García Cornejo, R. (2009). La negación y las palabras negativas nunca, ninguno, nada y nadie. *Verba*, 36: 353–95.
García Mayo, M. & R. Hawkins (2009). *The Second Language Acquisition of Articles*. Amsterdam: John Benjamins.
Genovese, E. (1967). *The Political Economy of Slavery: Studies in Economy and Society of the Slave South*. New York: Vintage Books.
Goodall, G. (2004). On the syntax and processing of *Wh*-questions in Spanish. In Schmeiser, B. Chand, V., Kelleher, V. & A. Rodríguez (eds.), *Proceedings of the 23rd West Coast Conference on Formal Linguistics*, 237–50. Somerville, MA: Cascadilla.
Gooden, S., Drayton, K. A. & M. Beckman (2011). Tone inventories and tune-text alignments: prosodic variation in "hybrid" prosodic systems. In Clements, J. C. & S. Gooden (eds.), *Language Change in Contact Languages: Grammatical and Prosodic Considerations*, 137–76. Amsterdam: John Benjamins.
Goodman, M. (1987). The Portuguese element in the American Creoles. In Gilbert, G. (ed.), *Pidgin and Creole Languages: Essays in Memory of John E. Reinecke*, 361–405. Honolulu: University Press of Hawaii.
Granda De, G. (1968). La tipología criolla de dos hablas del área lingüística hispánica. *Thesaurus*, 23: 193–205.
Granda De, G. (1970). Un temprano testimonio sobre las hablas "criollas" en África y América. *Thesaurus*, 25, 1: 1–11.
Granda De, G. (1974). Diatopía, diastratía y diacronía de un fenómeno fonético dialectal en el occidente de Colombia. *Thesaurus*, 29, 2: 221–53.
Granda De, G. (1976). Algunos rasgos morfosintácticos de posible origen criollo en el habla de áreas hispanoamericanas de población negra. *Anuarios de letras*, 14: 5–22.
Granda De, G. (1977). *Estudios sobre un área dialectal hispanoamericana de población negra: las tierras bajas occidentales de Colombia*. Bogotá: Publicaciones del Instituto Caro y Cuervo.
Granda De, G. (1978). *Estudios lingüísticos afrohispánicos y criollos*. Madrid: Gredos.
Granda De, G. (1988a). Los esclavos del Chocó: su procedencia africana (siglo XVIII) y su posible incidencia lingüística en el español del área. *Thesaurus*, 43, 1: 65–80.
Granda De, G. (1988b). *Lingüística e historia: temas afro-hispánicos*. Valladolid: Universidad de Valladolid.
Granda De, G. (1991). *El español en tres mundos: retenciones y contactos lingüísticos en América y África*. Valladolid: Universidad de Valladolid.
Granda De, G. (1994). *Español de América, español de África y hablas criollas hispánicas: cambios, contactos y contextos*. Madrid: Gredos.
Greenberg, J. H. (1963). Some universals of grammar with particular reference to the order of meaningful elements. In Greenberg, J. H. (ed.), *Universals of Language*, 73–113. Cambridge, MA: MIT Press.
Grimshaw, J. & V. Samek-Lodovici (1998). Optimal subjects and subject universals. In Barbosa, P., Fox, D., Hagstrom, P., McGinnis, M. & D. Pesetsky (eds.), *Is the Best*

Good Enough? Optimality and Competition in Syntax, 193–219. Cambridge, MA: MIT Press.
Guerra Rivera, A., Coopmans, P. & S. Baauw (2015). On the L2 acquisition of Spanish subject-verb inversion. *Procedia – Social and Behavioral Sciences*, 173: 37–42.
Guirao, R. (1938). *Obrita de la poesía afrocubana 1928–1937*. Havana: Ucar García.
Gutiérrez-Bravo, R. (2005). *Structural Markedness and Syntactic Structure*. New York: Routlegde.
Gutiérrez-Bravo, R. (2007). Prominence scales and unmarked word order in Spanish. *Natural Language and Linguistic Theory*, 25: 235–71.
Gutiérrez-Bravo, R. (2008). Topicalization and preverbal subjects in Spanish wh-interrogatives. In Bruhn de Garavito, J. & E. Valenzuela (eds.), *Selected Proceedings of the 10th Hispanic Linguistics Symposium*, 225–36. Somerville, MA: Cascadilla.
Gutiérrez-Rexach, J. & S. Sessarego (2011). On the nature of bare nouns in Afro-Bolivian Spanish. In Herschensohn, J. (ed.), *Romance Linguistics 2010*, 191–204. Amsterdam: John Benjamins.
Gutiérrez-Rexach, J. & S. Sessarego (2012). Bare nouns, reference and indefiniteness in a Spanish dialect. In Frath, P., Bourdier, V., Hilgert, E., Bréhaux, K., & J. Dunphy-Blomfield (eds.), *Reference, Consciousness and the Speaking Subject*, 339–50. Reims: Éditions et Presses Universitaires de Reims.
Gutiérrez-Rexach, J. & S. Sessarego (2014a). Morphosyntactic variation and gender agreement in three Afro-Andean dialects. *Lingua*, 151, Part B, 142–61.
Gutiérrez-Rexach, J. & S. Sessarego (2014b). N-Drop parallelisms in Afro-Bolivian Spanish and Standard Spanish: a microparametric account. In Orozco, R. (ed.). *New Directions in Hispanic Linguistics*, 188–216. Newcastle: Cambridge Scholars Publishing.
Guy, G. (1981). *Linguistic variation in Brazilian Portuguese: aspects of the phonology, syntax, and language history*. Ph.D. dissertation, University of Pennsylvania.
Guy, G. (2004). Muitas linguas: the linguistic impact of Africans in colonial Brazil. In Curto, J. C. & P. E. Lovejoy (eds.), *Enslaving connections: changing cultures of Africa and Brazil during the era of slavery*, 125–37. New York: Humanity Books.
Günther, W. (1973). *Das portugiesische Kreolisch der Ilha do Príncipe*. Marburg: Im Selbstverlag.
Hansen, A. (1991). *Conquest and colonization in the Colombian Chocó, 1510–1740*. Ph.D. dissertation, University of Warwick.
Harley, H. & E. Ritter (2002). Person and number in pronouns: A feature-geometric analysis. *Language*, 78: 482–526.
Herschensohn, J. (2000). *The Second Time around: Minimalism and L2 Acquisition*. Amsterdam: John Benjamins.
Hespanha, A. M. (2003). *Introduzione alla storia del diritto europeo*. Bologna: Il Mulino.
Hoetink, H. (1967). *The Two Variants in Caribbean Race Relations: A Contribution to the Sociology of Segmented Societies*. Cambridge: Cambridge University Press.
Holm, J. (1992). Popular Brazilian Portuguese: a semi-creole. In d'Andrade, E. & A. Kihm (eds.), *Actas do colóquio sobre crioulos de base lexical portuguesa*, 37–66. Lisboa: Colibrí.

Holm, J. (2004). *Languages in Contact: The Partial Restructuring of Vernaculars.* Cambridge: Cambridge University Press.

Holm, J. A. & P. L. Patrick (eds.), (2007). *Comparative Creole Syntax. Parallel Outlines of 18 Creole Grammars.* London: Battlebridge.

Holmberg, A. (2005). Is there a little *pro*? Evidence from Finnish. *Linguistic Inquiry*, 36: 533–64.

Hualde, J. I. (2005). *The sounds of Spanish.* Cambridge: Cambridge University Press.

Hualde, J. I. & A. Schwegler (2008). Intonation in Palenquero. *Journal of Pidgin and Creole Languages*, 23: 1–31.

Huang, Y. (1994). *The Syntax and Pragmatics of Anaphora: A Study with Special Reference to Chinese.* Cambridge: Cambridge University Press.

Hyman, L. (2003). Segmental phonology. In Nurse, D. & G. Philippson (eds.), *The Bantu Languages*, 42–58. London: Routledge.

Ionin, T., & S. Montrul (2010). The role of L1-transfer in the interpretation of articles with definite plurals in L2-English. *Language Learning*, 60, 4: 877–925.

Ionin, T., Ko, H., & K. Wexler (2004). Article semantics in L2-acquisition: the role of specificity. *Language Acquisition*, 12: 3–69.

Isabelli-García, C. (2010). Acquisition of Spanish gender agreement in two learning contexts: study abroad and at home. *Foreign Language Annals*, 43, 2: 289–303.

Jackendoff, R. (1997). *The Architecture of the Language Faculty.* Cambridge, MA: MIT Press.

Jackendoff, R. (2002). *Foundations of Language: Brain, Meaning, Grammar, Evolution.* Oxford: Oxford University Press.

Jacobs, B. (2012). *Origins of a creole: the history of Papiamentu and its African ties.* Berlin: De Gruyter.

Jacquot, A. (1962). Notes sur la phonologie du beembe. *Journal of African Languages*, 5: 232–42.

Jäger, A. (2008). *History of German Negation.* Amsterdam: Benjamins.

Jaeggli, O. (1986). Arbitrary plural pronouns. *Natural Language and Linguistic Theory*, 4: 43–76.

Jaramillo Uribe, J. (1963). *Esclavos y señores en la sociedad colombiana del siglo XVIII.* Bogotá: Universidad Nacional de Colombia.

Jespersen, O. (1917). *Negation in English and Other Languages.* Copenhagen: A.F. Høst & Son.

Jiménez Meneses, O. & E. Pérez Morales (2013). *Voces de esclavitud y libertad. Documentos y testimonios Colombia, 1701–1833.* Bogotá: Lemoine Editores.

Jiménez Sabater, M. (1975). *Más datos sobre el español español en la República Dominicana.* Santo Domingo: Ediciones Intec.

Johnson, J. & E. N. Newport. (1989). Critical period effects in second language learning: The influence of maturational state on acquisition of English as a second language. *Cognitive Psychology*, 21: 60–99.

Kayne, R. (1996). Microparametric syntax: some introductory remarks. In Black, J. & V. Motapanyane (eds.), *Microparametric Syntax and Dialect Variation*, IX–XXVIII. Amsterdam: John Benjamins.

King, J. (1939). *Negro Slavery in the Viceroyalty of New Granada.* Ph.D. Dissertation, University of California Berkeley.

Klein, H. (1967). *Slavery in the Americas: A Comparative Study of Virigina and Cuba*. Chicago: Chicago University Press.

Knaff, C., Sessarego, S., & R. Rao (2018). Future directions in the field: aspects of Afro-Hispanic prosody. In Sessarego, S. (guest ed.) *Current Trends in Afro-Hispanic Linguistics. Lingua Special Issue*, 202, 76–86.

Kohler, K. (2001). Plosive-related glottalization phenomena in read and spontaneous speech. A stød in German? In Grønnum, N. & J. Rischel (eds.), *To Honour Eli Fischer-Jørgensen. Travaux du Cercle Linguistique de Copenhague*, 174–211. Copenhagen: Reitzel.

Konetzke, R. (1953). *Colección de documentos para la historia de la formación social de Hispanoamérica, 1493–1810*. Madrid: Consejo Superior de Investigaciones Científicas.

Ladefoged, P. (1964). *A Phonetic Study of West African Languages*. Cambridge: Cambridge University Press.

Ladefoged, P. (2001). *A Course in Phonetics*. Boston: Heinle & Heinle.

Larrivée, P. & R. Ingham (eds.) (2011). *The Evolution of Negation. Beyond the Jespersen Cycle*. Berlin: De Gruyter Mouton.

Lasnik, H. (2001a). A note on the EPP. *Linguistic Inquiry*, 32: 356–62.

Lasnik, H. (2001b). Subjects, objects, and the EPP. In Davies, W. & S. Dubinsky (eds.), *Objects and Other Subjects: Grammatical Functions, Functional Categories, and Configurationality*, 103–21. Dordrecht: Kluwer Academic Publishers.

Laurence, K. (1974). Is Caribbean Spanish a case of decreolization? *Orbis*, 23: 484–99.

Levaggi, A. (1973). La condición jurídica del esclavo en la época hispánica. *Revista Historia del Derecho*, 1: 83–175.

Lindau, M. (1980). Phonetic differences in Nigerian languages. *UCLA Working Papers in Phonetics*, 51: 105–12.

Lipski, J. (1986). Convergence and divergence in bozal Spanish. *Journal of Pidgin and Creole Languages*, 1: 171–203.

Lipski, J. (1989). *The Speech of the Negros Congos of Panama*. Amsterdam: John Benjamins.

Lipski, J. (1992a). Spontaneous nasalization in the development of Afro-Hispanic language. *Journal of Pidgin and Creole Languages*, 7: 261–305.

Lipski, J. (1992b). El Valle del Chota: enclave lingüístico afroecuatoriano. *Boletín de la Academia Puertorriqueña de la Lengua Española*, 10: 21–36.

Lipski, J. (1993). On the Non-creole Basis for Afro-Caribbean Spanish. Albuquerque, NM: University of New Mexico Press. Available online at www.personal.psu.edu/jml34/noncreol.pdf

Lipski, J. (1994a). *Latin American Spanish*. New York: Longman.

Lipski, J. (1994b). A new perspective on Afro-Dominican Spanish: the Haitian contribution. *LAII Research Paper Series 26*, Albuquerque: University of New Mexico. Available online at www.personal.psu.edu/jml34/afrodom.pdf

Lipski, J. (1994c). El lenguaje afroperuano: eslabón entre Africa y América. *Anuario de Lingüística Hispánica*, 10: 179–216.

Lipski, J. (1995). [round] and [labial] in Spanish and the "free-form" syllable. *Linguistics*, 33: 283–304.

Lipski, J. (1998). El español bozal. In Pearl, M. and A. Schewgler (eds.), *América negra: panorámica actual de los estudios lingüísticos sobre variedades criollas y afrohispanas*, 293–327. Madrid/Frankfurt: Iberoamericana/Vervuert.

References

Lipski, J. (2000) *Spanish-based creoles in the Caribbean*. Available online at www .personal.psu.edu/jml34/ spcreole.pdf
Lipski, J. (2005). *A History of Afro-Hispanic Language: Five Centuries and Five Continents*. Cambridge: Cambridge University Press.
Lipski, J. (2006). Afro-Bolivian Spanish and Helvetia Portuguese: semi-creole parallels. *Papia*, 16: 96–116.
Lipski, J. (2007). Castile and the hydra: the diversification of Spanish in Latin America. Available online at www.personal.psu.edu/jml34/papers.htm
Lipski, J. (2008). *Afro-Bolivian Spanish*. Madrid/Frankfurt: Iberoamericana/Vervuert.
Llorens, E. (1929). *La negación en el español antiguo con referencias a otros idiomas*. Madrid: Anejo XI de la Revista de Filología Española.
Longobardi, G. (1994). Reference and proper names: a theory of N-movement in syntax and logical form. *Linguistic Inquiry*, 25: 609–65.
Lorenzino, G. (1993). Algunos rasgos semicriollos en el español popular dominicano. *Anuario de Lingüística Hispánica*, 9: 111–26.
Lucchesi, D., Baxter, A., & I. Riberio (eds.). (2009). *O português afro-brasileiro*. Salvador: EDUFBA.
Lucena Salmoral, M. (1994). *Sangre sobre piel negra*. Quito: Abya-Yala.
Lucena Salmoral, M. (1995). La esclavitud americana y las partidas de Alfonso X. *Indagación: Revista de Historia y Arte*, 1: 33–44.
Lucena Salmoral, M. (1996a). La instrucción sobre educación, trato y ocupaciones de los esclavos de 1789: una prueba del poder de los amos de esclavos frente a la debilidad de la corona española. *Estudios de Historia Social y Económica de América*, 13: 155–78.
Lucena Salmoral, M. (1996b). El original de la R.C. instrucción circular sobre la educación, trato y ocupaciones de los esclavos en todos sus dominios de indias e Islas Filipinas. *Estudios de Historia Social y Económica de América*, 13: 311–18.
Lucena Salmoral, M. (1999a). El derecho de coartación del esclavo en la América española. *Revista de Indias*, 59: 357–73.
Lucena Salmoral, M. (1999b). *Los códigos negros de la América española*. Alcalá de Henares: Universidad de Alcalá.
Lucena Salmoral, M. (2000a). *Leyes para esclavos: el ordenamiento jurídico sobre la condición, tratamiento, defensa y represión de los esclavos en la América española*. Madrid: Digibis.
Lucena Salmoral, M. (2000b). *Relatos de viajeros europeos en Iberoamérica, s. XV–XX*. Madrid: Digibis.
Lucena Salmoral, M. (2002). *La esclavitud en la América española*. Centro de Estudios Latinoamericanos, Warsaw: Uniwersytet Warszawski.
Lucena Salmoral, M. (2005). *Regulación de la esclavitud negra en las colonias de América Española (1503–1886): documentos para su estudio*. Alcalá de Henares: Universidad de Alcalá.
Macera, P. (1966). *Instrucciones para el manejo de las haciendas jesuítas del Perú, ss. XVII–XVIII*. Lima: Universidad Nacional Mayor de San Marcos.
Malpica de Barca, D. (1890). *En el Cafetal*. Havana: Tipografía de Los niños huérfanos.
Manzini, G. M. (1983). Apuntes acerca del español hablado en el Chocó (Colombia). *Annali dell'Istituto Universitario di Lingue Moderne*, 67: 127–43.
Marrone, M. (2001). *Lineamenti di diritto privato romano*. Turin: Giappichelli Editore.

References

Martohardjono, G. & J. W. Gair. (1993). Apparent UG inaccessibility in SLA:, isapplied principles or principled misapplications? In Eckman, F. R. (ed.), *Conference: linguistics, second language acquisition and speech pathology*, 79–103. Amsterdam: John Benjamins.

Marzahl, P. (1978). *Town in the Empire*. Austin, TX: University of Texas Press.

Mayén, N. (2007). *Afro-Hispanic linguistic remnants in Mexico: the case of the Costa Chica region of Oaxaca*, Ph.D. Dissertation, Purdue University.

McCarthy, C. (2008). Morphological variability in the comprehension of agreement: an argument for representation over computation. *Second Language Research*, 24, 4: 459–86.

McWhorter, J. (1997). *Towards a New Model of Creole Genesis*. New York: Peter Lang.

McWhorter, J. (2000). *The Missing Spanish Creoles. Recovering the Birth of Plantation Contact Languages*. Berkeley: University of California Press.

Megenney, W. (1984a). Traces of Portuguese in three Caribbean creoles: evidence in support of the monogenetic theory. *Hispanic Linguistics*, 1, 2: 177–89.

Megenney, W. (1984b). El habla bozal cubana ¿lenguaje criollo o adquisición imperfecta? *La Torre*, 33, 123: 109–39.

Megenney, W. (1985). La influencia criollo-portuguesa en el español caribeño. *Anuario de Lingüística Hispánica*, 1: 157–80.

Megenney, W. (1986). *El palenquero, un lenguaje post-criollo de Colombia*. Bogotá: Instituto Caro y Cuervo.

Megenney, W. (1990). *África en Santo Domingo: la herencia lingüística*. Santo Domingo: Museo del Hombre Dominicano.

Megenney, W. (1993). Elementos criollo-portugueses en el español dominicano. *Montalbán*, 15, 3–56.

Megenney, W. (1999). *Aspectos del lenguaje afronegroide en Venezuela*. Madrid/Frankfurt: Iberoamericana/Vervuert.

Meiklejohn, N. (1981). The implementation of slave legislation in eighteenth-century New Granada. In Tolpin, R. (ed.). *Slavery and Race Relations in Latin America*, 176–203. Westport, CT: Greenwood Press.

Meisner, C., Stark, E., & H. Völker (eds.) (2014). *Jespersen revisited: negation in Romance and beyond*. Special issue of *Lingua*, 147: 1–86.

Mena Mena, W. (2014). *Características de la entonación en el habla de Quibdó*. MA dissertation, Universidad Nacional de Colombia y Universidad Tecnológica del Chocó.

Michnowicz, J. & H. Barnes (2013). A sociolinguistic analysis of pre-nuclear peak alignment in Yucatan Spanish. In Howe, C., Blackwell, S., & M. Lubbers Quesada (eds.), *Selected Proceedings of the 15th Hispanic Linguistics Symposium*, 221–35. Somerville, MA: Cascadilla.

Mintz, S. (1971). The socio-historical background to pidginization and creolization. In Hymes, D. (ed.). *Pidginization and Creolization of Languages*, 481–98. Cambridge: Cambridge University Press.

Molinelli, P. (1984). Dialetto e italiano: fenomeni di riduzione della negazione. *Revista Italiana di Dialettologia*, 8: 73–90.

Montalbetti, M. (1984). *After binding: On the interpretation of pronouns*. Ph. D. dissertation, MIT Press.

Montes, J. J. (1962). Sobre el habla de San Basilio de Palenque. *Thesaurus*, 17, 1: 446–50.

Montes Giraldo, J. J. (1966). ¿'H' faríngea en Colombia? *Thesaurus*, 21, 2: 341–42.
Montes Giraldo, J. J. (1969). ¿Desaparece la ll de la pronunciación bogotana? *Thesaurus*, 24, 1: 102–4.
Montes Giraldo, J. J. (1974). El habla del Chocó: notas breves. *Thesaurus*, 39, 1: 409–28.
Montes Giraldo, J. J. (1982). El español de Colombia: propuesta de clasificación dialectal. *Thesaurus*, 37, 1: 24–92.
Montrul, S. (2004). *The Acquisition of Spanish*. Amsterdam: John Benjamins.
Montrul, S., Foote, R., & S. Perpiñán (2008). Gender agreement in adult second language learners and Spanish heritage speakers: the effects of age and context of acquisition. *Language Learning*, 58, 3: 503–53.
Montrul, S. & T. Ionin (2010). Transfer effects in the interpretation of definite articles by Spanish heritage speakers. *Bilingualism, Language and Cognition*, 13, 4: 449–73.
Montrul, S. & T. Ionin (2012). Dominant language transfer in Spanish heritage speakers and L2 learners in the interpretation of definite articles. *Modern Language Journal*, 96, 2: 70–94.
Mosquera, S. (2004). *Don Melchor de Barona y Betancourt y la esclavización en el Chocó*. Quibdó: Alto Vouelo Comunicaciones.
Mufwene, S. (1996). The founder principle in creole genesis. *Diachronica*, 13: 83–134.
Mufwene, S. (1994). On decreolization: the case of Gullah. In Morgan, M. (ed.), *Language, Loyalty, and Identity in Creole Situations*, 63–99. Los Angeles: Center for Afro-American Studies.
Mufwene, S. (2010). SLA and the emergence of creoles. *Studies in Second Language Acquisition* 32: 359–400.
Mufwene, S. (2014). Globalisation économique mondiale des XVIIe–XVIIIe siècles, émergence des créoles, et vitalité langagière. In Carpooran, A. (ed.). *Langues créoles, mondialisation et éducation*, 23–79. Vacoas, Mauritius: Éditions le Printemps.
Mufwene, S. (2015). Pidgin and Creole languages. In Wright, J. (ed.). *International Encyclopedia of the Social & Behavioral Sciences*, 2nd edition, Vol 18. 133–45. Oxford: Elsevier.
Murillo Mena, M. E. (2005). *El habla de Quibdó*. Medellín: Ediciones Zuluaga, Ltda.
Murillo Valencia, Y. (2013). *Análisis morfofonológico del habla de los habitantes de los barrios Futuro y Villa España de la zona norte del municipio de Quibdó, Chocó*. MA dissertation, Universidad Nacional de Colombia y Universidad Tecnológica del Chocó.
Naro, A. & M. M. Scherre. (2000). Variable concord in Portuguese: the situation in Brazil and Portugal. In McWhorter, J. (ed.), *Language change and language contact in pidgins and creoles*, 235–55. Amsterdam: John Benjamins.
Naro, A. & M. M. Scherre. (2007). *Origens do português brasileiro*. São Paulo: Parábola.
O'Rourke, E., (2004). Peak placement in two regional varieties of Peruvian Spanish intonation. In Auger, J., Clements, J., & B. Vance (eds.), *Contemporary Approaches to Romance Linguistics*, 321–41. Amsterdam: John Benjamins.
O'Rourke, E. (2005). *Intonation and language contact: a case study of two varieties of Peruvian Spanish*. PhD. dissertation, University of Illinois at Urbana-Champaign.
Ordóñez, F. & A. Olarrea (2006). Microvariation in Caribbean/non-Caribbean Spanish interrogatives. *Probus*, 18: 59–96.

Orozco, R. & G. Guy (2008). El uso variable de los pronombres sujetos: ¿qué pasa en la costa caribe colombiana? In Westmoreland, M. & J. A. Thomas (eds.), *Selected Proceedings of the 4th Workshop on Spanish Sociolinguistics*, 70–80. Somerville, MA: Cascadilla.
Ortiz López, L. (1998). *Huellas etno-sociolingüísticas bozales y afrocubanas*. Frankfurt/Madrid: Vervuert/Iberoamericana.
Ortiz López, L. (2010). *El español y el criollo haitiano. Contacto lingüístico y adquisición de segunda lengua*. Frankfurt/Madrid: Vervuert/Iberoamericana.
Otheguy, R. (1973). The Spanish Caribbean: a creole perspective. In Bailey, C. J. & R. Shuy (eds.), *New Ways of Analyzing Variation in English*, 323–39. Washington, DC: Georgetown University Press.
Pacheco, J. (1962). *Los jesuitas en Colombia*. Bogotá: Eduardus Briceño, S. I.
Páez Acevedo. D. (2009). *Análisis instrumental de las consonantes oclusivas posnucleares seguidas de consonantes en el dialecto del español del Chocó*. B. A. dissertation, Universidad Nacional de Colombia.
Park, S. (2013). Testing the interface hypothesis: acquisition of English articles by Korean L2 learners. In Cabrelli Amaro, J., Judy, T., & D. Pascual y Cabo (eds.), *Proceedings of the 12th Generative Approaches to Second Language Acquisition Conference*, 155–61. Somerville, MA: Cascadilla.
Parkvall, M. (2000). *Out of Africa: African Influences in Atlantic Creoles*. London: Battlebridge Publications.
Peralta Rivera, G. (2005). *El Comercio negrero en América Latina (1595–1640)*. Lima: Universidad Nacional Federico Villarreal Editorial Universitaria.
Perez, D. (2015). Traces of Portuguese in Afro-Yungueño Spanish? *Journal of Pidgin and Creole Languages*, 30: 2, 307–43.
Perl, M. (1982). Creole morphosyntax in the Cuban "habla bozal." *Studii și Cercetări Lingvistice*, 5: 424–33.
Perl, M. (1985). El fenómeno de la descriollización del "habla bozal" y el lenguaje coloquial de la variante cubana del español. *Anuario de Lingüística Hispánica*, 1: 191–202.
Perl, M. (1998). Introduction. In Perl, M. & A. Schwegler (eds.), *América negra: panorámica actual de los estudios lingüísticos sobre variedades hispanas, portuguesas y criollas*, 1–24. Madrid/Frankfurt: Iberoamericana/Vervuert.
Perl, M. & A. Schwegler (eds.) (1998). *América negra: panorámica actual de los estudios lingüísticos sobre variedades hispanas, portuguesas y criollas*. Madrid/Frankfurt: Iberoamericana/Vervuert.
Pesetsky, D. & E. Torrego (2007). The syntax of valuation and the interpretability of features. In Karimi, S., Samiian, V., & W. K. Wilkins, *Phrasal and Clausal Architecture: Syntactic Derivation and Interpretation*, 262–94. Amsterdam: John Benjamins.
Picallo, C. (1991). Nominals and nominalizations in Catalan. *Probus*, 3: 279–316.
Pienemann, M. (1998). *Language Processing and Second Language Development: Processability Theory*. Amsterdam: John Benjamins.
Pienemann, M. (ed.). (2005). *Cross-linguistic Aspects of Processability Theory*. Amsterdam: John Benjamins.

References

Pierrehumbert, J. & D. Talkin (1991). Lenition of /h/ and glottal stop. In Docherty, G. & R. Ladd (eds.), *Papers in Laboratory Phonology II*, 90–117. Cambridge: Cambridge University Press.

Pollard, C. & I. Sag (1994). *Head-Driven Phrase Structure Grammar*. Chicago: The University of Chicago.

Poplack, S. (1980). The notion of the plural in Puerto Rican Spanish: competing contrasts on (s) deletion. In Labov, W. (ed.), *Locating Language in Time and Space*, 55–67. New York: Academic Press.

Porter, R. (1989). *European activity on the Goald Coast, 1620–1667*. Ph.D. dissertation, University of South Africa.

Pound, R. (1910). Law in books and law in action. *American Law Review* 44: 12–36.

Ramat, P., Bernini, G., & P. Molinelli (1986). La sintassi della negazione germanica e romanza. In Lichem, K., Mars, E., & S. Knaller (eds.), *Parallela 2: atti del 3º incontro italoaustriaco di linguisti a Graz*, 237–70. Tübingen: Gunter Narr.

Rao, R. & S. Sessarego (2016). On the intonation of Afro-Bolivian Spanish declaratives: implications for a theory of Afro-Hispanic creole genesis. *Lingua*, 174: 45–64.

Rao, R. & S. Sessarego (2018). Intonation in Chota Valley Spanish: contact-induced phenomena at the discourse/phonology interface. *Studies in Hispanic and Lusophone Linguistics*, 11, 1: 163–92.

Redi, L. & S. Shattuck-Hufnagel (2001). Variation in the realization of glottalization in normal speakers. *Journal of Phonetics*, 29: 407–29.

Reinhart, T. (2006). *Interface Strategies: Reference-Set Computation*. Cambridge, MA: MIT Press.

Restall, M. (2000). Black conquistadors: armed Africans in early Spanish America. *The Americas*, 57, 2: 171–205.

Rickford, J. (2015). The creole origins hypothesis. In S. Lanehart (ed.), *The Oxford Handbook of African American Language*, 35–56. Oxford: Oxford University Press.

Rizzi, L. (1982). *Issues in Italian Syntax*. Dordrecht: Foris.

Rizzi, L. (1996). Residual verb second and the Wh-criterion. In Belletti, A. & L. Rizzi (eds.), *Parameters and Functional Heads*, 63–90. Oxford: Oxford University Press.

Rodríguez de Montes, M. L. (1972). Oclusivas aspiradas sordas en el español colombiano. *Thesaurus*, 27, 3: 583–6.

Rodríguez de Montes, M. L. (1981). *Muestra de literatura oral en Leticia, Amazonas*. Bogotá: Instituto Caro y Cuervo.

Rodríguez Tocarruncho, L. (2010). *La marca de plural y otros aspectos morfológicos y sintácticos del español del Pacífico de Colombia*. Madrid: Consejo Superior de Investigaciones Científicas.

Romero, F. (1987). *El negro en el Perú y su transculturación lingüística*. Lima: Editorial Milla Btres.

Romero, R. & S. Sessarego (2018). Hard come, easy go: linguistic interfaces in Istanbul Judeo-Spanish and Afro-Ecuadorian Spanish. In King, J. & S. Sessarego (eds.), *Language Variation and Contact-Induced Change: The Spanish Language across Space and Time*, 83–110. Amsterdam: John Benjamins.

Rothman, J. (2008). How pragmatically odd! Interface delays and pronominal subject distribution in L2 Spanish. *Studies in Hispanic and Lusophone Linguistics*, 1: 317–39.

Rothman, J., & R. Slabakova (eds.) (2011). Acquisition at the linguistic interfaces. *Lingua* (special issue) 121, 4: 567–687.

Rout, L. (1976). *The African experience in Spanish America: 1502 to the present day*. Cambridge: Cambridge University Press.

Rubio, R. & J. Pine (1998). Subject-verb agreement in Brazilian Portuguese: what low error rates hide. *Journal of Child Language*, 25: 35–59.

Ruiz García, M. (2000). *El español popular del Chocó, Colombia*. Ph.D. Dissertation, University of New Mexico.

Ruiz García, M. (2009). *El español popular del Chocó, Colombia*. Saarbrücken: VDM Verlag Dr. Müller.

Sánchez L. & M. J. Giménez (1998). The L2 Acquisition of definite determiners: from null to overt. *Proceedings of the 22nd Annual Boston University Conference on Language Development*, 640–50. Somerville, MA: Cascadilla.

Sandoval, A. de (1627) [1956]. *De instauranda aethiopum salute. El mundo de la esclavitud negra en América*. Bogotá: Biblioteca de la Presidencia de Colombia.

Schmitt, C. & A. Munn (1999). Against the nominal mapping parameter: bare nouns in Brazilian Portuguese. *Proceedings of NELS*, 29: 1–30.

Schuchardt, H. (1889). Beiträge zur Kenntnis des Kreolischen Romanisch IV. Zum Negerportugiesischen der Ilha do Príncipe. *Zeitschrift für Romanische Philologie*, 13: 461–75.

Schwegler, A. (1983). Predicate negation and word-order change: a problem of multiple causation. *Lingua*, 61: 297–334.

Schwegler, A. (1991a). La doble negación dominicana y la génesis del español caribeño. *Lingüística*, 3: 31–88.

Schwegler, A. (1991b). El español del Chocó. *América Negra*, 2: 85–119.

Schwegler, A. (1991c). Predicate negation in contemporary Brazilian Portuguese: a change in progress. *Orbis*, 34: 187–214.

Schwegler, A. (1993). Rasgos (afro-)portugueses en el criollo del Palenque de San Basilio (Colombia). In Díaz Alayón, C. (ed.), *Homenaje a José Pérez Vidal*, 667–96. La Laguna, Tenerife: Litografía A. Romero SA.

Schwegler, A. (1996). *"Chi ma nkongo" : lengua y rito ancestrales en el Palenque de San Basilio (Colombia)*. Madrid/Frankfurt: Iberoamericana/Vervuert.

Schwegler, A. (1999). Monogenesis revisited: the Spanish perspective. In Rickford J. & S. Romaine (eds.), *Creole Genesis, Attitudes and Discourse*, 235–62. Amsterdam: John Benjamins.

Schwegler, A. (2002). Review of "The Missing Spanish Creoles: Recovering the Birth of Plantation Contact Languages." *Language in Society*, 31: 113–21.

Schwegler, A. (2010). State of the discipline. Pidgin and creole studies: their interface with Hispanic and Lusophone linguistics. *Studies in Hispanic and Lusophone Linguistics*, 3, 2: 431–84.

Schwegler, A. (2014). Portuguese remnants in the Afro-Hispanic diaspora. In Amaral, P. & A. M. Carvalho (eds.), *Portuguese-Spanish Interfaces: Diachrony, synchrony, and contact*, 403–41. Amsterdam: John Benjamins.

References

Schwegler, A. (2018). On the controversial origins of non-canonical Spanish and Portuguese negation: case closed? In Sessarego, S. (guest ed.), *Current Trends in Afro-Hispanic Linguistics* (special issue of *Lingua*), 202, 24–43.

Schwenter, S. (2005). The pragmatics of negation in Brazilian Portuguese. *Lingua*, 115: 1427–56.

Sessarego, S. (2011a). *Introducción al idioma afroboliviano: una conversación con el awicho Manuel Barra*. Cochabamba/La Paz: Plural Editores.

Sessarego, S. (2011b). On the status of Afro-Bolivian Spanish features: decreolization or vernacular universals? In Michnowicz, J. & R. Dodsworth (eds.), *Proceedings of the Fifth Workshop on Spanish Sociolinguistics*, 125–41. Somerville, MA: Cascadilla.

Sessarego, S. (2012a). The contribution of Afro-Hispanic contact varieties to the study of syntactic microvariation. In González-Rivera, M. & S. Sessarego (eds.), *Current Formal Aspects of Spanish Syntax and Semantics*, 229–50. Newcastle: Cambridge Scholars Publishing.

Sessarego, S. (2012b). Non-creole features in the verb system of Afro-Hispanic languages: new insights from SLA studies. *International Journal of Linguistics*, 146–57.

Sessarego, S. (2013a). Afro-Hispanic contact varieties as advanced second languages. *IBERIA*, 5, 1: 96–122.

Sessarego, S. (2013b). *Chota Valley Spanish*. Madrid/Frankfurt: Iberoamericana/ Vervuert.

Sessarego, S. (2013c). On the non-creole bases for Afro-Bolivian Spanish. *Journal of Pidgin and Creole Languages*, 28, 2: 363–407.

Sessarego, S. (2013d). Chota Valley Spanish: a second look at creole monogenesis. *Revista Internacional de Lingüística Iberoamericana*, 22, 2: 129–48.

Sessarego, S. (2013e). Enhancing dialogue between quantitative sociolinguistics and minimalist syntax. *Studies in Hispanic and Lusophone Linguistics*, 5, 2: 79–97.

Sessarego, S. (2014a). *The Afro-Bolivian Spanish Determiner Phrase: A Microparametric Account*. Columbus, OH: The Ohio State University Press.

Sessarego, S. (2014b). On Chota Valley Spanish origin: linguistic and socio-historical evidence. *Journal of Pidgin and Creole Languages*, 29, 1: 86–133.

Sessarego, S. (2014c). Afro-Peruvian Spanish in the context of Spanish Creole genesis. *Spanish in Context*, 11, 3: 381–401.

Sessarego, S. (2015a). *Afro-Peruvian Spanish: Spanish Slavery and the Legacy of Spanish Creoles*. Amsterdam: John Benjamins.

Sessarego S. (2015b). Las lenguas criollas. In Gutiérrez-Rexach, J. (ed.). *Enciclopedia de Lingüística Hispánica*, 685–96. London/New York: Routledge.

Sessarego, S. (2016). On the non-(de)creolization of Chocó Spanish. *Lingua*, 184: 122–33.

Sessarego, S. (2017a). The legal hypothesis of Creole genesis: presence/absence of legal personality, a new element to the Spanish creole debate. *Journal of Pidgin and Creole Languages*, 32, 1: 1–47.

Sessarego, S. (2017b). Chocó Spanish double negation and the genesis of the Afro-Hispanic dialects of the Americas. *Diachronica*, 34, 2: 219–52.

Sessarego, S. (2017c). A feature-geometry account for subject-verb agreement phenomena in Yungueño Spanish. In Colomina-Almiñana, J. (ed.). *Contemporary Studies on*

Theoretical and Applied Linguistics of Spanish Variation, 265–82. Columbus, OH: Ohio State University Press.

Sessarego, S. (2018a). On the importance of legal history to Afro-Hispanic linguistics and creole studies. In Sessarego, S. (guest ed.) *Current Trends in Afro-Hispanic Linguistics* (Special issue) *Lingua*, 202, 13–23.

Sessarego (2018b). *La schiavitù nera nell'America spagnola*. Genoa: Marietti Editore.

Sessarego, S. (2018c). Enhancing dialogue in the field: some remarks on the status of the Spanish creole debate. *Journal of Pidgin and Creole Languages*. 33, 1: 197–203.

Sessarego, S. & L. Ferreira (2016). Spanish and Portuguese parallels: impoverished number agreement as a vernacular feature of two rural dialects. In Sessarego, S. & F. Tejedo (eds.), *Spanish Language and Sociolinguistic Analysis*, 283–304. Amsterdam: John Benjamins.

Sessarego, S. & J. Gutiérrez-Rexach (2011). A minimalist approach to gender agreement in the Afro-Bolivian DP: variation and the specification of uninterpretable features. In De Vogelaer, G. & M. Janse (eds.), *The Diachronic of Gender Marking* (Special issue of *Folia Linguistica*), 45, 2: 465–88.

Sessarego, S. & J. Gutiérrez-Rexach (2012). Variation, universals, and contact-induced change: language evolution across generations and domains. In González-Rivera, M. & S. Sessarego (eds.), *Current Formal Aspects of Spanish Syntax and Semantics*, 251–70. Newcastle: Cambridge Scholars Publishing.

Sessarego, S. & J. Gutiérrez-Rexach (2014). Bare nouns, plurality and (in)-definiteness in Afro Hispanic creoles. *Formal Approaches to Creole Studies 4 (FACS-4)*, Université Paris 8, Paris (France), November 2014.

Sessarego, S. & J. Gutiérrez-Rexach (2015). Nominal ellipses in an Afro-Hispanic language of Ecuador: the Choteño case. In Sessarego, S. & M. González-Rivera (eds.), *New Perspectives on Hispanic Contact Linguistics in the Americas*, 177–93. Madrid/Frankfurt: Iberoamericana/Vervuert.

Sessarego, S. & J. Gutiérrez-Rexach (2018). Afro-Hispanic contact varieties at the interface: a closer look at pro-prop phenomena in Chinchano Spanish. In King, J. & S. Sessarego (eds.), *Language Variation and Contact-Induced Change: The Spanish Language across Space and Time*, 63–82. Amsterdam: John Benjamins.

Sessarego, S. & R. Rao (2016). On the simplification of a prosodic inventory: the Afro-Bolivian Spanish case. In Cuza, A., Czerwionka. L., & D. Olson (eds.), *Inquiries in Hispanic Linguistics*, 171–90. Amsterdam: John Benjamins.

Sessarego, S. & R. Rao (In press). On Chota Valley Spanish declarative intonation: contact-induced phenomena at the discourse/phonology interface. *Studies in Hispanic and Lusophone Linguistics*.

Sharp, W. (1974). Manumission, libres and black resistance: the Colombian Chocó, 1680–1810. In Toplin, B. (ed.), *Slavery and Race Relations in Latin America*, 89–111. New York: Greenwood.

Sharp, W. (1976). *Slavery on the Spanish Frontier*. Norman: University of Oklahoma Press.

Slabakova, R. (2008). *Meaning in the Second Language*. Mouton de Gruyter, Berlin.

Slabakova, R. (2009). What is easy and what is hard to acquire in a second language? In Bowles, M., Ionin, T., Montrul, S., & A. Tremblay (eds.), *Proceedings of the 10th*

References

Generative Approaches to Second Language Acquisition Conference, 280–94. Somerville, MA: Cascadilla.

Sorace, A. (2000). Syntactic optionality in non-native grammars. *Second Language Research*, 16, 93–102.

Sorace, A. (2003). Near-nativeness. In Doughty, C. & M. Long (eds.), *The Handbook of Second Language Acquisition*, 130–53. Oxford: Blackwell Publishers.

Sorace, A., (2005). Selective optionality in language development. In Cornips, L. & K. Corrigan (eds.), *Syntax and Variation: Reconciling the Biological and the Social*, 55–80. Amsterdam: John Benjamins.

Sorace, A., & L. Serratrice (2009). Internal and external interfaces in bilingual language development: beyond structural overlap. *International Journal of Bilingualism*, 13, 2: 195–210.

Stevenson, W. B. (1828). *Voyage en Araucanie, au Chili, au Pérou et dans la Colombie, ou relation historique et descriptive d'un séjour de vingt ans dans l'Amérique du Sud, suivie d'un précis des révolutions des colonies espagnoles de l'Amérique du Sud.* Paris: Librairie universelle de P. Mongie.

Stolz, T. (1987). *In dubio pro substrato: ein Einblick in die Negation in portugiesisch-basierten Kreols.* Duisburg: Linguistic Agency of the University of Duisburg.

Suñer, M. (1983). "proarb." *Linguistic Inquiry*, 14: 188–91.

Suñer, M. (1994). V-movement and the licensing of argumental wh-phrases in Spanish. *Natural Language and Linguistic Theory*, 12: 335–72.

Tagliamonte, S. (2006). *Analyzing sociolinguistic variation*. Cambridge: Cambridge University Press.

Tannenbaum, F. (1947). *Slave and Citizen*. New York: Vintage Books.

Tavares, J. (1934). *Gramática da língua do Congo*. Luanda: Imprensa Nacíonal da Colonia de Angola.

Taylor, D. (1961). New languages for old in the West Indies. *Comparative Studies in Society and History*, 3: 277–88.

Thompson, R. W. (1961). A note on some possible affinities between the creole dialects of the old world and those of the new. In Le Page R. (ed.), *Creole Language Studies*, 2: 107–13.

Toribio, A. J. (2000). Setting parametric limits on dialectal variation in Spanish. *Lingua*, 110: 315–41.

Torrego, E. (1984). On inversion in Spanish and some of its effects. *Linguistic Inquiry*, 15, 102–29.

Tsurska, O. (2009). The negative cycle in Early and Modern Russian. In van Gelderen, E. (ed.), *Cyclical Change*, 73–90. Amsterdam: John Benjamins.

Valente, J. F. (1964). *Gramática umbundu: a lingua do centro de Angola*. Lisboa: Junta de investigações do Ultramar.

Valentín-Márquez, W. (2006). La oclusión glotal y la construcción lingüística de identidades sociales en Puerto Rico. In Sagarra, N. & A. J. Toribio (eds.), *Selected Proceedings of the 9th Hispanic Linguistics Symposium*, 326–41.

Valkhoff, M. (1966). *Studies in Portuguese and Creole*. Johannesburg: Witwatersrand University Press.

Vázquez Cuesta, P. & M. A. Mendes da Luz (1971). *Gramática portuguesa. Vols. 1–2*. Madrid: Gredos.

Vega, L. de. (1893). *Obras de Lope de Vega*. Madrid: Real Academia Española.

Villa-García, J. (2015). *The Syntax of Multiple-que Sentences in Spanish: Along the Left Periphery*. Amsterdam: John Benjamins.

Voorhoeve, J. (1953). *Voorstudies tot een beschrijving van het Sranan Tongo*. Amsterdam: Noord-Hollandsche U.M.

Watson, A. (1989). *Slave law in the Americas*. Athens: University of Georgia Press.

West, R. (1949). *The Mining Community on Northern New Spain*. Berkeley: University of California Press.

West, R. (1953). *Colonial Placer Mining in Colombia*. Baton Rouge: Louisiana State University Press.

West, R. (1957). *The Pacific Lowlands of Colombia*. Baton Rouge: Louisiana State University.

Whinnom, K. (1965). Origin of European-based creoles and pidgins. *Orbis*, 14: 510–27.

White, L. (1992). Subjacency violations and empty categories in L2 acquisition. In Goodluck, H. & M. Rochement (eds.), *Island Constraints*, 445–64. Dordrecht: Kluwer.

White, L. & A. Juffs. (1998). Constraints on wh-movement in two different contexts of non-native language acquisition: competence and processing. In Flynn, S., Martohardjono, G., & W. O'Neil (eds.), *The Generative Study of Second Language Acquisition*, 111–29. Mahwah, NJ: Lawrence Erlbaum.

White, L., Valenzuela, E., Kozlowska–Macgregor, M. & Y.-K. I. Leung. (2004). Gender and number agreement in nonnative Spanish. *Applied Psycholinguistics*, 25: 105–33.

Whitten, N. (1974). *Black Frontiersmen*. New York: Wiley.

Winks, R. (ed.) (1972). *Slavery: A Comparative Perspective*. New York: New York University Press.

Zamora Munne, J. & J. Guitart (1982): *Dialectología hispanoamericana: teoría, descripción, historia*. Salamanca: Ediciones Almar.

Index

abolition, 10, 127, 144, 147, 177
acculturation, 130, 141, 145, 186
Afro-Bolivian Spanish. *See* Bolivia
Afro-Cuban Spanish. *See* Cuba
Afro-Ecuadorean Spanish. *See* Ecuador
Afrogenesis, 3, 8, 38–41, 44, 47, 74, 127, 147, 150, 190
Afro-Panamanian Spanish. *See* Panama
Afro-Peruvian Spanish. *See* Peru
alcabala, 133, 172–173
almorjarifazgor, 133
Andean Highlands, 4
Antilles, 7, 8, 25, 30–31, 35, 151, 177, 191
Antioquia, 49, 58, 127, 128, 133
asientos, 38, 133, 137–139
assimilation, 192
Audiencia de Buenos Aires, 176
Audiencia de Santa Fe, 128

Bantu, 35, 58, 69, 122
Barlovento Spanish, 31, 44
Bolivia, 5, 15, 31, 44, 86, 103, 108, 122, 123, 188
bottleneck of acquisition, 114
Brazil, 28, 160
Brazilian Portuguese, 19, 35, 74, 76, 82, 88, 89, 91, 95, 114

Cali, 127
capataces, 141
Cartagena, 25–29, 35, 37–38, 52, 128, 133, 137–139, 173
Catholic Church, 40, 46, 153, 154, 160–161, 179, 181, 183, 185, 186, 188
Chincha, 8, 38, 44, 86, 141
Chocoanos, 4, 5, 67
Chota Valley, 8, 15, 32, 34, 38, 39, 40, 44, 63, 97
Christian doctrine, 166, 203, 204, 208
CJC. *See Corpus Juris Civilis*
coartación, 31, 155, 164, 171–174, 175
Code Noir, 157, 163

Company of Jesus, 11, 34, 37, 41, 142, 183, 184, 188
complaints, 163, 168–170, 208
Consejo de Indias, 170, 172, 178, 179
contact vernacular, 5, 38, 135, 190
Corpus Juris Civilis, 9, 45–47, 149, 151, 159
Cuba, 8, 17, 21, 28, 29, 32, 34–36, 57, 86, 90, 95, 162, 169–171
Cuban (Bozal) Spanish. *See* Cuba

decree, 163, 164, 170
decreolization, 3, 8, 10–15, 25, 30, 31, 36, 47, 54, 68, 74, 79, 89, 95, 99, 103–106, 107, 127, 139, 146–148, 150, 190
Dominican Republic, 8, 17, 28, 29, 89, 94, 114, 120
Dominican Spanish. *See* Dominican Republic
Dutch West India Company, 158

Ecuador, 5, 8, 9, 15, 17, 25, 32, 34, 39, 40, 44, 97, 108, 142, 181, 188
education, 4, 18, 31, 58, 78, 143, 147, 150, 152, 156, 162, 166, 180, 183, 186, 188, 191, 202–203
England, 155, 159, 162

fieldwork, 4, 74
Founder Principle, 135
France, 157, 159, 162
Franciscans, 129, 131

habla bozal, 30, 43, 60, 147
Haiti, 1, 10, 35
Haitian Creole. *See* Haiti
Haitian French. *See* Haiti
Hispaniola, 35, 135, 163

informants, 4, 32, 43, 58, 60, 67, 76, 77, 87, 115
integration, 157, 158, 175, 192, 193
interlanguage, 5, 110, 112, 120, 138

229

Index

Jamaica, 1, 10, 30
Jesuits. *See* Company of Jesus

Kikongo, 24, 92, 96
Kimbundu, 24, 92, 96
Kwa, 24, 58, 68, 69

language acquisition, 3–6, 30–32, 41, 43, 70, 106, 114, 166, 183, 188, 193
law in action, 9, 47, 150, 174–178, 181, 185–186, 188, 192
law in books, 9, 47, 150, 174–175, 178, 185, 186, 192
lawsuits, 45, 150, 154, 156, 182
Legal Hypothesis of Creole Genesis, 4, 6, 9, 44–47, 148, 149–189
legal personality, 9, 45–47, 153–161, 174, 175, 182, 184, 186, 188, 190
lexifier, 39, 91, 157
Leyes de Indias, 45, 46, 153–154, 168, 170, 181
LHCG. *See* Legal Hypothesis of Creole Genesis
licencias, 132, 195

Macau Creole, 13
manumission, 31, 47, 144–147, 153, 155, 158–164, 171–172, 178–179, 181–182, 184, 186–187, 191
Maya, 71, 122
Medieval Spanish, 87, 91
Mexico, 8, 39, 41, 176, 182
Minimalist Program, 111, 113, 114, 117, 126
monogenesis, 7, 13, 15, 17, 30, 36, 47, 54, 74, 89, 127, 150
monopoly, 31, 133
morphosyntax, 5, 11, 13, 25, 28, 31, 36, 42, 43–44, 74–99, 112, 123

Nine Years' War, 133

Palenquero, 1, 7, 8, 11, 15, 17, 25, 28, 32, 34–35, 39, 54, 121, 151, 190
Panama, 25, 128, 133, 135, 137
Papiamentu, 7, 8, 11, 13, 39, 151, 190, 191
peculium, 46, 152, 154, 156, 158, 159, 160, 166, 171, 183–184, 186–187
Peru, 5, 8, 9, 39, 41, 44, 51, 86, 108, 114, 141, 142, 177, 182, 188
Philippines, 13
placaaten, 158–159

Popayán, 127–139, 141, 143, 169
Portuguese-based pidgin/creole, 3, 7, 10, 13, 17, 21, 34, 36, 89, 139, 147, 190
protector de esclavos, 46, 154, 167, 175, 182
Puerto Rican (Bozal) Spanish. *See* Puerto Rico
Puerto Rico, 8, 10, 11, 17, 29, 34, 69

Quechua, 50, 71, 122
Quibdó, 4, 44, 49, 53, 66, 131

restructuring, 1, 36, 107, 193
rights, 9, 45–47, 149–150, 151, 152, 153, 154, 157, 159, 168, 174–175, 181–183, 186–188, 191

San Basilio de Palenque, 1, 7, 151, 191
São Tomé, 11, 13, 36, 89, 91
second-language acquisition. *See* language acquisition
segregation, 157
Siete Partidas, 45, 46, 153–155, 158, 162, 181
SLA. *See* language acquisition
Spanish creole debate, 5, 7, 10, 44, 151, 174, 188, 192
standard norm, 8, 77, 79, 103, 136
standard Spanish, 3–5, 10, 11, 25–28, 31, 36, 42, 49, 58, 67, 70, 74, 76–83, 85–90, 94, 98, 103, 110–113, 117–118, 123–125, 146, 147, 190–191
standardization. *See* standard norm
standards of living, 151, 178
stigmatization, 5, 8, 28, 58, 60
substrate, 8, 24–25, 28, 58–60, 67, 68–71, 76, 99, 106, 117, 121–123, 126
superstrate, 38

trials, 46, 167, 171, 181–182, 183–185

Umbundu, 24, 92, 96
Universal Grammar, 107, 114

Venezuela, 8, 9, 31, 39, 40, 44, 168, 176, 177
Veracruz, 8, 39, 41–42
Villa España, 4, 44, 78

War of Spanish Succession, 133
working conditions, 1, 40, 43, 143, 147, 161, 176, 178, 181, 187–188, 191

Yungueño Spanish, 31, 44

Lightning Source UK Ltd.
Milton Keynes UK
UKHW011508030622
403870UK00018B/492